ANALYSING QUALITATIVE DATA IN PSYCHOLOGY

ANALYSING QUALITATIVE DATA IN PSYCHOLOGY

EDITED BY
EVANTHIA LYONS AND
ADRIAN COYLE

SAGE Publications
Los Angeles • London • New Delhi • Singapore

Editorial arrangements © Evanthia Lyons and
Adrian Coyle 2007

Chapter 1 © Evanthia Lyons
Chapter 2 © Adrian Coyle
Chapter 3 © Jonathan A.
  Smith and Virginia
  Eatough
Chapter 4 © Lesley Storey
Chapter 5 © Sheila Payne
Chapter 6 © Sheila Hawker
  and Christine Kerr
Chapter 7 © Adrian Coyle
Chapter 8 © Chris Walton
Chapter 9 © Michele
  Crossley
Chapter 10 © Neil Harbison

Chapter 11 © Evanthia
  Lyons
Appendix 1 Preface © Arnie
  Reed
Appendix 2 Preface ©
  Adrian Coyle and
  Evanthia Lyons
Report 1 © Virginia Eatough
  and Jonathan A. Smith
Report 2 © Magi Sque and
  Sheila Payne
Report 3 © Mark Craven
  and Adrian Coyle
Report 4 © Michele Crossley

First published 2007

 SAGE Publications Ltd
1 Oliver's Yard
55 City Road
London EC1Y 1SP

SAGE Publications Inc.
2455 Teller Road
Thousand Oaks, California 91320

SAGE Publications India Pvt Ltd
B 1/I 1 Mohan Cooperative Industrial Area
Mathura Road
New Delhi 110 044

SAGE Publications Asia-Pacific Pte Ltd
33 Pekin Street #02-01
Far East Square
Singapore 048763

Library of Congress Control Number: 2006936969

British Library Cataloguing in Publication data

A catalogue record for this book is available from
the British Library

ISBN 978–1–4129–0782–8 (hbk)
ISBN 978–1–4129–0783–7 (pbk)

Typeset by Newgen Imaging Systems (P) Ltd, Chennai, India
Printed and bound in Great Britain by The Cromwell Press,
Trowbridge, Wiltshire
Printed on paper from sustainable resources

CONTENTS

LIST OF CONTRIBUTORS

Adrian Coyle is a Social Psychologist and Senior Lecturer in the Department of Psychology at the University of Surrey, where he fulfils the role of Research Tutor on the Practitioner Doctorate Programme in Psychotherapeutic and Counselling Psychology. He has been undertaking qualitative research since the mid-1990s, mostly using interpretative phenomenological analysis, grounded theory and discourse analysis. His research and publications have addressed a wide range of topics, including identity, bereavement, religion and spirituality and various issues within lesbian and gay psychology.

Mark Craven is a Chartered Counselling Psychologist, working with Surrey and Borders Partnership NHS Trust in both community forensic and acute in-patient psychiatric services. After a successful first career in the health industry, ontological curiosity and a passion for sense-making drew him back into higher education and eventually towards the 'psy disciplines'. He undertook his first degree in psychology and counselling at what is now Roehampton University, where he developed an interest in social constructionist and critical approaches to psychology. He went on to complete a Practitioner Doctorate in Psychotherapeutic and Counselling Psychology at the University of Surrey.

Michele Crossley is Professor of Social Work in the Faculty of Health and Applied Social Sciences at Liverpool John Moores University. Michele has published widely in narrative psychology, with specific application to the emerging field of critical health psychology and its application in various health domains. One of the core aims of her work has been to explore how people make sense of traumatizing and transitional health-related events through the use of narratives and how, in turn, these narratives connect to the historical, social and political context. This programme of work has important implications for health education and health promotion interventions.

Virginia Eatough is Lecturer in Psychology at Birkbeck University of London where she teaches social psychology and qualitative research methods. Before that she taught at Nottingham Trent University. Her main research interests are in phenomenological and social psychology, in particular emotions and emotional experience. These interests are represented in her recent studies investigating women's lived experiences of anger using interpretative phenomenological analysis. This work emphasized the role of feelings in emotion and how individuals make sense of their experiences. Currently, she is involved in a cross cultural study looking at how women talk about and understand hostility. She is also conducting research examining adult crying which focuses on the subjective experience and structure of crying episodes.

Neil Harbison is the pseudonym of a contributor who wishes not to reveal his identity.

Sheila Hawker received her BSc and PhD from the University of Southampton. She is a health services researcher who has worked on numerous projects, principally concerned with quality of life for older people and cancer care. These include a systematic review of qualitative literature concerned with inter-professional communication when older people are discharged from hospital, a study evaluating the feasibility of a nurse-specialist managed chemotherapy service and a multi-method examination of the provision of palliative care for older people in UK community hospitals. She is currently co-director of C&S Academic Services, a company offering qualitative interview and transcription services for social and health services research. Her publications include papers on 'End of life care in community hospitals: the perceptions of bereaved family members' (in *Palliative Medicine*, 2006) and 'Appraising the evidence: reviewing disparate data systematically' (in *Qualitative Health Research*, 2002).

Christine Kerr received her BSc and PhD from the University of Southampton. She has worked on research projects focusing on health care for older people. These include a systematic review of qualitative literature concerned with inter-professional communication when older people are discharged from hospital, a multi-method examination of the provision of palliative care for older people in UK community hospitals and an evaluation of out-of-hours care in community hospitals. Her latest project concerned incentives for health professionals taking part in clinical research trials. She is currently co-director of C&S Academic Services, a company offering qualitative interview and transcription services for social and health services research. Her most recent publication is 'Out of hours medical cover in community hospitals: implications for palliative care' (in the *International Journal of Palliative Nursing*, 2006).

Evanthia Lyons is a Senior Lecturer in Social Psychology and leads the Social Psychology European Research Institute (SPERI) at the University of Surrey. She obtained her degrees at Bedford College and the Institute of Education of London University. She teaches social psychology and qualitative research methods at masters and doctoral level. Her research interests include identity and social representational processes in the contexts of inter-group conflict and multi-cultural societies. She has used both qualitative and quantitative methods to study the development of national identities in children, the role of social memories in maintaining inter-group conflicts and the relationship between trust in political institutions and political participation amongst young people from different ethnic origins in seven European countries. She has also used qualitative research methods to challenge existing literature on the potential impact of stigma on the self amongst members of socially devalued groups such as people with mental illness and learning disabilities, older people and young mothers.

Sheila Payne is a Health Psychologist with a background in nursing. She currently holds the 'Help the Hospices' Chair in Hospice Studies at the Institute of Health Research at Lancaster University, working in collaboration with the International Observatory on End-of-Life Care. She has a long track record in palliative care research and scholarship and previously led the Palliative and End-of-Life Care Research Group at the University of Sheffield. Her research agenda focuses on palliative and end-of-life care for older people and bereavement support. She holds a number of major grants in these areas and supervises PhD students. She co-directs the National Cancer Research Institute-funded Cancer Experiences Collaborative with Professor Julia Addington-Hall and is also a Trustee of St Luke's Hospice, Sheffield. Sheila has published widely in academic and professional journals, has written ten books and, with Sandra Horn, edits the 'Health Psychology' book series published by the Open University Press.

Arnie Reed is a Chartered Counselling Psychologist based in Cardiff. He works in an NHS Trust Community Mental Health Team and also has a private practice. After a full and rewarding military career, he moved into psychology, graduating from the University of Surrey in 2001 with a Practitioner Doctorate in Psychotherapeutic and Counselling Psychology. He now provides psychological assessment and a wide range of short and long-term psychological treatments for all adult mental health difficulties, working from an integrative position. In addition, he teaches on Cardiff University's Practitioner Doctorate in Clinical Psychology and MSc in Psychiatry.

Jonathan A. Smith is Professor of Psychology at Birkbeck University of London where he teaches social psychology and qualitative research methods. Before that he taught at Keele University and the University of Sheffield. He has been developing and applying interpretative phenomenological analysis over the last 15 years. His primary research interests lie in health and social psychology. Much of his recent research has been on the psychosocial issues arising from the 'new genetics'. This includes analysis of individuals' understandings of genetics and genetic testing and an examination of the process of genetic counselling. He is currently involved in an NHS-funded project exploring how information about genetic test results is communicated through families. He has recently been an editor of *Psychology and Health* and has edited a number of books on research methods in psychology, most recently *Qualitative Psychology* (2nd edition) (in press) with Sage.

Magi Sque is a Senior Lecturer in the School of Nursing and Midwifery at the University of Southampton. She studied nursing at Guy's Hospital, London, and specialized in oncological nursing, working clinically in this field for 17 years at the Royal Marsden Hospitals, London and Sutton, and the Princess Margaret Hospital in Toronto. Supported by a British Department of Health Nursing Research Studentship, she completed a PhD in 1996. A member of the Cancer, Palliative and End of Life Care Research Group, Magi leads research focused on the psychological and social issues concerning organ donation, retention and transplantation, the role of family in end of life care, and the nature and quality of support given to them. Magi has an international reputation for her work on organ donation. Her forthcoming book *Organ and Tissue Donation: An Evidence Base for Practice* is co-edited with Sheila Payne.

Lesley Storey is a Research Development Coordinator for the UK National Cancer Research Institute. She obtained her PhD from the University of Surrey. Her research explored the importance of the past in the construction of 'Blackness' and the connection between Blackness and Britishness for people of African Caribbean descent and heritage in the UK.

Chris Walton is a Lecturer in Social Psychology in the Department of Psychology at Lancaster University. He obtained his PhD from the University of Surrey in 2004, having presented a critical discursive psychological analysis of masculinity and emotions. Since then, he has used qualitative research methods – primarily discursive approaches – to examine various other topics such as new genetic technologies and learning disabilities.

LIST OF BOXES

LIST OF TABLES

LIST OF FIGURES

Section 1

QUALITATIVE RESEARCH IN PSYCHOLOGY: SETTING THE SCENE

1

DOING QUALITATIVE RESEARCH: INITIAL QUESTIONS

Evanthia Lyons

This chapter will outline the aims of the book and provide an overview of the contents. It will describe the main decisions and uncertainties that researchers face when conducting qualitative research at the different stages of the research process and will raise some of the questions that you, as a reader, should bear in mind when you attend to each chapter to enable you to make the most effective use of the book.

Key terms

descriptive

discourse analysis

epistemology

evaluation criteria

explanatory

grounded theory approach

interpretative phenomenological approach

meaning-making

narrative analysis

social critique

Background to the book

As a teacher and a researcher, I have often been faced with excited and anxious students and colleagues who were either about to embark on or were in the midst of the process of conducting qualitative research. In talking about their anxieties and excitement, they have often commented on the uncertainties associated with making the decisions involved in the research process. Qualitative researchers soon realize that there are no universally agreed right answers to questions such as the style of interviewing they should use to collect their data or which approach to data analysis they should adopt or how they can identify a theme in their analysis or the exact **criteria** they should use to **evaluate** their research.

This book aims to provide both relatively novice and more experienced researchers with the necessary methodological tools and conceptual maps to navigate their way through the process of qualitative research. It describes the uncertainties surrounding qualitative research and the many dilemmas faced by researchers. It illustrates these by drawing on the experiences of researchers with varying degrees of expertise in qualitative research. It also provides the readers with the necessary background knowledge and raises their awareness of the questions they will need to address in order to make informed decisions about how to deal with such uncertainties and dilemmas.

Conducting qualitative research: Quandaries and uncertainties

Qualitative research methods do not easily provide firm and incontestable answers to questions about the research process and data interpretation. This in part results from their underlying philosophical assumptions concerning how we should produce psychological knowledge. Although 'qualitative research' is a term that covers a number of different methods, as a bare minimum, most of these methods share the assumption that there is no 'objective' reality or universal truth. Rather they are underpinned by the belief that knowledge, and the processes which lead to its production are context specific (Lyons, 2000; Willig, 2001). Furthermore, there is the assumption that researchers and participants, together with other related individuals and groups of individuals, ideologies and social structures, are integral and dynamic parts of the context of the phenomenon under investigation (Dallos and Draper, 2000; Harré and Secord, 1972). Therefore there is no formulaic way, no blueprint, of how qualitative research ought to be conceptualized and conducted as the choices and decisions made throughout the research process are likely to define and influence what is researched, what data are collected, how data are made sense of and the conclusions drawn.

However, it is important to emphasize that qualitative research is not a homogeneous domain: different research approaches and methods are based on different philosophical assumptions concerning how we should produce psychological knowledge and what can be known, and have different scientific goals and guidelines for good practice (Denzin and Lincoln, 2005a; Henwood and Pidgeon, 1994; Willig, 2001). Furthermore, they are based on differing conceptualizations of the relationship between language, cognitions and reality. These sets of assumptions are the focus of the domain of the philosophy of science which is referred to as **epistemology** (Benton and Craib, 2001). Chapter 2 provides a fuller discussion of what epistemology is and the various epistemological stances underlying the different research methods.

The assumption that the production of knowledge and how we make sense and talk about our social world is context specific together with the wide range of methods available to those who want to conduct qualitative research give rise to a number of questions at each stage of the research. For example, at the very beginning of the research journey, one deals with the issue of whether one should use qualitative or quantitative research methods to investigate a topic. If you do decide to conduct qualitative research, then you are faced with the decision of which particular approach you should use.

At the research design stage, one has to make decisions about how to use existing theory and empirical knowledge. Do we take this knowledge into account when we, for example, formulate our research questions and/or design our interview schedule or choose what texts will form the data we plan to analyse? Do we engage with existing knowledge before, during or after the interpretation stage and how do we ensure that pre-existing ideas do not overly influence how we make sense of what the participants tell us – or should we? Should we give theory the same status as that we give to the accounts that the participants or other texts provide us with? Furthermore, we need to reflect on how we conceptualize our role as a researcher. Do we see the role of the researcher as being a mere perceiver of the participants' meaning-making endeavours? Do we see the researcher as a perceiver and interpreter of what participants express? Do we see our role as being one of deconstructing and reconstructing textual accounts of a phenomenon, thus offering a **social critique** of the *status quo* and opening up alternative ways of constructing our social world?

Both relatively novice and more experienced researchers feel a sense of excitement, perhaps bewilderment, and quite often anxiety when they face the task of analysing pages and pages of qualitative data. They may of course have a textbook, which outlines a step-by-step guide and techniques of how to analyse qualitative data using their chosen analytic approach. But how does one apply these to one's own data? Qualitative researchers quickly come to realize that this is not a straightforward process. Irrespective of which approach to qualitative research is employed, identifying a 'theme' or a 'category' or a 'discourse' in the data is not easy. However clearly the analytical steps are described in a textbook, applying them to a data set is not a mechanical process. It is a **meaning-making** process. It requires the researcher to immerse themselves in the data, make sense of the data and identify the 'themes', 'codes', 'discourses' which would provide a recognizable and useful account of the data. However, what is recognizable and what is useful are to a great extent subjective judgements. In this sense, no one interpretation is the 'correct' or 'true' one. This does not mean *any* interpretation is a good interpretation. One could argue that a piece of qualitative research should be evaluated along two main dimensions: first, its rigour and quality and second, its usefulness (see Chapter 2 and Chapter 11 for more on this). So how does a researcher know what themes, codes or discourses are relevant and/or useful? Should their relevance and usefulness be determined by how good they are at providing a **descriptive** or an **explanatory** account of the data? Or should their relevance and usefulness be judged on how they engage with existing theoretical and empirical knowledge or their relative applicability to real life situations? In any case, should they be relevant and useful to those participating in the research or to those who fund it or to other potential users of the research findings?

Furthermore, qualitative researchers also face the task of disseminating their findings in a way that is recognized by the participants, colleagues and other interested audiences as making a useful contribution. Given the diversity of the potential audience, how we present our findings orally or in a written form again raises a lot of questions. For instance, how can we show the rigour and quality of our research so that our academic peers accept the credibility and usefulness of our findings? How do we make our findings accessible to the groups of people who participated in the research? How do we persuade policy makers to take notice of the findings of a research study which is based on perhaps just a few individuals, as often qualitative research involves small size samples? How can we ensure that our research has the desired political and social implications and avoid others exploiting the research for purposes we do not agree with?

These are only a few of the many issues that qualitative researchers face and we as a research community do not have precise and universally agreed answers. These issues are often resolved on the basis of the questions researchers seek to address and their exact assumptions about what can be known, what are valid ways of producing knowledge and the relationship between language, cognition and 'reality'.

The structure of the book

The contents of the book are organized in a way that reflects the three main objectives that Adrian Coyle and I had when we initially conceptualized this book. Our first objective was to provide readers with the necessary background knowledge and an awareness of the questions they will need to address in order to make informed decisions about whether to conduct qualitative rather than quantitative research and, if they decide to follow a qualitative path, which particular qualitative approach(es) would best suit their research goals. Our second objective was to equip readers with the basic tools to carry out their analysis by providing detailed, contextualized coverage of the practicalities of each of the following four qualitative methods/approaches: interpretative phenomenological analysis (Smith, 1996, 2004), grounded theory (Glaser and Strauss, 1967; Strauss and Corbin, 1990, 1998), discourse analysis (Parker, 1992; Potter and Wetherell, 1987) and narrative analysis (Crossley, 2000a). In addition, the book includes accounts of an actual analysis of a specific data set in a step-by-step manner using the four approaches.[1] Our third objective was to provide the reader with guidance as to how to write up qualitative research in general and how to report studies employing each of the four approaches in particular.

Thus, in addition to this chapter, Section 1 includes a chapter by Adrian Coyle which gives an account of the historical development of qualitative research methods in Britain and discusses in some detail some of the central issues underlying qualitative research. The chapter aims to sensitize the reader to issues such as the value of qualitative research in psychology, the relationship between epistemology and method and how qualitative research might be evaluated. The chapter provides a general background to qualitative research and raises questions that the reader may want to bear in mind when reading the theoretical and analytic chapters included in Section 2 in order to note how each of the four approaches deals with them.

Section 2 includes four chapters (Chapters 3, 5, 7 and 9) outlining the theoretical underpinnings and methodological issues involved in employing each of the four approaches to qualitative research that are focused on in this volume. These chapters contextualize the discussion of these issues by giving ample examples of the main issues faced by researchers who employ each of the analytical approaches and examples of how these issues were dealt with in particular projects.

Each theoretical chapter is followed by a chapter describing the reflections of a member of a group that analysed a specific data set using the approach described in the theoretical chapter. The main aim of these chapters are twofold. First, they reflect on the experiences of relatively novice researchers who used each method and second, they provide a comparative context within which the reader can explore the similarities and differences amongst the four approaches. The data set used in this exercise can be found in Appendix 1.

The final chapter in Section 2 (Chapter 11) offers some reflections on the similarities and differences between the four focal analytic approaches. It extends the discussion on some of the issues raised in both the introductory chapters as well as the subsequent theoretical and analytic chapters. In that chapter, I summarize and compare the position each approach takes on these issues. Also, I consider the political implications of the choices we make in the research process, especially in relation to how we conceptualize the relationship between ourselves, as the researchers, and the participants.

Finally, Appendix 2 includes examples of published work by researchers who used each of the research methods, with commentaries on the writing-up process. These reports provide the reader with useful examples of and tips on how to write up qualitative research, thus completing the research process.

Doing qualitative research is certainly an exciting and challenging process. Its appeal is partly due to the rich data it produces and the opportunities it opens up for exploring the complex, ambivalent and often contradictory ways we make sense of and construct our social worlds. Reading this volume will, we hope, make it easier to explore issues which are important not only in a social and political sense but to you personally. However, it does not promise to answer all your questions as there are many that remain unanswered by the research communities and there are others that are specific to particular research methods and that could not be covered in the space available in this book.

Summary

This chapter has emphasized the diversity of the research methods covered under the umbrella of qualitative research and has described some of the common assumptions these methods share. It argued that assumptions regarding meaning-making processes and processes involved in how we produce knowledge as context specific make researchers feel uncertain about how to conduct research and present their analytic accounts. The chapter has raised some of the questions that qualitative researchers often grapple with and has outlined the structure of the book.

Further reading

A volume which covers many approaches to qualitative research and deals with debates and tensions within the qualitative research paradigm is Norman Denzin and Yvonna Lincoln's (2005b), *The SAGE Handbook of Qualitative Research*. Carla Willig's (2001) *Introducing Qualitative Research in Psychology: Adventures in Theory and Method* and Jonathan Smith's (2003), *Qualitative Psychology: A Practical Guide to Research Methods* provide very clear and rigorous accounts of some widely used qualitative research methods and of the methodological debates within the field of qualitative research.

Note

1 The data set in question (see Appendix 1) was analysed by three groups of postgraduate students using **interpretative phenomenological analysis**, **discourse analysis** and **narrative analysis** under the guidance of expert facilitators at an Economic and Social Research Council (ESRC) 'Advanced Training in Social Psychological Research Methods' workshop which was organized by the editors in July 2002. The same data set was also analysed by a group of postgraduates using grounded theory in 2002, again working under the guidance of an expert facilitator. Three of the group facilitators have authored the chapters on their specific research methods in this book (Jonathan A. Smith, Sheila Payne and Michele Crossley). The fourth facilitator was Carla Willig, who guided the discourse analytic group.

2

INTRODUCTION TO QUALITATIVE PSYCHOLOGICAL RESEARCH

Adrian Coyle

This chapter introduces the reader to some key issues in qualitative psychological research. It begins by reviewing the assumptions made by the standard 'scientific method' within psychology concerning *how* we can know and *what* we can know. These are contrasted with the assumptions that underpin different qualitative methods. This discussion includes an outline historical account of the development and use of qualitative research in psychology. Attention then turns to some of the relative benefits of qualitative methods and also the potential danger of becoming too focused on methods rather than research questions. The issue of how qualitative work might be evaluated is examined. Finally, some areas of qualitative inquiry that require further development are considered.

Key terms

coherence
commitment
context
empiricism
epistemology
hypothetico-deductivism
idiographic
impact and importance
integration of qualitative and
   qualitative research methods
longitudinal qualitative research

methodolatry
nomothetic
phenomenological
positivism
rigour
scientific method
sensitivity to context
social constructionism
speaking position
transparency

Introduction

The methodological repertoire of psychological research has undergone a remarkable transformation over the last couple of decades. I recall that when

I was an undergraduate in the mid-1980s, we received a very clear message from our lecturers that acceptable psychological research involved, among other things, the careful measurement of variables, the control of other variables and the appropriate statistical analysis of quantitative data. The possibility of conducting psychological research using qualitative methods was never entertained. Indeed, I remember thinking that qualitative work was something done by some of my unfortunate peers in sociology, who, I thought, did not seem to realize that their research could never be properly 'scientific'. How times have changed – and how quickly.

My own moment of transformation came after completing a PhD based upon a lengthy structured questionnaire, with the data analysed through factor analysis and multiple regression. At that time, I heard about a workshop on qualitative methods for psychologists and this aroused my interest because of some experiences I had had during my PhD. As my doctoral research progressed, I had become increasingly uneasy about the way in which the response categories of my questionnaire often seemed too limiting for my participants, despite extensive preparative work and piloting. They would often scribble caveats and qualifiers beside ratings they had given and responses they had ticked. Of course, I then ignored these in my analysis because I could not find a way of meaningfully accommodating them. Even when participants took the trouble to write their own understandings of their experiences in the 'Other' category that was provided at the end of each question's response categories, these data were coded and quantified and then disappeared in the analysis because there were few instances of each coded category. These considerations made me wonder at the credibility of the findings I had obtained. My findings seemed to represent gross commonalities but without the complexity and nuances of individual stories that would reveal the range of ways in which these common features operated in lived experience. The workshop on qualitative methods provided some welcome answers to my questions about how the complexity and nuances of lived experience might be brought centre stage in psychological research. The result of this was that I became a committed advocate of qualitative methods thereafter (although my understanding of the relationship between qualitative data and 'lived experience' has become less straightforward since then).

Of course, I may not have pursued my interest in qualitative psychological work with such vigour had I not received institutional support and I may not have received that support had British psychology not developed a much greater openness to qualitative work in recent years. This can be seen, for example, in the frequency with which psychology conference papers and symposia feature qualitative work without methodology being a focal issue, the increasing number of qualitative articles in many peer-reviewed psychology journals, the plethora of books on the use of qualitative methods in psychology and the establishment of modules within psychology degree programmes and entire courses devoted to qualitative methods. Qualitative work has become a standard feature of many branches of psychology, especially in social psychology, health psychology, feminist psychology, psychotherapeutic and counselling psychology, clinical psychology and educational psychology. As a result, it is fair to say that psychology students in British universities today have a rather different methodological socialization compared to the one I experienced as an undergraduate, although coverage of qualitative methods can sometimes be tokenistic and there are some outposts where qualitative methods are still resisted.

This chapter examines this upsurge of psychological interest in qualitative methods in historical context, looking at the benefits that psychology gains from qualitative research at present and also what additional benefits might come from potential future developments in qualitative methods. First, we will consider a vitally important matter that cannot be overlooked in any consideration of qualitative research – epistemology.

Epistemology and the 'scientific method'

At its most basic, qualitative psychological research may be regarded as involving the collection and analysis of non-numerical data through a psychological lens (however we define that) in order to provide rich descriptions and possible explanations of people's meaning-making – how they make sense of the world and how they experience particular events. As Carla Willig (2001: 9) notes, qualitative researchers 'aim to understand "what it is like" to experience particular conditions (e.g. what it means and how it feels to live with chronic illness or to be unemployed) and how people manage certain conditions (e.g. how people negotiate family life or relations with work colleagues)'; the chapters outlining the principles and practicalities of the four focal methods in this volume specify the kinds of research questions that each method most readily addresses. However, qualitative psychological research involves more than this.

Qualitative research is bound up with particular sets of assumptions about the bases or possibilities for knowledge, in other words, **epistemology**. The term 'epistemology' refers to a branch of philosophy that is concerned with the theory of knowledge and that tries to answer questions about *how* we can know and *what* we can know. The epistemological position adopted by a research study specifies what kinds of things that study can find out. Different research approaches and methods are associated with different epistemologies. It is important to bear this in mind because otherwise it is easy to assume that we are talking about a homogenous domain when we refer to 'qualitative research'. Instead, the term 'qualitative research' covers a variety of methods with a range of epistemologies, resulting in a domain that is characterized by (potentially creative) difference and tension (Denzin and Lincoln, 2005a). In this section and the next, we shall examine the main epistemologies associated with both quantitative and qualitative research.

11

The epistemology adopted by a particular study can be determined by a number of factors. Researchers may have a favoured epistemological position and may locate their research within this, choosing methods that accord with that position (or that can be made to accord with it). Alternatively, the researchers may be keen to use a particular qualitative method in their research and so they frame their study according to the epistemology that is usually associated with that method (although note that many qualitative methods have some degree of epistemological flexibility). Whatever epistemological position is adopted in a study, it is usually desirable to ensure that this position (with its assumptions about the sort of knowledge that the research is producing) is maintained consistently throughout the write-up in order to help produce a coherent research report. Sometimes, however, a more flexible position on this is needed – for example, when using methods with different epistemologies within the same study. We shall return to this issue later.

Researchers and students who come to qualitative research methods for the first time sometimes think that this concern with epistemology is something that unnecessarily complicates the qualitative research process. If they have been using experimental approaches to research or other research designs in which they have been gathering and analysing quantitative data, they may not have encountered major discussion about epistemology. This does not mean that those types of research have no epistemological position. It just means that those research approaches adopt an epistemology that is often taken for granted both in research and in life more generally. That epistemology can be referred to as positivist-empiricist and hypothetico-deductive, although, strictly speaking, positivism and empiricism are slightly different.

Positivism holds that the relationship between the world (i.e., events, objects and other phenomena) and our sense of perception of the world is straightforward: there is a direct correspondence between things in the world and our perception of them, provided that our perception is not skewed by factors which might damage that correspondence, such as our vested interests in the things we are perceiving. Thus, it is thought possible to obtain accurate knowledge of things in the world, provided we can adopt an impartial, unbiased and objective viewpoint. The related domain of **empiricism** holds that our knowledge of the world must arise from the collection and categorization of our sense perceptions/observations of the world. This categorization allows us to develop more complex knowledge of the world and to develop theories to explain it.

Few scientists today adopt an unqualified positivist or empiricist outlook because it is generally recognized that our observations and perceptions do not provide pure and direct 'facts' about the world. These processes are never wholly objective: in our observation and perception, we are always selective, attending to some aspects of whatever we are looking at more than others. The point of debate concerns the extent to which we can move towards objective knowledge or truth about the world. Yet one fundamental claim remains central for empiricists, namely the idea that the development of knowledge requires the collection and analysis of data. This is something shared by qualitative researchers, although, compared with empiricists, we have very different ideas about what constitutes appropriate data and about how those data should be collected and analysed.

Researchers and students who have been exposed to a traditional methodological socialization within psychology (especially experimental psychology) will be very familiar with the theory of knowledge that developed in response to the shortcomings of positivism and empiricism – **hypothetico-deductivism**. The figure most closely associated with the development of hypothetico-deductivism, Karl Popper (1969), believed that no scientific theory could be definitively verified. Hence, the aim is not to obtain evidence that supports a theory but rather to identify theoretical claims (hypotheses) that are false (involving a process of deduction) and ultimately theories that are false. Research which adopts a hypothetico-deductive stance therefore operates by developing hypotheses from theories and testing these hypotheses. The assumption is that by identifying false claims, we can develop a clearer sense of the truth.

As psychology developed as a discipline, it became identified with the assumptions of positivism, empiricism and hypothetico-deductivism – in short, the **'scientific method'**. This was characterized by a striving for objectivity and neutrality and for precise measurement in hypothesis-testing, with the assumption that this would enable the researcher to obtain accurate, unclouded information about the psychological and social worlds. It was believed that objectivity and neutrality could be attained by having researchers remain detached from their research so that they would not contaminate the research process with whatever personal investments they may have had in the research topic. So, for example, contact between researchers and participants was either minimized or standardized so that each participant received the same instructions. In writing up research reports, the researcher was usually erased from the research process by the use of the passive voice rather than personal pronouns. Hence, rather than saying 'I developed a questionnaire', researchers would write 'A questionnaire was developed', erasing the agent in the process and creating the impression that the work was 'untainted' by human involvement on the researcher's side. Precision in measurement was assumed to be possible for any psychological dimension that existed. As Anne Constantinople (1973: 389) pointed out, 'Students in psychology often learn a famous dictum that expresses a fundamental axiom in psychological measurement: "Everything that exists, exists in some quantity, and if it exists in some quantity, it can be measured."' It was assumed that, through the development of progressively refined tests and measures, it was possible to measure any psychological dimension with precision. If something appeared to be impossible to measure in a satisfactory way, its very existence could be contested.

Where qualitative work was undertaken within the 'scientific method', this was very much as a preliminary step before the 'real' research. For example, when researching an area that had not been researched before or that had been minimally researched, qualitative work might be conducted to identify the key elements in that area which could then form the basis of measurement instruments such as questionnaires. However, a few qualitative research methods embraced the 'scientific method' and all its apparatus. One example is Klaus Krippendorf's (2004) structured form of content analysis, although it is debatable whether this constitutes a truly qualitative method because it categorizes and quantifies qualitative data very systematically and is concerned with reliability in a way that is not shared by other qualitative methods. We shall return to this later.

Resistance to the 'scientific method': Alternative epistemologies

The positivist-empiricist, hypothetico-deductive approach to psychological research has been resisted in some branches of the discipline. For example, in versions of psychotherapeutic psychology, from its early days emphasis was placed on qualitative case studies as a means to knowledge development (e.g., Freud, 1909/1955). However, the truly 'scientific' status of these domains was constructed as dubious by the arbiters of scientific practice and they remained the methodological exception rather than the rule. Beginning in the 1960s and 1970s but becoming more evident in the latter part of the 1980s and the 1990s, there was an incremental but discernible shift in British psychology as the discipline moved towards acceptance of at least some versions of qualitative research. This was the culmination of a long history of debate about what sort of knowledge psychologists can and should aim for in research (in other words, epistemological debate), even if this debate did not occur in the foreground of mainstream psychology.

In their historical account of the development of qualitative psychology, Karen Henwood and Nick Pidgeon (1994) trace this debate back to the work of Wilhelm Dilthey in 1894 who argued that the human sciences should aim to establish understanding rather than causal explanation (see also Norman Denzin and Yvonna Lincoln's (2005a) review of the history of qualitative research across disciplines). This challenge proved persistent and it can be heard echoed in the nomothetic–idiographic debate of the 1950s and 1960s. This debate concerned the relative merits of **nomothetic** research approaches which seek generalizable findings that uncover laws to explain objective phenomena and **idiographic** approaches which seek to examine individual cases in detail to understand an outcome. Researchers such as Gordon Allport (1962) argued that we cannot capture the uniqueness of an individual's personality simply by abstracting dimensions from aggregate statistical scores. These themes are also readily discerned within some influential early texts that advocated a shift towards qualitative methods within psychology. For example, in their 1972 text, *The Explanation of Social Behaviour*, Rom Harré and Paul Secord expressed concern about the reductionism that was implicit in the manipulation of variables and the dominance of quantification within psychological research. They saw this as reflecting a limited, mechanistic model of human beings. In their classic 1981 text, *Human Inquiry*, Peter Reason and John Rowan drew upon these and other ideas to advocate what they called a 'new paradigm' for psychology and especially a co-operative, participative, action-focused approach to inquiry. Similarly, in their 1985 text, Yvonna Lincoln and Egon Guba called for a 'naturalistic' paradigm based upon the search for detailed description, aiming to represent reality through the eyes of research participants and being attentive to the complexities of behaviour and meaning in context.

These concerns were also characteristic of psychological research informed by second-wave feminism in the 1960s and 1970s. One of the chief aims of feminist psychology is to reveal and challenge the ways in which male power has operated within psychology and the ways in which it has overlooked or misrepresented women's experiences. For example, psychology has long evaluated women's experiences in terms of male norms and, unsurprisingly, has found that women 'fall short'. It has also looked for 'sex differences' in various domains and has turned up differences that construct women as inferior to men, except when those differences are in domains that allow women to excel in their 'natural' roles as wives and mothers (Wilkinson, 1996). In a desire to explore women's experiences on their own terms and to allow women's voices to be presented without imposing pre-existent, ill-fitting frameworks of meaning, many feminist psychologists turned to qualitative methods that had a **phenomenological** emphasis. Such methods focus on obtaining detailed descriptions of experience as understood by those who have that experience in order to discern its essence. These methods are not concerned with producing an objective statement of an experience but rather with obtaining an individual's personal perception or account of the experience. For example, one explicitly feminist qualitative method that was developed was the voice relational method, which has as one of its aims as the hearing of voices that have often been suppressed and silenced such as those of adolescent girls (McLean Taylor et al., 1996). It does this through a careful, guided 'listening' to interview transcripts.

Some of the research methods focused on in the present volume can be seen as practical responses to the concerns raised by these critics of the use of the 'scientific method' within psychology. For example, interpretative phenomenological analysis (IPA) has an explicitly phenomenological commitment to discerning individual meaning-making within qualitative data and has a clear idiographic emphasis (see Chapter 3). However, feminist and other psychological researchers also sought approaches which allowed not just a phenomenological understanding of experience but also a critical understanding of the social and economic factors which determined experience. Both the voice-relational method and IPA permit this but the major focus for those who wished to undertake thoroughly critical work was research methods that were located within a radically different epistemology – **social constructionism**.

The milestone in the popularization of a social constructionist approach to psychological research was the publication of Jonathan Potter and Margaret Wetherell's book *Discourse and Social Psychology: Beyond Attitudes and Behaviour* in 1987. This was to have a profound and unsettling influence on social psychology and sparked much debate and controversy not only within this but in other branches of the discipline too, as it challenged the very foundations of what was regarded as legitimate psychological research. In broad terms, the social constructionist perspective adopts a critical stance towards the taken-for-granted ways in which we understand the world and ourselves, such as the assumption that the categories we use to interpret the world correspond to 'real', 'objective' entities (Burr, 2003). From a social constructionist perspective, the ways in which we understand the world and ourselves are built up through social processes, especially through linguistic interactions, and so there is nothing fixed or necessary about them: they are the products of particular cultural and historical contexts. Research conducted within a social constructionist framework focuses on examining the ways of constructing social reality that are available within a particular cultural and historical context, the conditions within which these ways of constructing are used and the implications they hold for human experience and social practice (Willig, 2001).

To this extent, social constructionism contrasts with the epistemology of other approaches to qualitative research which tend to assume that there is some relationship between the outcome of the analysis of research data and the *actualities* of which the analysis speaks. So, for example, if I were to analyse qualitative data from men on their experiences of expressing emotion, many analytic approaches would assume that the resultant analysis reflects some sort of underlying 'truth' or 'reality' about these experiences. Many approaches may see the correspondence between the analysis and those experiences as not being an exact one because the men may have forgotten some of the details of what they described or because they engaged in particular self-presentations or because the analysis is seen as representing an interaction between the data and the interpretative framework (consisting of both personal and professional investments) that the researcher brought to bear on the data. Nevertheless, some relationship is usually assumed between the analysis and 'truth' or 'reality'. Social constructionism views things rather differently. Some qualitative methods that adopt a social constructionist epistemology hold on to the idea of data representing things that have an existence outside the data; others are largely disinterested in whether there is a reality existing 'out there' to which qualitative data correspond because of the difficulties in ascertaining this. So, to return to our example, data on emotions are not seen as reflecting some reality about emotions but as representing accounts that construct emotions in particular ways and that use 'emotion talk' to perform particular social functions. Social constructionism can be quite difficult to grasp as its understandings run counter to so much that we take for granted in our world and in much psychological research. Those who are interested in finding out more about it should turn to Chapters 7 and 8 in this volume which examine the main social constructionist research approach – discourse analysis.

When you see how radically qualitative methods can differ from the standard 'scientific method' in terms of epistemology, it is hardly surprising that the growing acceptance of qualitative methods in psychological research has met with some resistance. This has been directed at both qualitative methods in general and at specific methods. Qualitative research within psychology has been represented as and criticized for being subjective, anecdotal, lacking rigour, being unable to offer anything that could readily address 'real life' problems, resembling journalism and – the most heinous crime of all – being almost indistinguishable from sociology. As qualitative methods do not seek to control what experimental approaches would regard as potentially 'confounding' variables, qualitative analysis has even been likened to doing 'surgery in a sewer' (Shevlin, 2000), which, of course, constructs experimental psychological research as precise and practically important like surgery. Some of these criticisms represent the pangs of pain felt by exponents of the scientific method within psychology as the methodological terrain of the discipline shifts beneath them. However, some criticisms merit serious consideration, such as the question about the practical utility of qualitative research. We shall return to this later.

Contextualized understandings through qualitative psychology

We have noted that psychologists have turned to qualitative research methods owing to dissatisfaction with the version of the 'scientific method' that was for so long regarded as the 'gold standard' in psychology and in a desire to obtain research participants' accounts of their own experiences on their own terms or to adopt a thoroughly critical analytic stance towards research topics. However, one other noteworthy potential benefit that may flow from using qualitative methods in psychology is that these may help researchers to attend to the key factor of **context** in all its complexity and fluidity. As we noted earlier, the desire for research to achieve contextualized understandings of phenomena was one reason why Lincoln and Guba (1985) called for the adoption of a 'naturalistic' paradigm in research.

'Context' is one of those terms which is often invoked in psychological work (especially within social psychology) but is not always conceptualized or explored in an optimally fruitful way. Drawing upon systemic theory (Dallos and Draper, 2000), I tend to view context in terms of the social systems and feedback loops in which an individual is embedded and through which they make sense of, construct and are constructed by their worlds. Thus, instead of being mere 'background', context becomes a constituent part of whatever it is we are researching. Within this framework, at a micro-social level, context refers to partnerships, family relationships, occupational networks and friendship networks, for example. This level influences and is influenced by broader social systems such as gender, social class, ethnicity and sexuality and these in turn are permeated by macro-social ideologies or narratives.

A thoroughly contextual analysis aspires to attend to all these levels and to trace their changing reverberations and implications for individual participants and for their positions within the social systems of which they are part. Such an analysis would be a prime concern for a social psychologist but the development of a properly contextual understanding would also be of enormous benefit within research in other psychological domains such as health psychology, counselling psychology and clinical psychology. Producing such an analysis is no easy matter for any research method but, in the hands of skilful researchers, many qualitative methods can readily permit us to trace the operation of these contextual considerations as expressed through the subjectivities of our research participants. Alternatively, from a social constructionist perspective, we could talk about the possibility of exploring texts created by and with participants to examine the ways in which particular contexts of talk open up some discursive options and close off others (in other words, make some things sayable and others unsayable). This is not to say that quantitative research cannot provide important information on context. However, it is limited in the extent to which it can capture the complexity and fluidity of context on participants' own terms.

One aspect of context that is either ignored, downplayed or regarded as contaminating in most quantitative research is the role of the researcher in generating data and producing the analysis. In contrast, many qualitative methods are characterized by an expectation that the researcher will make explicit their **'speaking position'** – that is, the interpretative framework which shaped their research questions and informed their analysis – and that they will reflect upon this process.

In some research, there is a tokenistic engagement with this, where researchers present a mini-biography and fail to identify which aspects of their speaking position were salient in their research and in what ways these commitments influenced the research process and the research product (to the extent that this is available to the researcher's conscious awareness). However, properly done, this can acknowledge the role of the researcher and it can increase the transparency of the research process and so help readers to understand and evaluate the work. Research is itself a social process and this helps to clarify the nature of that process for the reader. For an example of reflection by a researcher upon their speaking position, see Box 2.1. Incidentally, the conceptualization of research as a social process can be extended to include the research participants as co-researchers who actively shape the research product, as in some co-operative inquiry approaches (Heron, 1996). The reader or consumer of research can also be included in this as many qualitative methods invite readers to check interpretations against the data that are presented, although the opportunities to contest and reshape a published analysis are usually rather limited.

Box 2.1   RESEARCHERS' REFLECTIONS UPON THEIR SPEAKING POSITIONS

In an unpublished study of men's experiences of living apart from their children after divorce or separation, the counselling psychologist Natalie Chambers offered some reflections upon how different aspects of what she brought to the research process affected how she saw her participants, the accounts they offered during interviews and the people of whom they spoke (Chambers, 2006). For example, she wrote that one challenge she faced related to 'my status both as a woman and as a daughter. Even though they were talking to a female researcher, participants did not seem to hold back in their accounts of their ex-partners and I found it disheartening to hear that women or indeed people can behave so cruelly towards one another, seemingly in some cases with no regard for the bigger picture (namely their children's well-being). As a daughter who particularly cherishes her relationship with her own father, I found it difficult to conceive that some children would not want to have a relationship with their dad. Perhaps if the men had been abusive or neglectful, I would have understood but the men whom I interviewed did not seem to fall into this category. Of course, I was all too aware that the men's accounts represented only one side of the story and that each of the other "characters" (that is, the men's children and their ex-wives and ex-partners) may well have held a different view. In one case, I found myself doubting elements of a participant's account, thinking that there must be more to it for his ex-partner to have responded in the way that he said she did. On reflection, I suspect I just didn't want to believe that someone could be so cruel.'

   Reflections such as these can be readily incorporated within qualitative studies undertaken by undergraduate and postgraduate students, especially in disciplines such as counselling psychology and clinical psychology where personal reflectiveness is usually expected. Students can work these reflections into their research narrative at appropriate points. For example, the reflections above could be located within an account of the analytic procedure and process. The only difficulty with this is that, if the rest of the account is written in a more detached style, the use of 'I' in the personal reflections can be rather jarring. In this case, it is necessary to think carefully about how best to achieve a consistent tone throughout the research report – for example, by writing in a more personal way throughout. Alternatively, personal reflections can be kept separate from the main body of the text. This, however, runs the risk of suggesting that the personal dimension is not really very important or that it somehow contaminates the qualitative research process and so has to be kept separate from the 'real' business of the research (i.e., the analyses). Instead, the personal dimension is an integral aspect of many qualitative methods.

(Continued)

(Continued)

While personal reflections can and should be included in student research reports, it is usually a different matter when writing for publication. Relatively few academic journals carry articles which feature analyses that include consistent personal reflections. Hence, researchers may need to explore the extent to which and the form in which personal reflections are permitted by any given journal and hope that, over time, the parameters may slowly be shifted so that consistent personal reflection becomes an expected part of a journal article reporting qualitative work. Of course, there is an optimal level of personal reflection: too much personal reflection can create the impression that an analysis is more about the researcher than the researched.

Although qualitative methods potentially carry many benefits for psychologists, there are some benefits that are occasionally ascribed to them that are questionable. The impression may be created that many qualitative methods somehow provide access to the pure and unadulterated subjectivities of research participants. This is not the case because all research products are the result of a dynamic and inescapable interaction between the accounts offered by participants and the interpretative frameworks of the researchers. Also questionable is the often implicit assumption that qualitative methods somehow lead automatically to a democratization of the research process. Addressing the power differential between the researcher and the researched involves much critical, honest, reflective dialogue and flexibility: it is not miraculously conferred simply by adopting a qualitative research method. Nor is qualitative research necessarily radical. Indeed, as Norman Denzin and Yvonna Lincoln (2005a) have noted, far from being inherently radical, qualitative research outside psychology has been intimately tied up with processes of colonization. Also, as we have noted, while many qualitative methods do embody challenges to the taken-for-granted assumptions within psychological research, some methods embody the same assumptions as quantitative research. Real radicalism is conferred more by the frameworks and theories within which research is located rather than the methodologies that are used.

Evaluative criteria for qualitative research

Having considered one way in which qualitative methods can benefit the research endeavour, an associated question arises concerning how consumers of qualitative research (whether they be students, academics or psychological service providers) can evaluate the worth of a qualitative study. Positivist–empiricist, hypothetico-deductive, quantitative psychological research tends to be assessed in terms of criteria such as reliability and internal and external validity. These rely on an assumption of objectivity – that the researcher and the research topic can be independent of each other. Hence the aim in this research paradigm is to limit researcher 'bias', with 'bias' being defined in terms of deviation from some definitive truth or fact. Given the contention in most qualitative research that the researcher is inevitably present in their research, any evaluative criteria that relate to strategies for eliminating 'bias' are inappropriate.

However, some qualitative methods have sought to use versions of these traditional criteria to evaluate their research products and hence the research process. We have already noted that structured forms of content analysis do this, although whether they are really qualitative methods is questionable. An indisputably qualitative method that adopts versions of these evaluative criteria is the 'data display' method. This is an empiricist approach which holds that 'social phenomena exist not only in the mind but also in the objective world – and that some lawful and reasonably stable relationships are to be found among them' (Miles and Huberman, 1994: 4). The analytic process involves collecting and reducing qualitative data, displaying data and drawing and verifying findings. The management and presentation of data in an accessible way are key considerations: data are displayed in summarizing tables, matrices, flow charts and figures. This can be a valuable approach, especially for researchers who might feel overwhelmed by the task of structuring what may be a daunting amount of qualitative data, although researchers need to consider whether they can 'buy' the method's epistemology. This epistemology leads Matthew Miles and Michael Huberman (1994) to present criteria for evaluating data display analyses which represent an overlap between traditional evaluative criteria and alternative ones developed specifically for qualitative research, such as trustworthiness and authenticity (for more on these, see Lincoln and Guba, 1985). However, as Karen Henwood and Nick Pidgeon (1994) note, there are tensions between the different understandings of the research process that underpin these criteria, which are difficult to resolve.

Qualitative research is sometimes evaluated using inappropriate traditional criteria and, unsurprisingly, is found wanting. It is as if a music critic who was a specialist in heavy metal evaluated an opera in terms of its pounding, driving rhythm and loud elemental physical sound, expecting fast and furious screaming guitar lines. For this reason, in their research reports qualitative researchers may wish to specify alternative criteria by which they wish their research to be evaluated. There is now a variety of such criteria that have been developed. One of the most systematic evaluative schemes was produced by Robert Elliott and colleagues (1999). Through a thorough process of consultation, they developed 'evolving guidelines' for evaluating qualitative research in psychology. These consisted of criteria that are deemed common to qualitative and quantitative methods (explicit scientific context and purpose; appropriate methods; respect for participants; specification of methods; appropriate discussion; clarity of presentation; contribution to knowledge) and criteria that are particularly pertinent to qualitative research (owning one's perspective; situating the sample; grounding in examples; providing credibility checks; coherence; accomplishing general versus specific research tasks; resonating with readers). Some qualitative researchers have expressed reservations about these criteria (Reicher, 2000) and have favoured other looser evaluative schemes such as that of Lucy Yardley (2000), although her criteria do overlap with those of Elliott et al. (1999) in some respects.

Yardley held that good qualitative research should embody elements of 'sensitivity to context', 'commitment and rigour', 'transparency and coherence' and 'impact and importance'. By **'sensitivity to context'**, she means that, among other matters, the research should make clear the context of theory and the understandings created by previous researchers using similar methods and/or analysing similar topics; the socio-cultural setting of the study (e.g., the normative, ideological, historical, linguistic and socio-economic influences on the beliefs, objectives, expectations and talk of all participants, including the researchers); and the social context of the relationship between the researchers and the participants (see Box 2.2). **'Commitment'** is said to involve demonstrating prolonged engagement with the research topic and **'rigour'** relates to the completeness of the data collection and analysis. **'Transparency'** entails detailing every aspect of the processes of data collection and analysis and disclosing/discussing all aspects of the research process; **'coherence'** refers to the quality of the research narrative, the 'fit' between the research question and the philosophical perspective adopted, and the method of investigation and analysis undertaken. **'Impact and importance'** relate to the theoretical, practical and socio-cultural impact of the study.

Box 2.2   'SENSITIVITY TO CONTEXT' IN A STUDY OF PERCEPTIONS OF BYSTANDERS HELD BY PEOPLE WHO EXPERIENCED WORKPLACE BULLYING

To take an example of what one of Yardley's (2000) evaluative criteria might refer to in practice, let us consider a qualitative study which sought to develop an understanding of how people who had been bullied in the workplace perceived the role played by bystanders to this experience – that is, workmates who witnessed the bullying or were aware of it but did not intervene to prevent it. Let us say that the researcher obtained his/her data by conducting individual interviews with people who reported that they had been subjected to workplace bullying.

In order for this study to demonstrate 'sensitivity to context', it would need to relate the study to other relevant research and theory on bullying in general, workplace bullying in particular and the bystander phenomenon. We would expect the analysis to note not only where the findings echo this previous work but also where they differ from it and to suggest new ways of conceptualizing the bystander effect in workplace bullying.

We would also expect that the participants and the researcher would be placed in context. This would involve describing the participants' demographic and other

(Continued)

relevant 'background' details (such as sex, age, ethnicity, educational attainment and occupational history) and, in presenting the findings, orienting to how these factors may have shaped the reports that participants provided. So, for example, a female employee may not have expected male bystanders to intervene when she was subjected to bullying by a male supervisor for 'not being competitive enough' because she may have perceived the bully and the bystanders to share the same ideas about the necessity of a competitive ethic in the workplace and about women not being ideally suited to this. We would also expect the researcher to disclose whether he/she had experienced bullying in the workplace or in other settings and, if so, to suggest how these experiences might have shaped their expectations of the study and influenced the analysis.

We may also wish to see the researcher reflect upon the social context of his/her relationship with the participants, especially in terms of any power differentials. Although research participants have power during interviews as they possess something that the researcher wants, the researcher is usually on familiar terrain in the interview context and may use this familiarity to exert control. In this particular study, we would expect the researcher to be carefully attuned to issues of power because, if the researcher were overly controlling, the participant may experience this as replicating the bullying that they are talking about. Hence, we would hope to see the researcher discussing how issues of power were managed during the interviews and afterwards (e.g., the researcher may have sent draft analyses to participants to allow them to play an active role in interpreting the data).

As yet, there is no consensus about the best criteria for evaluating qualitative research, although there are recurrent themes among the criteria that have been developed relating to the provision of contextualized accounts of the participants, detailed accounts of the analytic process, an account of the researcher's 'speaking position' and how this influenced the analysis and the consistent grounding of interpretations in research data. Indeed, it could be claimed that reaching consensus is impossible because of the heterogeneity of qualitative methods. Hence it may be enough to have at our disposal a range of potential evaluative criteria so that a researcher can select those which are most appropriate to their study, justify their choice of criteria and allow readers to assess that rationale and, if they agree, evaluate the study using those criteria.

One criterion that appears in the schemes of Elliott et al. (1999) and Yardley (2000) relates to something that I mentioned earlier concerning critical questions about qualitative psychology that deserve serious consideration. I singled out the question about the practical utility of qualitative research, which overlaps with Elliott et al.'s criterion about resonating with readers and is part of

Yardley's 'impact and importance' criterion. This is sometimes referred to as the 'So what?' question, which arises from the assertion that 'The best psychological research should inform, amongst other things . . . professional practice [and] the delivery of public services' (Bruce, 2002: 620). For example, a clinical psychologist specializing in working with people with chronic conditions may enjoy reading a detailed qualitative analysis of an account offered by one person of their experience of living with Parkinson's disease (see Bramley and Eatough, 2005). However, they may then wonder 'So what? What does this tell me about the experiences of the many people with Parkinson's disease whom I encounter in my work? How can my practice be improved by this study?' Given that relatively few qualitative studies can confidently claim to have charted the full diversity of their research topic, these 'So what?' questions can be frequently encountered. Of course, the researcher could question the assumption that research needs to have practical utility in order to be seen as valuable and could point to the value of knowledge for its own sake. However, if the premise of the question is accepted, various responses are possible. The researcher could explain that a more general picture of a research topic is progressively built up through a series of complementary qualitative studies, with each adding something new to that developing picture. Hence, an individual study represents a step in the process of building up a more general picture that could be used to inform therapeutic intervention. In addition, it has been contended that there is the possibility of glimpsing something of the universal through the particular (Warnock, 1987).

Areas for future development in qualitative psychology

Although qualitative research methods are now relatively well established within psychology, there are some methodological areas that have been identified through experience as being in need of further development (and undoubtedly, further experience with qualitative research will uncover additional areas for development). In this section, I will focus on two that seem to be ongoing salient concerns within the methodological field.

One such area concerns the **integration of qualitative and quantitative research methods**. Although the qualitative and quantitative research paradigms tend to be associated with quite different epistemologies, they need not be conceptualized as incompatible: quantitative methods need not be wedded to a positivist–empiricist, hypothetico-deductivist epistemology and qualitative methods are not necessarily hostile to positivism–empiricism and hypothetico-deductivism. Earlier we noted that structured content analysis is located within this epistemology. Although we suggested that it could not really be deemed a qualitative method, it could be represented as embodying one way of combining qualitative and quantitative aspects within a single method – what we might call a 'hybrid' approach (Fielding and Schreier, 2001).

However, note that this method does not integrate qualitative and quantitative aspects because integration requires that different methods, which are oriented to the same research goal or question, are given equal weight (see Moran-Ellis et al., 2006). There are many possible ways of integrating methods. For instance, a study could consist of relatively discrete qualitative and quantitative elements, with each equally contributing something different to the task of answering the research question(s). For example, see Richard Shepherd and colleagues' (forthcoming) report of a project which examined public attitudes to new genetic technologies through a quantitative national survey, a quantitative study involving vignettes and qualitative studies using data from focus group interviews and the media.

Various benefits have been identified as potentially arising from a meaningful combination of methods. For example, it has been claimed that quantitative methods could gain greater proximity to their research participants (Mayring, 2001) and qualitative methods could produce findings with greater generalizability. However, it should not be assumed that a combination of qualitative and quantitative methods is inherently superior to a single-paradigm approach: the sorts of research questions that are presented in the chapters on the focal methods (and in the empirical reports in Appendix 2) in this volume could not have been addressed using quantitative methods without losing richness and detail. The decision to use a combination of qualitative and quantitative methods should be determined by how best to answer the research question(s). For some time, consideration has been given to the question of exactly how qualitative and quantitative methods might be best combined and how tensions between them might be handled (e.g., see Brannen, 1992; Schreier and Fielding, 2001) but this is an ongoing discussion that requires further work (Todd et al., 2004).

Another area that is evolving is the development of **qualitative methods for longitudinal research**, following individuals over time and interviewing them at different time points to explore change and development. Qualitative studies have tended to explore change over time by asking participants to talk about their experiences retrospectively. There are disadvantages associated with this; for example, participants may tend to view the past from the perspective of their present situation and viewpoint. Some of the particular challenges raised by longitudinal qualitative research have been discussed by Rachel Thomson and Janet Holland (2003) in their reflections upon a nine-year study of transitions to adulthood. At the end of this study, approximately 100 young people will have been interviewed individually six times and will have taken part in at least one focus group interview and other research activities. Among the challenges they identify is the pressure that participants may feel to produce accounts that speak of progress and development rather than difficulty and failure over time. Another issue is the provisional nature of the interpretations of the data that can be offered at any one stage of analysis; interpretations offered at one stage may need to be revised in light of data that emerge at a later stage.

Also, if the study is being conducted by a research team, staff changes may make it difficult to maintain a continuity of interpretation as a new researcher may find him/herself drawn to different aspects of the data set than his/her predecessor. However, any challenges seem to be outweighed by the potential benefits, such as the chance to gain better understandings of individual participants through interviewing them on several occasions at different times. If the research question is focused on a dimension that is better understood as an unfolding process rather than as something static (such as identity, for example), a longitudinal qualitative approach is ideal. Of course, some challenges associated with longitudinal research *per se* are also faced by longitudinal qualitative research, such as how to retain participants and also the financial cost of the work. The value of charting change as it unfolds (in terms of developing knowledge about psychological and social processes and using this to inform relevant services) is such that longitudinal work will surely become a standard part of the qualitative repertoire in the future. However, this will require new developments in some existing qualitative methods in order to equip the researchers who use them to meet the challenges of longitudinal work.

Guarding against 'methodolatry' and advocating methodological flexibility in qualitative research

Having rejoiced at the start of this chapter because British psychology has developed a greater openness to qualitative research in research years, I will end the chapter with a warning about what could happen as greater methodological diversity becomes the norm. In her reflections upon her evolving understanding of the research process, Carla Willig (2001) has talked about how, as an undergraduate, she thought of research methods as 'recipes'. These recipes specified the right ingredients (e.g. a representative sample, a suitable measurement instrument and a relevant statistical test) and the order in which they had to be used to produce the right outcome. However, over the years, through her experience of research, she has come to view the research process as a much more creative enterprise centred not on the correct application of techniques but on the best ways of answering research questions. For her, the focus has shifted from the method to the questions that the research seeks to answer. As was suggested when we looked at the prospects of combining qualitative and quantitative methods, this prioritization of the research question is vital. Those of us who find methodology fascinating can sometimes lose sight of what is ultimately important in research and can become more concerned with using as pure a version of our favoured methods as possible. We can become guilty of 'methodolatry' – a slavish attachment and devotion to method.

This, of course, raises a question about what this book aims to do. With its focus on presenting the principles and practicalities of four qualitative research methods that are increasingly used in psychology, does this book run the risk of promoting qualitative methodolatry within psychology? The answer to that depends partly on the way in which the material in this book is used. For students and researchers who are using a particular qualitative method for the first time, it can be useful to have a set of steps that can be followed. Otherwise, lacking a clear sense of where to begin and how to move an analysis forward, students or researchers may experience anxiety about whether what they are doing qualifies as a legitimate version of whatever method they are using. This can lead to the researcher becoming analytically immobilized. Hence, each of the four chapters which present the focal methods in this book (Chapters 3, 5, 7 and 9) outlines steps or strategies that can be useful 'road maps' to guide the student or researcher who is new to these methods. However, continuing the analogy, it is important to remember that each of these maps represents only one route to an analysis. If the researcher becomes fixated on that route and regards it as the only possible way to achieve a legitimate analysis using that particular method, he/she is in danger of falling prey to a methodolatrous stance. The researcher is also in danger of producing a limited analysis, which could have been improved if he/she had explored different analytic routes which might have taken them along more creative and unexpected paths. It is worth noting that there is a theme of flexibility running across the four chapters which present the focal methods. Each of the writers on these methods acknowledges that there is more than one acceptable way to conduct an analysis using their approach. Of all the contributors, Michele Crossley makes this most explicit in her chapter on narrative analysis (Chapter 9). She presents narrative analysis as an interpretative art that involves putting together a coherent and convincing analytic story and that cannot and should not be reduced to step-by-step guidelines.

Yet, there are limits to the extent to which researchers can amend and adapt particular methods. The more a researcher amends a given method, the greater is the risk that his/her analysis will not be seen as a legitimate example of that method. Exactly where the boundaries to methodological flexibility lie with any particular method is quite difficult to say. The nature of the innovation process is that new developments may at first be resisted by some exponents of a method but, if these changes are found to be useful and appropriate and if they are taken up by other researchers using that method, over time they may become an accepted variant of the method. Perhaps the best way to achieve credible change to an existing method is to alter it bit by bit over time rather than changing it radically and expecting others to accept that change. With experience, researchers can develop a sense of the limitations of a given method and the issues that it does not deal with clearly or well and can develop possible strategies for addressing such limitations in order to answer research questions more effectively. For example, in my early attempts at using IPA (see Chapter 3), I became unsure of how to employ existing psychological theory in an analysis without violating the method's commitment to foregrounding the meaning-making of research participants. After experimenting with various options, I developed a way of having theory inform the research rather than driving it, employing theory with (what I hope is) a lightness of touch to add psychological depth to the analysis (see Box 4.2 in Chapter 4; for more on the use of theory in qualitative research, see Anfara and Mertz, 2006). Research papers which have used this approach have been published and have been cited approvingly by the originator of IPA, which suggests that it has been deemed an acceptable version of the method.

Another possible way of developing new approaches is to combine existing qualitative methods or aspects of those methods. As with the combination of qualitative and quantitative methods, this can extend the scope of a research approach and enable it to provide more complete and more useful answers to research questions and perhaps to address a wider range of research questions. Yet again as with the combination of qualitative and quantitative methods, the process of combining (aspects of) qualitative methods can be tricky, especially if the methods are based on different epistemologies. In that case, the researcher could end up producing an approach that lacks epistemological coherence – assuming that epistemological coherence is a necessary quality in all research, which is open to debate. For example, there is no reason why a research study could not produce an analysis using IPA which has a social constructionist slant. As well as focusing on participants' meaning-making in research interviews, such an analysis would consider how the categories that participants use in their talk have been built up through social processes and the social functions that are performed by participants' talk. However, it would be necessary to find a way of doing this which would allow the study to retain IPA's central understanding that participants' talk bears some relation to the actuality of which it speaks.

So, it is fair to say that this book does not necessarily contribute to methodolatry, provided its chapters are not regarded as presenting the sole and definitive ways of applying the focal methods. Instead, the chapters should be seen as providing useful initial routes through the methods for novice researchers. With time and experience, these researchers should devise their own 'takes' on these methods and might even creatively develop the methods for future researchers.

Summary

This chapter has presented a number of issues that are relevant to and, in some cases, will help to contextualize the four qualitative research methods that are focused on in this volume. Readers who attend carefully to the material presented in this volume and who consult other important work that is cited here will find themselves equipped to undertake good qualitative research. However, the key factors in determining the ultimate quality of their research will be the skill and creativity with which they apply the principles of the various methods.

Further reading

Those who are coming to qualitative research for the first time are in a fortunate position because there are now many good quality books available that provide a background to the emergence of qualitative research in psychology and details of specific methods (although none has the practical and comparative focus of the present volume). The 'magnum opus' of qualitative research across disciplines is Norman Denzin and Yvonna Lincoln's (2005b) edited volume, *The SAGE Handbook of Qualitative Research*. In the UK, a less comprehensive but very user friendly early book in this tradition is John Richardson's (1996) edited *Handbook of Qualitative Research Methods for Psychology and the Social Sciences*. Subsequent noteworthy examples include Carla Willig's (2001) *Introducing Qualitative Research in Psychology: Adventures in Theory and Method* and Jonathan Smith's (2003) edited book, *Qualitative Psychology: A Practical Guide to Research Methods*. Useful texts have also appeared on qualitative research in specific fields of psychology such as health psychology (see Michael Murray and Kerry Chamberlain's (1999) edited volume, *Qualitative Health Psychology: Theories & Methods*) and psychotherapeutic and counselling psychology (see John McLeod's (2000) *Qualitative Research in Counselling and Psychotherapy*).

Section 2

APPROACHES TO DATA ANALYSIS

PREFACE

Evanthia Lyons and Adrian Coyle

As was indicated in Chapters 1 and 2, there are a large number of research methods that fall under the umbrella of qualitative research and that have been used in studies within psychology. These include content analysis (Krippendorf, 2004), the data display approach (Miles and Huberman, 1994), protocol analysis (Gilhooly and Green, 1996; Green and Gilhooly, 1996), grounded theory (Glaser and Strauss, 1967), interpretative phenomenological analysis (Smith, 1996, 2004), the voice relational method (McLean Taylor et al., 1996), discourse analysis (Potter and Wetherell, 1987) and conversation analysis (Hutchby and Wooffitt, 1998). Furthermore, some of these are not unitary methods/approaches; rather they exist in several different forms. No single book could hope to cover in depth all the qualitative methods that have been used or could be used in psychological research.

In this volume, we chose to focus on four methods/approaches: interpretative phenomenological analysis, grounded theory, discourse analysis and narrative analysis. The reasons for our choice of methods were twofold. First, each of these methods is widely used by researchers in many sub-disciplines within psychology. Second, these methods vary in terms of their underlying epistemological assumptions. We expect the comparison of these methods to facilitate an understanding of the relationship between epistemology and method and, in turn, its impact on different aspects of the research process.

The principles and practicalities of each approach are discussed first by researchers with considerable experience of using them in their own work. Interpretative phenomenological analysis (IPA) is presented by Jonathan A. Smith and Virginia Eatough, grounded theory by Sheila Payne, discourse analysis by Adrian Coyle and narrative analysis by Michele Crossley. It is worth noting that Jonathan A. Smith was the creator of the method that he discusses and Michele Crossley has played a leading role in popularizing narrative analysis in the UK.

These chapters present a detailed discussion of the epistemological and methodological issues pertaining to each method. They introduce the theoretical and philosophical backgrounds to the method and, where there are different versions of the method, they discuss these in relation to their favoured version. For example, in Chapter 5, Sheila Payne talks about the historical development of grounded theory and distinguishes between the approach first put forward by Glaser and Strauss in 1967 and subsequent versions developed independently by Glaser and by Strauss, as well as more recent developments such as Rennie's (2000) methodical hermeneutics, Clarke's (2003) postmodern version and Charmaz's (2006) social constructivist version. In Chapter 7 on discourse analysis, Adrian Coyle distinguishes between the two major variants in the UK – discursive psychology (Edwards and Potter, 1992) and Foucauldian discourse analysis (Parker, 1992) – while attending also to a synthesis of the two.

Each of the chapters that present the methods includes a discussion of the type of research questions that their focal method is best suited to addressing and gives examples of research questions that have been explored. They also consider the type of data that are most amenable to analysis using the particular method. For example, in Chapter 3, Jonathan A. Smith and Virginia Eatough discuss in some detail different types of interviewing and argue that semi-structured interviewing is the most appropriate method of data collection for IPA. Hence, readers should consult that chapter for some useful material on qualitative interviewing, although the basic principles outlined there may need to be altered in light of the demands of other methods. In Chapters 5 and 9, Sheila Payne and Michele Crossley discuss the optimal ways of collecting data for grounded theory and narrative analysis respectively; in Chapter 7, Adrian Coyle considers the process of selecting texts for discourse analysis. Each of these chapters also gives an invaluable step-by-step guide to the analytic process and illustrates different analytic principles and strategies by giving examples from past research projects.

Each of the methods presented in this book has been applied to a common data set by different groups of postgraduate students, working under the guidance of an expert in the method. The aim of this was to allow a clear comparison between the methods in terms of how the analytic focus was framed, what the analytic task involved and what was produced at the end of the process. The interview transcripts used for this exercise are presented in Appendix 1, together with an introduction to the data set by Arnie Reed, who collected the data for research that he conducted as part of his doctoral training in Counselling Psychology at the University of Surrey. The research project was a qualitative study of ex-soliders' accounts of renegotiating their identities after leaving the army. Prior to this exercise, most of these postgraduate students had relatively little experience of using the method that they applied to the data set.

One or more members of each analytic group wrote up their analysis in the form of 'Doing . . .' chapters and reflected on their experiences of the analytic process. All of these authors recognize that, inevitably, their account is their personal interpretation of that process, although attention is consistently paid to debates, disagreements and analytic insights within the group. For example, in Chapter 4 which discusses the application of IPA, Lesley Storey points to a debate within her group about the role of theory in their analysis and also draws on existing IPA research to show how theory has been used there. In Chapter 6 which reflects on the use of grounded theory, Sheila Hawker and Christine Kerr share their insights into the importance of being able to demonstrate a study's 'decision trail', which begins at the outset of the study and ends with the final emergent theory, by keeping a record of all the ideas, codes, meanings, categories and discrepancies generated during the analysis. They argue that the ability to be transparent about the analytic process helps to promote the rigour and validity of the analysis. In Chapter 8, Chris Walton reports on the application of discourse analysis and reflects on how one reconciles some of the assumptions of Foucauldian discourse analysis with issues such as the implications of the research findings for action and practice and their engagement with existing theory. In Chapter 10, Neil Harbison discusses the application of narrative analysis and raises questions about the predominance of the use of textual data in qualitative research and the theoretical choices that are made when work is presented through different genres (academic, theatrical, etc.).

These writers have not been hesitant in pointing to the difficulties their groups encountered and the ways in which they tried to overcome these difficulties. It is almost as if the initial chapters on each method present the 'theory' of what it is like to analyse data using these approaches whereas the 'Doing . . .' chapters suggest, through the practical experience of novice researchers, what it is *really* like to grapple with these methods! We recommend that readers study both chapters on each approach together so that they can get a more complete picture and understanding of the method. In order to follow the 'Doing . . .' chapters fully, though, it is important that readers familiarize themselves with the data set in Appendix 1 first.

Finally in this Section, in Chapter 11 Evanthia Lyons discusses the major similarities and differences between the four approaches. She pays particular attention to how each of the four approaches conceptualizes and deals with the way researchers should use existing psychological knowledge and their personal experiences and speaking positions in the process of conducting qualitative research. She also discusses the goals of psychological enquiry and the question of what are the most appropriate criteria for evaluating research conducted within each approach.

Across the chapters in this Section, the reader will find detailed discussion of the theoretical and philosophical underpinnings of the four research methods as well as rich and detailed technical information on how to apply these in research projects. We invite the reader to pay equal attention to each of these aspects and, perhaps most importantly, to reflect on the relationship between them.

3

INTERPRETATIVE PHENOMENOLOGICAL ANALYSIS

Jonathan A. Smith and Virginia Eatough

This chapter outlines the theoretical underpinnings of interpretative phenomenological analysis (IPA). It discusses the type of research questions for which IPA is suitable and considers sampling and data collection methods. Finally it offers some guidelines to conducting an IPA study, including the interviewing and analytic processes.

Key terms

case study	idiographic
cool cognition	interpretation
double hermeneutic	meaning-making
hermeneutics	phenomenology
hot cognition	semi-structured interviews
identity	themes

Theoretical underpinnings

Each of the three words making up IPA has a long intellectual history. However, over the last ten years or so this particular configuration of the three terms has produced a distinctive approach to psychological research, supported by a growing corpus of psychological studies. The main theoretical toughstones for IPA are **phenomenology** (Moran, 2000), **hermeneutics** (Palmer, 1969) and idiography (Smith et al., 1995). IPA also connects with a traditional concern with personal accounts and subjective experience in psychology (Allport, 1942; James, 1890) and with symbolic interactionism (Blumer, 1969).

The aim of IPA is to explore in detail individual personal and lived experience and to examine how participants are making sense of their personal and social world. The main currency for an IPA study is the meanings that particular experiences, events and states hold for participants. For example, IPA is particularly well suited to exploring topics within health, social and clinical psychology where there is a need to discern how people perceive and understand significant events in their lives. This reflects its phenomenological lens (Giorgi and Giorgi, 2003), which orients to an individual's personal perception or account of an object or event as opposed to attempting to produce an objective statement of the object or event itself.

At the same time, IPA also emphasizes that research is a dynamic process with an active role for the researcher in that process. Access to the participant's experience depends on and is complicated by the researcher's own conceptions and indeed these are required in order to make sense of that other personal world through a process of interpretative activity. Thus a two-stage interpretation process, or a **double hermeneutic**, is involved. The participant is trying to make sense of his/her world and the researcher is trying to make sense of how the participant is trying to make sense of his/her world. This double hermeneutic neatly illustrates the dual role of researcher. In one sense the researcher is like the participant, drawing on mental faculties they share. At the same time, the researcher is different to the participant, always engaging in second order sense-making of someone else's experience (see Palmer, 1969, for a history of hermeneutics).

It is also possible to look at this double hermeneutic another way as IPA combines an empathic hermeneutics with a critical hermeneutics (Ricoeur, 1970). Thus, consistent with its phenomenological origins, IPA is concerned with trying to understand what it is like from the point of view of the person, to take their side, to stand as far as possible (which is never completely possible) in the shoes of the participant. At the same time, a detailed IPA analysis can also involve standing a little back from the participant and asking curious and critical questions of their accounts – for example, 'What is the person trying to achieve here?', 'Is something leaking out here that wasn't intended?', 'Do I have a sense of something going on here that maybe the person him/herself is less aware of?' Both styles of interpretation can be parts of sustained qualitative inquiry and IPA studies will often contain elements of both. Allowing for both aspects in the inquiry is likely to lead to a richer analysis and to do greater justice to the totality of the person, 'warts and all'.

IPA has a theoretical commitment to the person as a cognitive, linguistic, affective and physical being and assumes a chain of connection between people's talk and their thinking and emotional state. At the same time, IPA researchers realize this chain of connection is not at all straightforward. People struggle to express what they are thinking and feeling; there may be reasons why they do not wish to self-disclose. The researcher has to interpret the person's mental and emotional state from what he/she says. In practice, this involves the researcher adopting different ways of thinking interpretatively about the data – for example, moving between building up rich experiential descriptions heavily grounded in the participant's own words and developing a more interrogative alternative account. IPA also recognizes that any analytic account will be partial: we cannot imagine it could ever be the final word on the topic.

The holism inherent in this portrait of the person also connects IPA with humanistic psychology (Graham, 1986) which developed in the 1960s and 1970s as a reaction against the conceptualization of the person within the experimental and laboratory paradigm. Humanistic psychology also had a political commitment to personal and social activity outside the academic world, promoting, for example, self-actualization, group therapy and connections with eastern philosophy. IPA has a humanistically informed holistic model of the person but is still oriented to research within academia and within psychology as a discipline. Thus IPA is trying to change psychology from within, to broaden its conceptualization both of what the person is and of how research on this person is to be conducted.

IPA's emphasis on sense-making by both participant and researcher means that it can be described as having cognition as a central analytic concern and this suggests an interesting theoretical alliance with the dominant cognitive paradigm in contemporary psychology. However while IPA does share with cognitive psychology and social cognition (Fiske and Taylor, 1991) a concern with mental processes, IPA strongly diverges from mainstream psychology when it comes to deciding the appropriate methodology for examining such phenomena. While mainstream psychology is still strongly committed to quantitative and experimental methodology, IPA employs in-depth qualitative analysis. In this context, it is interesting to see an alignment with Bruner (1990), who was one of the founders of the cognitive approach and who regrets how it swiftly moved from a central concern with meaning and meaning-making into the science of information processing.

IPA is an **idiographic** mode of inquiry as opposed to the nomothetic approach which dominates in psychology (Smith et al., 1995). In a nomothetic study, analysis is at the level of groups and populations and only probabilistic claims about individuals can be made – for example, that there is a 70 per cent chance that person X will respond in this way. In an idiographic study, because it has been derived from the examination of individual case studies, it is also possible to make specific statements about those individuals. Thus, for IPA, the analysis always begins with the detailed reading of the single case. The case can then be written up as a **case study** or else the researcher then moves to an equally attentive analysis of the second case and so on. Assuming the analysis is of a group of individuals, a good IPA study will always allow itself to be parsed in two different ways. It should be possible to learn something about both the important generic themes in the analysis but also still about the narrative life world of the particular participants who have told their stories. For more on the theoretical foundations of IPA, see Smith (1996, 2004).

Over the past ten years, IPA has developed into a fully articulated qualitative psychological approach and it is possible to identify particular themes from the body of published work which, it can be argued, is a consequence of IPA's focus on how people think about and understand significant events and people in their lives. These themes include a focus on participants' **meaning-making** and interpretation, a concern with **identity** and a sense of self and an attention to bodily feeling within lived experience.

Research questions, sampling and data collection

As has been stated above, IPA is concerned with the in-depth exploration of personal and lived experience of the individual and with how he/she is making sense of that lived experience. This therefore helps define the type of research question that is suitable for an IPA study. Box 3.1 illustrates some specific research questions that guided IPA projects and which have resulted in subsequent publication.

Box 3.1   EXAMPLES OF PSYCHOLOGICAL RESEARCH QUESTIONS ADDRESSED IN IPA STUDIES

- How does being HIV impact on personal relationships? (Jarman et al., 2005)
- How do people with genetic conditions view changing medical technologies? (Chapman, 2002)
- What role, if any, do spiritual beliefs play in helping older people come to terms with the death of a partner? (Golsworthy and Coyle, 1999)
- How do parents experience a rare illness affecting their child? (Smith et al., 2006)
- What theoretical models are used by mental health nurses? (Carradice et al., 2002)

As can be seen, IPA studies are usually concerned with 'big questions', questions of considerable importance to the participant either on an ongoing basis or at a particular critical juncture. Often these issues are transformative and often they are about identity because individual accounts of significant experiences or events almost always impact on personal and social identity. IPA studies can be concerned with questions which are apparently quite particular or well defined (e.g., how does a person decide whether to take a genetic test or not?) or much broader (e.g., how will changing career affect this person's life more generally?). IPA questions can tap into 'hot cognition', engaging with issues that are urgent, emotive and dilemmatic, or 'cool cognition', involving longer-term reflection across the life course. Studies can be single snap shots or can follow participants longitudinally. What all of these studies and all of these research questions would have in common is a concern with the detailed exploration of the personal and social experience of the participant in the study.

IPA studies are conducted with relatively small sample sizes. The priority is to do justice to each case and the detailed case-by-case analysis of individual transcripts or accounts takes a long time. This means that, early on, the researcher needs to make some crucial choices, asking him/herself 'Do I want to say something detailed and nuanced about the particular person or do I want to say something more general about groups and populations?' Methodology and design will then follow from the answer to that question. Sometimes students try to 'play safe' by having a larger sample size, hoping they will therefore overcome the anxieties of examiners who might be more comfortable with quantitative research. In our experience, this almost always misfires: it is too easy to end up in the trap of being swamped with data and only producing a superficial qualitative analysis but still not having an adequate sample to satisfy quantitative criteria.

Before continuing on the question of sample size, we should say that recently we have increasingly been arguing the case for a sample of one (see, for example, Smith, 2004). Consequently, there is a growing number of published single person case studies on topics which include the experience of living with Parkinson's disease (Bramley and Eatough, 2005), the subjective experience of anger (Eatough and Smith, 2006), genetic testing (Smith et al., 2000) and consensual, sadomasochistic and dominant–submissive sexual games (Weille, 2002). This is indeed a logical step if the idiographic project is taken seriously. The single case study has been sorely neglected in psychology (Radley and Chamberlain, 2001; Smith, 1993; Yin, 1989) and we would argue that it has an important intellectual role to play in its own right. Of course, if work is being submitted for a degree, conducting a single case study is a high-risk strategy and should not be undertaken lightly. Pragmatically, it makes sense to be careful in the selection of the case that is put under such intense scrutiny. However increasingly postgraduate students are finding that there is value in sticking with a fascinating, troubling, complex case and attempting to do justice to it in its own right before moving on to another.

The value of a detailed case study like this is two fold. Obviously a great deal is learned about that particular person and his/her response to this specific situation. There is also space to see connections between different aspects of the participant's account. However, Warnock (1987) makes the important and profound point that delving deeper into the particular also takes us closer to the universal. We are thus better positioned to think about how we and other people might deal with the particular situation being explored, how at the deepest level we share a great deal with a person whose personal circumstances may at face value seem entirely separate and different from our own. Thus in some ways the detail of the individual also brings us closer to significant aspects of the general; connecting with his/her individual unique life also connects with a shared humanity.

However, assuming you resist the temptation of sticking with a single case study, how many participants should be included? There is no *right* answer to this question. It partly depends on the degree of commitment to the case study level of analysis and reporting, the richness of the individual cases and the constraints in operation. IPA studies have been published with samples ranging from one to 42 with the norm being towards the lower end. There seems to have been some convergence in clinical and health psychology postgraduate programmes that six to eight is an appropriate number for an IPA study (Turpin et al., 1997). For the present, we think this is acceptable. It provides enough cases to examine similarities and differences between participants but not so many that the researcher is in danger of being overwhelmed by the amount of data generated. However, it is important that a certain figure or band does not become a fixed expectation. As we have said above, in certain cases, an 'n of 1' can be argued for; in other cases, a detailed examination of convergences and divergences within a set of three cases would be the best way to proceed. Our experience tells us that a set of three cases works very well for undergraduate projects, encouraging students to do justice to the data and at the same time giving them a sense of how patterns can be discerned across the material.

IPA researchers usually try to find a fairly homogenous sample. The basic logic is that if you are interviewing, for example, six participants, it is not very helpful to think in terms of random or representative sampling. IPA therefore goes in the opposite direction and, through purposive sampling, finds a more closely defined group for whom the research question will be significant. How the specificity of a sample is defined will depend on the study. In some cases, the topic under investigation may itself be rare and/or under-researched and will thus define the boundaries of the relevant sample – for example, the experience of living with a rare genetic disorder such as juvenile Huntington's Disease. In other cases where a less specific issue is under investigation, the sample may be drawn from a population with similar demographic/socio-economic status profiles – for example, if you are interested in how people responded to government advice on healthy eating.

The logic is similar to that employed by the social anthropologist conducting ethnographic research in one particular community. The anthropologist then reports in detail about that particular culture but does not claim to be able to say something about all cultures. In time, of course, it will be possible for subsequent studies to be conducted with other groups and so gradually more general claims can be made but with each founded on the detailed examination of a set of case studies.

It is also possible to think in terms of theoretical rather than empirical generalizability. In this case, the reader makes links between the findings of an IPA study, his/her own personal and professional experience and the claims in the extant literature. The power of the IPA study is judged by the light it sheds within this broader context.

As ever, these issues must be tempered with a strong dose of pragmatism. Your research sample selects itself in the sense that potential participants are or should be free agents who choose to participate or not. So you may have to adapt or redraw the criteria for inclusion as it transpires that you are unable to persuade enough members of the originally defined group to agree to take part in your study.

What about the method of data collection? The vast majority of IPA studies have been conducted on data obtained from **semi-structured interviews** and this form of data collection might be considered the exemplary one for this type of research. The advantage of semi-structured interviewing for IPA is that the researcher is, in real time, in a position to follow up interesting and important issues that come up during the interview. However, it is important not to be doctrinaire about this. It is possible to collect rich verbal accounts by other means. For example, participants can be asked to write autobiographical or other personal accounts or to keep diaries for a period of time. The first author used all these forms of data collection during a study of the transition to motherhood and the diaries in particular were an important source for the analysis (Smith, 1999).

Semi-structured interviewing

The continuum of interviewing styles

Given that most IPA studies at present use one-to-one semi-structured interviewing, we will concentrate on the practicalities of this form of data collection here. However, it is also possible to conduct interviews with groups of participants, although this 'focus group' approach tends not to be used in IPA work because of the difficulty in tracking individual meaning-making in group interviews (for more on focus group interviewing, see Cronin, 2001; Millward, 2006). While it is probably obvious that semi-structured interviewing lies on a continuum from unstructured to structured, just what people mean by these terms can vary considerably. Therefore to assist in understanding the particular features of what IPA means by 'semi-structured', we will contrast it with structured interviewing.

The structured interview shares much of the rationale of the psychological experiment. Generally the investigator decides in advance exactly what constitutes the required data. Sometimes the investigator will provide the respondent with a set of possible answers to choose from and the questions are constructed in such a way as to elicit answers corresponding to and easily contained within predetermined categories which can then be numerically analysed. In other cases the respondent is allowed a free response which can then be categorized subsequently. In order to enhance reliability, the interviewer is supposed to stick closely to the interview schedule and behave with as little variation as possible between interviews. While the structured interview offers maximal control to the investigator, the format clearly puts considerable constraints on the encounter between researcher and participant.

With semi-structured interviews, the investigator will have a set of questions on a schedule but the interview will be *guided* by the schedule rather than dictated by it, so the order of asking questions is less important. The interviewer is freer to probe interesting areas that arise and can follow the participant's interests or concerns.

These differences follow from the basic concerns of IPA. The investigator has an idea of the area of interest and some questions to pursue. At the same time, there is a wish to try and enter the psychological and social world of the participant as far as is possible. Therefore the participant is an active agent in shaping how the interview goes. The participant can be seen as the experiential expert and should therefore be allowed maximum opportunity to tell his/her own story. Of course, this form of interviewing reduces the control the investigator has over the situation.

Constructing the interview schedule

Although a researcher conducting a semi-structured interview is likely to see it as a co-determined interaction in its own right, it is still important when working in this way to produce an interview schedule in advance. Why? Producing a schedule beforehand forces you to think explicitly about what you think/hope the interview might cover. It also enables you to think of difficulties that might be encountered – for example, in terms of question wording or addressing sensitive issues – and to give some thought to how these difficulties might be handled. When it comes to the interview itself, having thought in advance about the different ways the interview may proceed allows you to concentrate more thoroughly and more confidently on what the participant is actually saying. As an example, Box 3.2 presents the first half of a schedule from a project of the authors on women's experience of anger and aggression.

Box 3.2   INTERVIEW SCHEDULE (ABRIDGED)

1   Can you tell me about what your life was like as a child and when you were growing up?
    Prompt: Might want focus on particular age points (child/teenager/young adult) and contexts (family/school/college/work/relationships).
    What about more recently?
2   Can you tell me about times when you have been involved in a conflictual situation when you were growing up?

(Continued)

> Prompt: Maybe focus on particular age points/contexts (family/school, etc.) description/cause/protagonist/actions/affect/cognitive response, then What about more recently?

3 Can you tell me what the word 'anger' means to you?

4 Can you tell me about times when you've been angry when you were growing up?

> Prompt: Maybe focus on particular age points/contexts (family/school, etc.) description/cause/protagonist/actions/affect/cognitive response, then What about more recently?

5 Can you tell me how you have acted on that anger?

> Prompt: age points/contexts.

In this type of interviewing, you as the interviewer are trying to encourage the person to speak about the topic with as little prompting as possible from you. Good interview technique therefore often involves a gentle nudge from the interviewer rather than being too explicit. You may well find that, in the course of constructing your schedule, your first draft questions are too explicit (for example, 'How bad did you feel when you were made redundant?'). With redrafting, these become gentler and less loaded but sufficient to let the participant know what the area of interest is and to recognize that they have something to say about it (e.g., 'Can you describe the day you were made redundant, starting with when you first became aware it might happen?'). The intention is to assure the participant of the value of what they have to say about the topic in the context of their lives in order to facilitate the giving of rich experiential accounts.

Sometimes participants may have difficulties in understanding or responding to questions. For example, for some, a particular question may be too open. To prepare for this, you can construct prompts which are framed more explicitly. Indeed some of your first draft questions may be able to act as these prompts. You do not have to prepare prompts for every question – only those where you anticipate there may be some difficulty and where this cannot be easily addressed by rewording the question. So, for example, in Box 3.2, question 1 has prompts relating to areas the participant may wish to consider. Questions 2 and 4 have a set of reminders to the interviewer of domains that it may be useful to ask the participant about.

Thus the interviewer starts with the most general possible question and hopes that this will be sufficient to enable the participant to talk about the subject. If the participant has difficulty, says he/she does not understand or gives a short or tangential reply, then the interviewer can move to the prompt which is more specific. Hopefully this will be enough to get the participant talking. The more specific level questions are there to deal with more difficult cases where the participant is more hesitant. It is likely that a successful interview will include questions and answers at both general and more specific levels and will move between the two fairly seamlessly.

Having constructed your schedule, you should learn it by heart – like a play script – before beginning to interview so, when it comes to the interview, the schedule acts as a mental prompt, if needed, and not something to which you are constantly referring.

Interviewing

Semi-structured interviews generally last for an hour or more and can become intense and involved, depending on the particular topic. It is therefore advisable to try to ensure that the interview can proceed without interruption as far as possible, so it is usually better to conduct the interview with the participant on their own. Of course there will be exceptions to this. For example, this may not be advisable or possible with young children. Where the interview takes place can also affect the ambience. People usually feel most comfortable in a setting they are familiar with – for example, in their own home – but again there may be times where this is not practicable or appropriate.

At the beginning of the interview, you need to put the participant at ease, to enable her/him to feel comfortable talking to you before any of the substantive areas of the schedule are introduced. Hopefully then, this positive and responsive 'set' will continue through the interview.

The interview does not have to follow the sequence on the schedule nor does every question have to be asked or asked in exactly the same way of each participant. Thus the interviewer may decide that it would be appropriate to ask a question earlier than it appears on the schedule because it follows on from something the participant has just said. Similarly how a question is phrased and how explicit it is will partly depend on how the interviewer feels the participant is responding.

The interview may well move away from the questions on the schedule. It is quite possible that the interview may enter an area that had not been predicted by the investigator but which is extremely pertinent to and enlightening of the project's overall question. Indeed these novel avenues are often the most valuable, precisely because they have come unprompted from the participant and therefore are likely to be of particular importance for him/her. On the other hand, of course, the interviewer needs to ensure the conversation does not move too far away from the agreed topic.

It is important to try to establish a slow and comfortable pace to the interview. Try not to rush in too quickly. Give the participant time to finish answering a question before moving on. Often the most interesting questions need some time to respond to and fuller answers may be missed if the interviewer jumps in too quickly. Also ask one question at a time. Multiple questions can be difficult for the participant to unpick.

Finally you need to monitor how the interview is affecting the participant. It may be that the participant feels uncomfortable with a particular line of questioning and this may be expressed in their non-verbal behaviour or in how they reply. You need to be ready to respond to this, for example, by backing off and trying again more gently or deciding it would be inappropriate to pursue this area with this participant. For more on interviewing, see Burgess (1984), Kvale (1996) and Taylor and Bogdan (1998).

For IPA, it is necessary to record (on audio tape or by using digital recording equipment which gives a much clearer recording) and transcribe the whole interview, including the talk of the interviewer. Leave a wide enough margin on both sides of the transcript to make your analytic comments. However, for IPA, you do not need the more detailed transcription of prosodic features of the talk which are required in conversation analysis (Drew, 2003) and in some forms of discourse analysis. Transcription of tapes takes a long time, depending on the clarity of the recording and one's typing proficiency. As a rough guide, you need to allow at least seven hours of transcription time per hour of interview.

Analysis

IPA is not a prescriptive approach; rather it provides a set of flexible guidelines which can be adapted by individual researchers in light of their research aims. This is particularly true when it comes to analysis. This section describes the analytic steps we went through in the anger and aggression study in order to help the reader to see how the analysis unfolds but this should not be treated as the 'correct recipe' for doing IPA. Rather it should simply be seen as an illustration of *one* way of doing it.

This project was a detailed, idiographic examination of participants' experience of anger and aggression, its interpersonal context and models of etiology. In brief, the analytic stages involved (a) several close and detailed readings of the data to obtain a holistic perspective so that future interpretations remained grounded within the participants' accounts; (b) initial themes were identified and organized into clusters and checked against the data; (c) themes were then refined, condensed and examined for connections between them; (d) a narrative account of the interplay between the interpretative activity of the researcher and the participants' account of their experiences in their own words was produced (Smith and Osborn, 2003).

The stages used throughout the analysis were as follows and were applied to the transcript of each participant. First, during transcription, the interviewer kept a record of initial thoughts, comments and points of potential significance. It was felt that these might be useful to return to and check against later interpretations during analysis. Second, each transcript was read several times and the left hand margin was used to make notes on anything that appeared significant and of interest. With each reading, the researcher should expect to feel more immersed in the data, becoming more responsive to what is being said. This stage is like a free textual analysis; notes may take the form of comments on the use of particular language styles or forms, initial attempts to spell out what the participant means and identification of convergences and contradictions in his/her talk.

The following extract demonstrates this stage of analysis for a small section of the interview with Debbie (a pseudonym) who was the first woman interviewed. The interviewer ('Int.') is responding to a topic introduced by the participant:

	Int. Can you tell me about an argument with your sister?
	Debbie: I've got a system, I mean I do it now, I always wash glasses first and my sister just came along with cups full of tea and coffee and poured them straight into
Lost my temper – instant	the sink and I just lost my temper. I just remember I
Anger	was so angry with her I wasn't going to let her push
Switched roles – Debbie the aggressor	me around any more that I just did a role reversal
	with her. And I just sort of pinned her against the
Physical aggression	wall and started slamming her head against the wall
Wants her sister to feel the same	to see how she felt like, to see what it felt like to her.
	Int. What happened next?
	Debbie: I don't know whether it was because I'd done it to
Broke into tears	my sister but I just broke up into tears and I just had
Get out – desire to escape	to *get out*. I mean, I've never had a fight with my
Verbal aggression	sister like that since. We have like verbal fights but
	I just felt like, I had a lot of mixed emotions after
Felt happy	I'd done that. I felt happy that I'd stuck up to myself
Felt annoyed	with her but I also felt annoyed with myself because
Felt happy again	I'd hurt her and then I felt happy again because
Wants sister to feel like her	she'd got a taste of her own medicine and knew
	how I felt. It's dead weird. I'd so many emotions in
Multiple emotions	one go that I'd never felt so many at the same time
Strange, unusual experience	before. It was a really strange feeling. But I broke
Tears	down into tears and I knew then I had to get out.
Left the situation	And I just went for a walk.

The next stage involved returning to the transcript and using the right hand margin to transform initial notes and ideas into more specific **themes** or phrases. This stage calls upon psychological concepts and abstractions. The researcher is attempting to capture more concisely the psychological quality inherent in the initial notes and in the participant's own words. Caution is essential at this point so that the connection between the participant's own words and the researcher's interpretations is not lost:

Int.   Can you tell me about an argument with your sister?

Debbie: I've got a system, I mean I do it now, I always wash
               glasses first and my sister just came along with cups
               full of tea and coffee and poured them straight into   *Rapid emotional*

	the sink and I just lost my temper. I just remember	*shift into anger*
	I was so angry with her I wasn't going to let her push	
	me around any more that I just did a role reversal with her.	*Power dynamics*
	And I just sort of pinned her against the wall and started	
	slamming her head against the wall to see how she felt like,	*Physical aggression*
	to see what it felt like to her.	
Int.	What happened next?	
Debbie:	I don't know whether it was because I'd done it to my	
	sister but I just broke up into tears and I just had to *get out.*	*Crying*
	I mean, I've never had a fight with my sister like that since.	*Desire for escape*
	We have like verbal fights but I just felt like, I had a lot of	*Verbal aggression*
	mixed emotions after I'd done that. I felt happy that I'd	
	stuck up to myself with her but I also felt annoyed with	*Conflicting emotions*
	myself because I'd hurt her and then I felt happy again	*Projection of self-*
	because she'd got a taste of her own medicine and knew	*feelings*
	how I felt. It's dead weird. I'd so many emotions in one go	
	that I'd never felt so many at the same time before. It was a	*Multiple emotions*
	really strange feeling. But I broke down into tears and I	*Crying*
	knew then I had to get out. And I just went for a walk.	*Avoidance*

The next stage consists of further 'reducing' the data by establishing connections between the preliminary themes and clustering them appropriately (see Box 3.3). As part of this process, you can 'imagine a magnet with some of the themes pulling others in and helping to make sense of them' (Smith, 2004: 71). This process is inevitably selective so that some of the themes may be dropped either because they do not fit well with the emerging structure or because, within the emerging analysis, they do not have a strong enough evidence base.

Box 3.3   CLUSTERING OF THEMES

Physical aggression
Verbal aggression

Rapid emotional shift into anger
Crying
Conflicting/multiple emotions
Desire for escape

Power dynamics
Projection of self-feelings

Finally, a Table is produced which shows each superordinate theme and the themes which comprise it (see Box 3.4). These clusters are given a descriptive label (superordinate theme title), which conveys the conceptual nature of the themes therein. Key words from the participant are used as reminders of what prompted the themes.

This Table is the outcome of an iterative process in which the researcher has moved back and forth between the various analytic stages ensuring that the integrity of what the participant said has been preserved as far as possible. If the researcher has been successful, it should be possible for someone else to track the analytic journey from the raw data through to the end Table. This is referred to as an independent audit (Smith and Osborn, 2003). It is also the case that during this process, the analysis becomes more interpretative as the researcher is coming to a more integrated sense-making of the participant's experience. As the interpretation continues, the researcher is likely to draw on their mental set of psychological constructs to help the sense-making process. However in IPA it is important that the participant's account is always attended to carefully, always kept foregrounded and that any psychological theory is drawn on because it is triggered by the personal account (see Smith, 2004, for more on levels of interpretation in IPA). Only after we felt some measure of gestalt had been reached for each participant was a cross case analysis carried out and a final Table of superordinate themes put together which represented the whole data set. For more details of this cross case analysis, see Smith and Osborn (2003). Because IPA has an idiographic commitment, the researcher should – even when presenting an analysis from a number of participants – endeavour to convey some of the details of the individual experience of those participants.

Box 3.4   FINAL TABLE OF THEMES

Forms of aggression

Physical aggression	*I just sort of pinned her against the wall*
Verbal aggression	*We have like verbal fights*

The anger experience

Rapid emotional shift into anger	*I just lost my temper*
Crying	*I just broke up into tears*
Conflicting/multiple emotions	*I'd so many emotions in one go*

Relationship between self and other

Power dynamics	*I just did a role reversal with her*
Projection of self-feelings	*She'd got a taste of her own medicine*

Analysis continues into the formal process of writing up a narrative account of the interplay between the interpretative activity of the researcher and the participant's account of their experience in their own words. The aim is to provide a close textual reading of the participant's account, moving between description and different levels of **interpretation**, at all times clearly differentiating between account and interpretation. Enough data should be presented for the reader to assess the usefulness of the interpretations. Box 3.5 shows a very short piece from the final write-up; within it is the extract from Debbie which helped generate one of the themes illustrated in Box 3.4. The extract comes from the middle of the write-up and begins with some consideration of a different participant, Angela, before moving to Debbie. For a more complete example of how an analysis might be written up, see Report 1 in Appendix 2 in this volume.

Box 3.5   SHORT EXCERPT FROM FINAL WRITE-UP

When emotions are felt intensely, such as extreme anger and grief, they can feel unbearable:

> I was thinking I want to get rid of this anger and I think what do I do so I just lay in the bed and I could feel it building up and my heart was killing me.

Angela's anger combined with her grief at the loss of her child is deeply felt. The experience is centred in her heart and she indicates that the experience is one of actual physical pain. Feeling several emotions at a single time is a tumultuous experience in itself. The effect is one of confusion, which is enhanced when the emotions are antagonistic:

> I had a lot of mixed emotions after I'd done that. I felt happy that I'd stuck up to myself with her [sic] but I also felt annoyed with myself because I'd hurt her I and then I felt happy again because she got a taste of her own medicine and knew how I felt. It's dead weird. I'd so many emotions in one go that I'd never felt so many at the same time before. It was a really strange feeling.

In this extract, Debbie is describing how she felt after a fight with her sister. As with the previous episode, happiness accompanied anger but there is a lot more going on besides. Debbie has conflicting feelings, which shift from annoyance to satisfaction and it appears that some form of internal dissonance ('weird' and 'strange') further complicates the emotional confusion.

Summary

This chapter has:

- presented the theoretical foundations for IPA – phenomenology, hermeneutics and idiography
- considered how to design an IPA study – appropriate research questions, sampling and data collection
- illustrated how to conduct an IPA analysis.

The chapter began with a presentation of the theoretical underpinnings of IPA and then went on to consider practical procedures, illustrated with material from one of our own studies. We hope that the reader now feels he or she knows something of the particular qualities of IPA, a sense which will be facilitated by a comparison with the other approaches in this book. Hopefully too, after reading this chapter, the empirical presentation in Chapter 4 and the IPA study in Appendix 2, some readers will feel inspired and more confident to have a go at conducting an IPA project themselves.

Further reading

For more on the theoretical basis of IPA, see Smith (1996, 2004). For more on the more general intellectual context for this type of qualitative work, see Ashworth (2003). For more on the practicalities of doing IPA, see Smith and Osborn (2003) and Smith and Dunworth (2003). For examples of IPA studies, see the references in Box 3.1.

4

DOING INTERPRETATIVE PHENOMENOLOGICAL ANALYSIS

Lesley Storey

This chapter presents an account of one researcher's experience of working in an analytic group which applied the principles of interpretative phenomenological analysis (IPA) to one interview transcript. This interview had been conducted with an ex-solider and examined his experiences of being in and leaving the army and his post-army life. The chapter describes the application of the different steps in IPA, illustrating these with reference to the data, and offers some reflections upon the analytic process. It also considers some broader issues raised by IPA, such as the role of theory in the analysis.

Key terms

connections	superordinate themes
interpretative frameworks	themes
notes	transparency
overall theme	

Introduction

Qualitative methods have a number of advantages over quantitative methods in some areas of research. As Willig (2001: 9) has pointed out, they are concerned with meaning, sense-making and subjective experience rather than the 'imposition of preconceived "variables."' Qualitative methods involving interaction between researchers and participants (usually face-to-face interaction in individual or group interview contexts) avoid the need to specify the meaning of core research concerns in advance. Instead, participants can determine (and revise) these meanings themselves during data collection and, in that process, potentially contest the researcher's interpretations of these core concerns. This openness and dialogue (which, of course, is not intrinsic to qualitative methods but depends upon the researcher's skills) also mean that the researcher is less likely to misinterpret participants' responses.

In this chapter, I discuss aspects of these advantages in relation to interpretative phenomenological analysis (IPA). I then focus on the practicalities of applying IPA to interview data from an ex-soldier which examined his experiences of being in and leaving the army and his post-army life (see Appendix 1 in this volume). Thus the chapter considers what it was like to apply the principles outlined by Jonathan A. Smith and Virginia Eatough in Chapter 3 and offers some 'hands-on' observations from the research 'coalface'. For this analysis, I worked as part of a group of six female researchers of different ages from different educational establishments who had not met prior to working on the data over the course of two days. We had different levels of experience with qualitative research in general and with IPA specifically. Throughout this chapter, although I talk about the work of our group, these are my personal interpretations of the group process and other group members may have interpreted the group's processes in a different but equally valid way.

It is worth noting that, early in the analytic task, the group decided to focus attention on one interview transcript because we felt that, within the limited analytic time available to us, we would have difficulty in completing a meaningful analysis of more than one transcript. The adoption of a case study approach accords readily with the idiographic commitment of IPA, which, when aiming for a group-level analysis, begins with the analysis of an individual case and moves from there to the analysis of further cases. Therefore we felt that this chapter would provide readers who have not used IPA before (and who are considering applying it to more than one transcript in a non-case-study analysis) with a good sense of what it may be like to conduct the important first analysis in the IPA process.

Stage 1: Initial readings of the transcript

One of the most challenging aspects of dealing with qualitative data can be knowing how and where to start. Often the researcher is presented with a mass of text which can feel overwhelming and it can seem an impossible task to find any sort of coherent meaning in the transcript (this may sometimes also be due to the nature of the data: see Box 4.1). The identification of central concerns within the data is a principal aim of many versions of qualitative analysis (e.g., in the form of superordinate themes in IPA, core categories in grounded theory and narrative themes in narrative analysis). Even in discourse analysis, with its concern with variability across and within the data set, there is a need to identify commonalities and significant points of construction and rhetorical function that can constitute themes within the analysis (see Chapter 7 in this volume). IPA offers a series of steps – albeit not in a prescriptive way – that are designed to allow the analyst to identify central concerns within the data.

Therefore, even if their data set appears overwhelming and even if they initially doubt whether they will ever be able to discern coherent meaning in it and present this as superordinate themes, it is important for the analyst to trust the analytic process and trust that eventually meaning will be created from the data; otherwise they may never dare to begin the analysis!

Box 4.1   DEALING WITH FRAGMENTED INTERVIEW DATA

Some interview transcripts can be quite fragmented, with the participant covering many seemingly unrelated issues, darting from issue to issue and apparently contradicting him/herself. This can result from a poorly focused interview guide or interview schedule, in which case the guide/schedule can be revised before the next interview if the project is still in progress. However, it may also happen with a well-organized guide/schedule, despite the interviewer having done his/her best to keep the participant focused on the research topic. Most qualitative researchers will attempt to do this with a lightness of touch, trying to strike a balance between ensuring that the issues specified on the interview guide/schedule are covered and allowing the participant to identify and pursue issues relevant to the research topic that were not considered when the guide/schedule was compiled. Still, some research participants may use the interview setting as a chance to rehearse other issues that are either unrelated or only tangentially related to the research topic. This may occur if the participants are suffering from a physiological, neurological or psychological disorder that has detrimentally affected their processing and attentional capacities. It may also occur if the research is dealing with a particular aspect of a topic that might be considered sensitive and if the participant has never or seldom had the opportunity to discuss the general topic with an attentive listener before. In this case, the participant may wish to relate *all* of their experience and may have difficulty in organizing such substantial information. As well as following standard ethical procedures during the interview and revisiting recruitment criteria for future interviews (Coyle and Olsen, 2005), the researcher may subsequently have to apply the analytic procedures to the transcript to whatever extent is possible or, in a worst case scenario, disregard highly fragmented interview data. The interview transcript analysed in this chapter posed no such problems.

IPA starts with an iterative process of reading and re-reading a transcript with a view to getting an overall 'feel' for the interview. This may result in the identification of an **overall theme** which encapsulates the whole interview, though it is rare that the complexities of human experience can be so easily and immediately summed up. With the transcript of the interview with David, despite the fact that we were analysing data that we had not collected, our emotional reactions to him were of different strengths and valences as a result of the account that he provided in the interview. It is possible that these reactions were a result of varying degrees of identification with David and his circumstances. Identification can potentially cause problems in analysis: an over-identification with an interviewee on the basis of shared or analogous experiences may lead the analyst to force the data to conform to *his/her* experiences or a negative disidentification with the interviewee can make it difficult to empathize (or at least sympathize) with the interviewee and thus attain the sort of 'insider' perspective on the research topic to which IPA aspires.

The analysts' predominant reaction to the transcript was one of sadness for David who seemed to have been abandoned by the army which had been his home for many years. However, our sadness was counterbalanced by frustration, as David seemed to feel that all his problems would be solved if only he were able to return to army life. We discussed the fact that these reactions were very much *our* reactions to the data, whereas we had initially hoped to identify a clear 'feel' for the transcript from David's perspective. Nevertheless, we felt that it was useful to have identified these responses and to have considered their origins because this alerted us to aspects of the **interpretative frameworks** which we would bring to bear upon the data. We were able to consider how some aspects might prove useful in the analytic process in terms of furthering our understanding of David's experiences and how others might prove problematic and would have to be closely monitored (e.g., in causing us to dismiss some of David's reactions to the situations he described). This process of reflecting upon and acknowledging the interpretative framework that the analyst applies to the data is important as it helps to increase the **transparency** of the analysis, although some aspects of an analyst's framework may be unconscious and so may not be readily identifiable by him/her. We were fortunate to have had a group context in which to consider these issues and question each other closely and we wondered about the extent to which we could have done this if we had been working alone.

Following the initial reading, the analysis continued by re-reading the transcript to produce wide-ranging **notes** that arose as responses to the text; we carried out this task as a group. These notes/questions were recorded in the left-hand margin of the transcript. For example, the powerful passage in which David referred metaphorically to seeing ghosts (lines 105–107) elicited the words 'death' and 'bereavement', although we were not clear at this stage who we felt had died or been bereaved.

In Box 4.1, it was noted that data can sometimes be fragmented and contradictory. However, contradictions can be discerned in many interviews without this being associated with problematic fragmentation. One observation that the group made following the initial reading related to the contradictions that analysts had observed within David's account. There were occasions when David identified a quality or a skill which had been useful in the army and which he had grown to value over the years. Sometimes consciously and in other places perhaps less consciously, the same quality or skill was represented as a handicap in the new, post-army phase of his life. There was a tragi-comic self-realization some way into the interview when David was talking about how having been in the army gave him a sense of self-confidence when it came to job interviews but he recognized some of the downsides:

> Where it hinders me is the fact that I like things in lines. I like things in neat pack-ages and so when I go – like when I was driving the truck, when I used to come back at night, I used to park all the wagons up so all the bumpers were level. (lines 238–241)

This attention to detail had undoubtedly been important in the regimented world of the army but it may have appeared unusual and may even have been negatively evaluated in a civilian context. At this stage, we simply noted this observation and set it aside as a possibly fruitful line of inquiry that might be followed later.

Stage 2: Identifying and labelling themes

The next stage of analysis involved returning to the transcript and using the notes that had previously been made in the left-hand margin to produce **themes** in the right-hand margin. This can involve using theoretical con-cepts to make maximum psychological sense of the data, although there is a need always to ensure a clear connection between themes and the data. Identifying themes in what the participant says and by using theoretical constructs to analyse the participant's phenomenology, the researcher takes the analytic process a step beyond a journalistic summarizing of the inter-view transcript.

However, we spent some time discussing the possible disadvantages of using theoretical constructs in our analysis. This was because some group members were concerned about the possibility of violating IPA's phenome-nological commitment if we were to over-emphasize its interpretative aspect and overwrite David's subjectivity with our pet theories. Other researchers who have used theory in IPA have faced the same dilemma concerning how best to avoid having it overwrite participants' phenomenologies in the analysis (see Box 4.2).

Box 4.2   STRATEGIES FOR USING THEORY IN IPA WORK

Researchers who have used IPA to analyse qualitative data and who wished to make explicit use of psychological theory in their analysis but also to avoid vio-lating participants' meaning-making have responded to this dilemma in various ways. The standard response has been to invoke theory when discussing the

(Continued)

> *(Continued)*
>
> findings arising from an analysis of participants' meaning-making undertaken, as far as possible, on their own terms (e.g., Flowers et al., 1997; Senior et al., 2002). Hence the theory does not influence the analysis in an explicit way but is invoked in a *post hoc* fashion. A variant of this has involved identifying a range of potential theoretical perspectives from which the data could be interpreted before the analysis began but refusing to privilege any single perspective in advance of engaging with the data (e.g., Vignoles et al., 2004). A more *a priori* theoretically committed approach has involved choosing a single theory in advance but using it to inform rather than drive the analysis (so no attempt is made to test the theory) (e.g., Coyle and Rafalin, 2000; Turner and Coyle, 2000). For more on the use of theory in qualitative research, see Anfara and Mertz (2006).

Ultimately we decided that, as we were conducting psychological research for a psychological audience, it was necessary to use concepts derived from psychological theory, where appropriate, in order to produce an analysis that would be credible and possibly useful to our audience. We adopted two strategies in order to reduce the risk of violating David's subjectivity. The first was to use theoretical constructs in an eclectic way in our interpretations rather than restrict ourselves to one particular theory because we felt that an over-investment in any single theory would make us more liable to squeeze David's data into that theory. 'Locus of control', 'possible selves', 'self-efficacy' and psychodynamic approaches were all suggested as possible theoretical concepts and approaches for making psychological sense of the data. Second, we resolved to ensure that any theoretical interpretation arose clearly from the data. As a result, during the analysis, I clearly recall the questions 'But is it in the text?' and 'Where does it say that in the transcript?' being voiced recurrently in relation to possible theoretical interpretations.

In the case of David's interview, there was one particular section of text which was interpreted from different theoretical perspectives. One of the issues which came up in discussion of the data was the way in which joining a total institution like the army at a relatively young age can create problems for soldiers when it comes to dealing with the complexities of adult life on discharge. Researchers operating from different theoretical perspectives interpreted this situation in terms of 'the army as mother', 'external locus of control', 'army as disempowering and emasculating', 'lack of self-efficacy' and 'external attribution of power'. It was exciting to pursue these interpretations and to see how far the data would allow us legitimately to 'stretch' them because we felt that here we were moving beyond a literal interpretation of the data into a more psychological interpretation. Nowhere in the transcript did David say that he saw the army as a substitute mother but he did ascribe to the army various nurturing qualities which are often associated with parenting, such as authority and the provision of protection, material shelter and comforts. It might be considered surprising that the group specified 'the army as mother' rather than 'the army as parent', especially as the stereotype of father as disciplinarian might seem closer to the army's image. However, David particularly commented on the deficits left by his mother's early death, and the practical skills which he said he had acquired in the army (such as cooking and cleaning) seemed to us to be more associated with a traditional maternal role. This allowed us to explore the idea that leaving the army was experienced by David as a form of extreme separation anxiety or even bereavement.

Following agreement on how to use theoretical constructs, we identified, as individuals, what we felt to be the most important themes in the transcript and then discussed them as a group. We all used different ways of describing themes and one of the major differences was in the level of analysis represented by our suggested theme titles. Some group members suggested very general themes such as 'loss', while others identified much more detailed themes around the specifics of the army's exit programme. Following discussion, we agreed on five initial themes, which were as follows:

- What the army gave David.
- What the army took away from David.
- The differences between army and civilian life.
- The similarities between army and civilian life.
- Identity transition as a work in progress/absence of closure.

We were aware that the aim of the interview had been to look at identity issues and we were concerned that only one of our themes at this stage seemed directly to concern identity. However, recognizing that an interview characterized by openness on the part of the interviewer may well elicit useful material which was not originally considered to be relevant to the research topic or research question(s), we decided to set this concern aside and concentrate on (our readings of) David's meaning-making in the transcript.

Stage 3: Linking themes and identifying thematic clusters

During this stage, **connections** were identified between the preliminary themes. This enabled us to amalgamate some themes and, where appropriate, to incorporate into other themes material from those themes which had been jettisoned. For example, we decided that the two themes concerning differences and similarities between army and civilian life fitted within the two themes concerning gains and losses associated with (leaving) army life. This was because the elements which we drew upon to provide examples of differences and similarities were actually illustrating the way in which David identified what he had gained and lost through (leaving) army life. For example, his sense that he had lost a sense of team membership when he left the army was exemplified by his identification of differences between the collective sense of 'team' in the army ('I was a member of a team and I was an important member of a team' – lines 17–18) and the more narrowly defined sense of 'team' in his civilian job ('You're not a team member within the school because you're not a teacher' – lines 48–49). We also felt that the provisional theme relating to 'Identity transition as a work in progress/absence of closure' was better dealt with as a sub-theme within a broader overarching theme entitled 'The end of a relationship'. We felt that this broad theme also allowed us to explore some of the emotional issues which had been raised and identified during the initial read-through of the transcript. So, our three final **superordinate themes** were as follows:

- What the army gave David.
- What the army took away from David.
- The end of a relationship.

We had some concerns that the first two themes might simply be two sides of the same coin and so one might turn out to be redundant or the themes might need to be combined. However, when we identified each theme's constituent sub-themes during the analysis, we found them to be sufficiently distinctive, with each relating to different aspects of the interview and, therefore, worthy of separate inclusion. This is a vital point because it showed us as a group how important it was to 'try out' an analysis in order to see whether or not it worked. If we could not identify data from the transcript to support a potential theme (or sub-theme), we dropped it.

We found the experiential aspect of the analytic exercise to be fundamental. We learned as much from actually doing the analysis and resolving analytic problems and dilemmas *in vivo* as we did from discussing it as a group. For example, we had initially identified 'absence of closure' as an overarching theme but we were only able to find one data extract which referred to this. We felt that this was a significant issue but would work better as a sub-theme rather than as a major theme.

Stage 4: Producing a summary table of themes with illustrative quotations

At the end of our analysis, we organized our superordinate themes into a Table, together with their constituent sub-themes and illustrative quotations (see Table 4.1).

Table 4.1 Superordinate themes and constituent sub-themes

Superordinate theme	Sub-themes	Example of illustrative quotation
Theme 1: What the army gave David	A sense of being someone special	
	A structure to his life which allowed him to plan	
	Confidence and pride	'It gave me more confidence. As a nipper when I joined the army, first I wasn't confident at all.' (lines 4–5)
	Sense of belonging and being part of a team	
	Parenting	
Theme 2: What the army took away from David	Health	
	Ability to relate to civilians	
	Practical skills	
	A future/sense of purpose	'sometimes I don't feel as though there's a purpose to it . . . thinking "What the hell am I doing here? Bugger this" . . . But I've got to do this yet again, today and tomorrow. And you think to yourself, "This is me for the rest of my life".' (lines 218–223)
	(Almost) his marriage	
Theme 3: The end of a relationship	Abandonment and betrayal	'Once you're out that gate, that's it. I know I can't even get back into the camp where, not ten minutes ago, I was a serving sergeant. I can't get back in. You know, you . . . it's like they're throwing you outside and locked the gate, you know, and that's it – you're on your own. That was painful.' (lines 95–99)
	Bereavement/death	
	No closure	

Presentation of the analysis in narrative form

A summary of the group's IPA analysis of the transcript is provided below. Given the time constraints under which we worked, this is not in any way intended to be read as a complete in-depth IPA analysis (for a much more extended and detailed example of such an analysis, see Report 1 in Appendix 2 in this volume). Rather, it is designed to convey the essence of our analysis of David's transcript and is presented in a simplified form. Each section starts with a superordinate theme, followed by sub-themes and then a brief discussion (see Box 4.3).

Box 4.3   THE STRUCTURE OF THE ANALYTIC NARRATIVE

The themes and associated quotations in our analytic narrative do not follow the chronology of the interview. Data from different parts of the transcript are used to exemplify any individual theme. There is a sense in which the interview is reconstructed to form a coherent analytic narrative, which is perfectly acceptable provided the meaning of data excerpts is not misrepresented or distorted. Great care needs to be taken with this because there can be a temptation to extort maximum evidence in support of a central or favoured theme by citing data out of context. As we reflected upon this in our analytic group, we realized that, if assessors of qualitative interview-based analyses have the core study's interview transcripts available to them, they would do well to check at least some of the quotations that have been used to illustrate themes to ensure that they have been used appropriately and have not been taken out of context.

Theme 1: What the army gave David

We know that David felt that the army gave him a lot and it was easy to identify these elements because they were clear and unambiguously stated. It gave him:

Sub-theme: A sense of being someone special

'I was an important member of a team and I was recognized as doing something for my country.' (lines 17–18)

Sub-theme: A structure to his life which allowed him to plan

'Like, we've got days when we're on exercise for a few weeks. Get there and you could plan your life. You knew you were going on exercise and you thought, um, you knew that 18 weekends out of the 52 . . . you knew you were going to kill a few beers and you knew you were going to have a good time.' (lines 313–317)

Sub-theme: Confidence and pride

'It gave me more confidence. As a nipper when I first joined the army, I wasn't confident at all.' (lines 4–5)

'so we were important and I was proud of that.' (lines 29–30)

The reference to having lacked confidence before joining the army would seem to be particularly relevant as it indicates that David does not have a positively evaluated prior possible self to draw on from his life before joining the army when it came to constructing a new identity in civilian life.

Sub-theme: Sense of belonging and being part of a team

> 'It's like, as I say, I had an identity and I belonged to somewhere.' (lines 22–23)

> 'I was a member of a team and I was an important member of a team.' (lines 17–18)

David compares his high status within his collective army team membership with his current position as a school caretaker. Having been a sergeant in the army and a member of the driving corps, he is now what he considers to be a lowly member of the school staff:

> 'You're not a team member within the school because you're not a teacher.' (lines 48–49)

> 'as if to say, "Ah, it's only the caretaker and his staff – they'll do it." It annoys me because being part of a team as we should be, as we were in the army, you know, we would have all helped right from the top all the way down.' (lines 54–57)

However, there is a suspicion that his memories of team spirit in the army are somewhat rose-tinted and later he does make a distinction between the way the officers and ordinary soldiers are treated at the end of the careers:

> 'You know, I think some of the officers at the top don't realize just how hard it is for someone to get out because I know when they finish, they don't really finish.' (lines 188–190)

Here we have an indication that it is not merely team membership that is important to him; it also matters which team he is a member of and what position he holds within that team's hierarchy.

Sub-theme: Parenting

> 'Yeah, I think I learned a great majority of them [values] being in the army. Ah, I wouldn't say I could have learned them at home because my mother died when I was young, when I was little, you know, um, so being brought up by my grandmother, right, I don't think she had a great deal of time so, so yeah, I think I got a lot of them being in the army.' (lines 69–74)

This nurturing also included training in practical skills which again he might otherwise have expected to have learned from his mother. There is something almost childlike in his listing of his practical skills, which is emphasized by his repeated use of the words 'I can':

> 'I can make my breakfast, I can make my dinner, I can sew, I can iron, I can wash.' (lines 208–209)

Theme 2: What the army took away from David

While we had a very strong sense that the army took away as much as it had given David, these losses were less explicitly stated and needed to be teased out from the text.

Sub-theme: Health

'I got damaged knees and other things and I'm knackered.' (lines 122–123)

Sub-theme: Ability to relate to civilians

'Well one of the reasons why I think I was moonlighting was to get to know my civilian counterparts and try and get into how they thought and how they worked and how they operated.' (lines 368–370)

David presents this as though he were an anthropologist exploring an alien civilization. He puts this in stronger terms a few lines later and emphasizes his sense of being excluded by his use of a simile in which he likens his attempts to join a civilian organization (in this case as a lorry driver) to those of a Black person trying to join a racist organization:

'it's how can I put it, a bit like a Black trying to join the Klu Klux Klan [sic], you know.' (lines 375–376)

Sub-theme: Practical skills   While we see above that the army provided him with the skills needed by a young person which he might not otherwise have learned, having lost his mother at an early age, later on it became clear that the army did not give him the practical skills to enable him to take on a more adult role outside the army. He discovered this in dramatic terms when buying a house:

'You just had to go out and try and find your own feet and make lots of mistakes – expensive ones at that.' (lines 261–263)

'what you see on paper and what happens on the ground are two different things. Um, we bought a house and it collapsed and we lost everything.' (lines 271–273)

Sub-theme: A future/sense of purpose

'sometimes I don't feel as though there's a purpose to it . . . thinking "What the hell am I doing here? Bugger this" . . . But I've got to do this yet again, today and tomorrow. And you think to yourself, "This is me for the rest of my life."' (lines 218–223)

Earlier in the interview, David had described how he had known exactly what lay ahead when he was in the army, which had enabled him to plan and had been evaluated in positive terms. However, knowing what the future holds for him in his present job is seen negatively. This suggests that it is not simply the ability to plan which is important to him: the content of the plan is equally significant.

Sub-theme: (Almost) His marriage

'I tended to be a little wild for about a couple of months after I got out, which one does. Uh, it nearly broke the marriage up at one stage.' (lines 135–137)

Our research group was entirely female and we were all struck by the paucity of references by David to his wife and children: they are practically invisible in the transcript. The fact that the difficulties he experienced after leaving the army jeopardized his marriage was dealt with in only one sentence – something that did not endear him to us. I do not know whether it was solely gender that prompted this reaction, despite comments such as 'typical man' from group members, but we did have to work to find strong grounds for empathizing with David after this. Once again, this offers an example of how the reactions that data elicit in an analyst need to be monitored and worked with if it is felt that they could adversely affect the analysis. Here, our reaction served to alert us to the near-absence of references to David's wife and children in the data.

Theme 3: The end of a relationship

Having discussed earlier the contention that the army gave him a sense of parenting which had been missing following the premature death of his mother, there is also a sense that, for David, leaving the army had much more emotional significance than might be associated simply with the end of a career. The sub-themes, which are discussed here, all relate to emotions commonly felt at the end of a deeply important personal relationship. Having theorized that the army fulfilled a motherly role for him, it seems therefore that having to leave the army against his will (we infer because of restructuring) has resulted in a sense of a second bereavement with which he has not yet come to terms.

Sub-theme: Abandonment and betrayal

> 'Once you're out that gate, that's it. I know I can't even get back into the camp where, not ten minutes ago, I was a serving sergeant. I can't get back in. You know, you . . . it's like they're throwing you outside and locked the gate, you know, and that's it – you're on your own. That was painful.' (lines 95–99)

> 'And you know they don't realize that you've given the best time of your life to them and you give, which I did, I gave 150 per cent.' (lines 120–122)

There is no sense in the interview that David left the army of his own volition. He specifies that his demobbing was under 'Options for change' but there is a very strong flavour of having been abandoned and indeed betrayed by the army. There is a very strong visual image generated by being locked out and physically excluded from the army premises showing how, despite attempts at negotiating a transition from army to civilian life, there comes a point at which the separation is crystallized and becomes final.

Sub-theme: Bereavement/death

> 'like we were saying, you walk round and you walk down the street and you see ghosts. You know, you walk down the streets where you walked down as a serving soldier and you can see all these ghosts.' (lines 105–107)

David does not use the words 'death' or 'bereavement' to describe his feelings but he does refer twice to seeing ghosts. We interpreted this as the ghost of his former life but it also sets up a metaphorical separation between the world of the dead and the world of the living and we felt that David felt himself to be more dead than alive.

Sub-theme: No closure

'I think we're still in the army.' (line 461)

This statement comes very near the end of the interview and seems to indicate clearly that, despite his articulate way of describing his situation, it is a situation which has not yet been resolved, emphasized by his use of the present tense. In Chapter 3 in this volume, Jonathan A. Smith and Virginia Eatough state that 'a detailed IPA analysis can also involve standing a little back from the participant and asking curious and critical questions of their accounts – for example, "What is the person trying to achieve here?", "Is something leaking out here that wasn't intended?", "Do I have a sense of something going on here that maybe the person him/herself is less aware of?"' On the whole we were cautious about reading too much into the words of the interviewee but in this case we felt that David's statement about still being in the army possibly indicated a need for psychological closure. We felt it was possible that, because in the interview he focuses on the practical problems of leaving the army, he has not yet had an opportunity or the support he needs to address the emotional legacy of leaving the army.

Our outline of our analysis ends here. Usually in IPA work, having analysed the first transcript, the researcher would proceed to analyse transcripts from other interviewees, conduct cross case comparisons and produce a final group-level table of superordinate themes. However, here we opted to focus on one case only and, in doing so, developed a real familiarity and engagement with his story, even within the relatively short time for which we worked on the data. I hope that my reflections on our analysis will provide both guidance and reassurance to those who are considering using IPA in their own research in the future.

Summary

This chapter has focused on providing some reflections on the process of applying the principles of IPA to one interview transcript within a group context and within a limited time frame. Readers have been taken through the analytic stages so that they can understand how the final superordinate themes, which reflect the core concerns of the interview (and the analysts' interpretative frameworks), were identified. Some general issues raised by the analytic process (the problem of fragmented data, the use of theory and the structure of the analytic narrative) were also explored. These have relevance beyond an IPA context and it is hoped that researchers using other qualitative methods may find these useful.

5

GROUNDED THEORY

Sheila Payne

This chapter starts by introducing the philosophical background and historical development of grounded theory. It highlights the different versions of the method produced by Glaser and Strauss (1967) and the tensions between them. The majority of the chapter discusses the principles and practice of grounded theory analysis, including the sorts of research questions best suited to this approach, the types of data and sampling approach to use, the timing of data collection and the distinctive analytic procedures. The chapter ends by considering the development and testing of new theory, the assessment of quality and how to present a grounded theory study. Throughout the chapter, examples are drawn from a current research project in order to illustrate analytic decisions.

Key terms

axial coding	open coding
categories	reflexivity
coding	research questions
constant comparison	saturation
core category	substantive coding
definitions	symbolic interactionism
emergent theory	theoretical coding
goodness of fit	theoretical sampling
interviews	theoretical sensitivity
memos	transcription

The origins of grounded theory

Grounded theory developed out of a research programme concerned with exploring the experience of dying patients in American hospitals during the 1950s and 1960s (Glaser and Strauss, 1965). At this time, medical practice was predominantly paternalistic and information about the diagnosis and the dying prognosis was not routinely shared with patients. The research team therefore had the difficult dilemma of how to investigate a phenomenon that was not openly acknowledged, although it was physically present in the trajectories of dying patients. The lack of 'grand' theories and the inappropriateness of survey methods (which were popular at the time in sociology) provided the impetus for the development of new ways of doing qualitative research.

Glaser and Strauss's (1967) book *The Discovery of Grounded Theory* offered a critique of a number of features of research practice at the time, including the hypothetico-deductive method in which research was designed to test existing theory. Instead they proposed a method of developing or 'discovering' theory inductively from close examination of data. They were also critical of the way qualitative research was regarded as merely descriptive and sought to demonstrate the analytical and explanatory power of qualitative analysis.

It is widely believed that grounded theory has derived its philosophical roots from pragmatism and symbolic interactionism (Bartlett and Payne, 1997). The ideas of Dewey, Cooley, James and Mead provide the foundation, in particular the notions explicated by Mead (1934) that individuals are self-aware and that intersubjectivity influences behaviours. **Symbolic interactionism** takes the position that social interactions are meaningful and these shared meanings are influential in society. According to Rennie (2000: 492), 'pragmatism holds that knowledge production is a matter of perspective and that warrants to truth are a matter of consensus among the members of the community of inquirers'. Strauss's background in the 'Chicago school' of sociology was influential in the use of in-depth case studies and ethnographic methods.

Early formulations of grounded theory have been regarded as based on the epistemological position of positivism, in which it is assumed that there is a straightforward relationship between objects in the world and our perception of them (see Chapter 2 in this volume). From this position, it is regarded as possible to describe what is 'out there' and that there is an ultimate 'truth'. Glaser and Strauss (1967) suggested that hypotheses derived from a grounded theory may be empirically tested and that methods of verification should rely on external objective procedures. Later formulations have emphasized a more interpretative stance (Strauss and Corbin, 1990). Henwood and Pidgeon (1994) highlighted the tension between the epistemological positions of 'realism' in that grounded theory inductively reflects participants' accounts and 'constructivism' because it is the researcher who creates and interprets the data to develop new theory.

Different versions of grounded theory: Variations on a theme

It was some time before grounded theory methodology was widely taken up (Turner, 1981) but, in the last 15–20 years, it has become one of the most popular methods of qualitative research. It has now spread across a number of disciplines (e.g., psychology, education, social work and nursing) and has been developed in a number of ways. The following section will briefly summarize the diversity of grounded theory methods.

The joint publication of Glaser and Strauss (1967) is regarded as the original version and, by some, as the 'classic' account of the method. However, the methodological procedures are poorly articulated and there are ambiguities in how researchers should conduct analyses. Since then, Glaser and Strauss have appeared to have divergent views on what constitutes 'correct' approaches to analysis. A more explicit version of the analytic procedures was published by Strauss and Corbin (1990) that departed in some ways from the original version. This was greeted by an angry reaction from Glaser who considered their approach to be too prescriptive. It is not my intention to offer a full account of the history of this conflict as others have summarized the key issues (e.g., Willig, 2001). The main differences in opinion have been around the role of induction, the degree to which theory 'emerges' or is 'forced' from the data, and procedural variations (see Box 5.1: the meaning of some terms used there will become clear later in the chapter). Where they influence analytic processes, I have highlighted them in this chapter. There have been numerous others who have contributed to the development of the grounded theory method, resulting, for example, in Charmaz's (1990, 2006) social constructivist version, Rennie's (2000) methodical hermeneutics version and Clarke's (2003) postmodern version.

Box 5.1 KEY DIFFERENCES IN THE CONCEPTUALIZATION AND CONDUCT OF GROUNDED THEORY ANALYSIS

Version advocated by Glaser and followers:

- places great value on simple systematic procedures to allow emergence of theory
- argues that theory generation arises directly and rigorously out of the data (Glaser is critical of Strauss for 'forcing' coding by having preconceived ideas; Glaser describes this as full conceptual description of data rather than an emergent theory)
- argues for verification of theory by returning to the data
- rejects interpretivism (the contention that there are multiple realities of phenomena, that these can differ across time and place and that the meaning of action can be understood from actors' perspectives)
- places great emphasis on the final stage of theoretical coding
- attaches great importance to memo writing
- advocates a simple version of theoretical sampling.

Version advocated by Strauss and followers:

- offers fairly complex analytic procedures
- advocates direct questioning during development of theory

(Continued)

(Continued)
- articulates an array of techniques to facilitate constant comparison
- proposes complex tools for theoretical comparison
- places less emphasis on final stage of selective coding
- suggests a number of types of memos including code notes, theoretical notes and logical notes
- offers more complex types of theoretical sampling.

Method and methodological issues

Having considered the philosophical basis for grounded theory and reviewed some of the debates on how grounded theory has developed since its inception, the remainder of the chapter offers practical suggestions about how to 'do' grounded theory analysis. In common with some writers on other qualitative methods (see especially Michele Crossley on narrative analysis in Chapter 9 in this volume, for example), in my view it is not helpful to present grounded theory as a fixed method in which there is only one 'right' way to conduct an analysis. Instead, I offer suggestions as to how researchers might proceed if they wish to label their method as 'grounded theory'. At the outset, it is important to recognize that, in this chapter, I will be describing the procedures that characterize research which aims to develop a new theory (the full version – Willig, 2001) and not the modified version in which only initial open coding is used. The latter is often described as a grounded theory approach to analysis too (see Foster et al., 2004, for a good example).

The following section is presented in linear order. There are early decisions and steps that need to be conducted in sequence but one of the unique features of grounded theory analysis is the dynamic interplay of data collection and analysis. To illustrate some of these issues, I will draw on data from a study exploring the understandings of cancer and end-of-life care of older Chinese people resident in the UK (Payne et al., 2004). The research design is described in Box 5.2.

Box 5.2   EXPLORING AND UNDERSTANDING THE VIEWS OF OLDER CHINESE PEOPLE ABOUT CANCER AND END-OF-LIFE CARE (PAYNE ET AL., 2004)

Rationale for study

Minority ethnic groups make up about six per cent of the population of Britain, with Chinese people constituting about five per cent of all minority ethnic people

---

(Continued)

living in the United Kingdom. There are concerns about equity of access to cancer and palliative care services for black and ethnic minority groups. Issues of English language competence, socio-economic deprivation, institutional ageism and cultural insensitivity may mean that older Chinese people are multiply disadvantaged in accessing acceptable cancer and end-of-life care services. Little is known about their understanding of cancer and end-of-life care.

Research question

What are older Chinese people's beliefs and perceptions regarding cancer and its treatment, and their preferences (if any) about end-of-life care?

Research design

Qualitative study using grounded theory analysis.

Phase 1

Formation of focus groups with members of existing community groups to elicit understandings of cancer and develop culturally appropriate vignettes.

Phase 2

Individual interviews using vignettes as prompts to explore understandings and preferences. Both focus groups and individual interviews were conducted in participants' preferred Chinese dialect (Cantonese, Hakka or Mandarin).

Research design

Types of research questions

All research should seek to address one or more specific **research questions**. For pragmatic reasons, by focusing on specific objectives, the research is more likely to be achievable within the constraints of finite resources such as time, money and energy. Students and new researchers may find this to be one of the most demanding aspects of designing their research but it is essential that a clear focus on a topic area is defined before embarking upon data collection. Because grounded theory is suitable for exploratory research, the research question may become more refined and specific during the course of data collection and analysis as the researcher gains a greater awareness of the key issues. The wording of the research question and research objectives should make it clear 'what, who, when and how' will be researched. Typically, research questions that seek to explore processes and/or meanings lend themselves to grounded theory analysis (see Box 5.3). If the research questions are predominantly concerned with 'how many' or 'how often', these may be better answered using quantitative methods of inquiry.

Box 5.3   EXAMPLES OF RESEARCH QUESTIONS ADDRESSED IN GROUNDED THEORY STUDIES

- How does chronic illness impact on perceptions of the self? (Charmaz, 1990)
- How do women with advanced breast or ovarian cancer cope with palliative chemotherapy? (Payne, 1992)
- How do families of deceased people decided whether to donate their loved one's organs for transplantation? (Sque and Payne, 1996: see Report 2 in Appendix 2 in this volume for more details)
- What expectations do patients and physiotherapists hold about the process of rehabilitation following stroke? (Ashburn et al., 2004)

When to use grounded theory?

Researchers may consider using grounded theory when:

- relatively little is known about the topic area
- there are no 'grand' theories to explain adequately the specific psychological constructs or behaviours under investigation
- researchers wish to challenge existing theories
- researchers are interested in eliciting participants' understandings, perceptions and experiences of the world
- the research aims to develop new theories.

The aims of grounded theory analysis are to develop inductive theory which is closely derived from the data rather than deductive theory which is supported by hypothesis testing. Therefore grounded theory is a suitable method for exploratory research and explanatory research but it should be more than descriptive. If the intention of your research is merely to describe a set of behaviours, perceptions or experiences, then thematic analysis (Joffe and Yardley, 2004) is likely to be a better option. With reference to the study described in Box 5.2, we selected grounded theory analysis because not only were we interested in describing older Chinese people's views but we wished to develop theoretical explanations about why they held these views and how they influenced behaviours such as seeking screening and treatment for cancer. For example, we wished to account for preferences about the role played by Western medicine and Chinese traditional medicine in cancer.

When to review the literature?

In many paradigms, it is usual to conduct a literature review and plan all stages of the research before gathering data but in grounded theory there is debate about the extent and nature of literature reviewing that are desirable and appropriate before embarking upon data collection. It has been argued that the researcher should commence data collection early and delay the literature review to enhance their naivety and their sensitivity to the issues emerging from the data. An alternative view is that some awareness of the existing literature and relevant theories is required if only to confirm that the topic is not already theoretically well developed and understood (Willig, 2001). Researchers should be sufficiently aware of the literature as to be sure that their research will contribute new knowledge. Awareness of the empirical and theoretical literature is essential during the latter stages of the analysis to ensure that new theoretical constructs are linked to existing work. In my view, novice researchers need to spend some time doing a preliminary search of the literature and they also need to be aware of the preconceptions and assumptions based upon disciplinary background that they bring to their data collection and analysis (see more about this and reflexivity later). Another pragmatic reason to undertake some reviewing of the literature is that this is often a requirement for students in presenting research proposals and for all researchers in obtaining ethical approval for their study. If external funding is being sought for the project, a literature review will also be an essential requirement.

With regard to the study with older Chinese people, we undertook a preliminary literature review during the process of developing the application for funding and as part of the procedures required to obtain ethical approval. However, we delayed the writing of a full literature review so that it ran concurrently with data collection during the initial focus groups in Phase 1. We considered that this strategy allowed us to comply with external constraints (e.g., funding bodies and ethical committees) while retaining some openness to new ideas and concepts during initial data collection and analysis. By undertaking the literature review concurrently with data collection in Phase 1, we were able to use both emerging analytic insights and existing theoretical and empirical information to shape the Phase 2 interviews.

Data collection

Types of data

There are four common types of qualitative data:

- Language in the form of written text or spoken words
- Observations of behaviours (involving talk and non-verbal interactions)
- Images which may be dynamic events (captured digitally, on videos or films, photographs, drawings or paintings)
- Artefacts such as sculptures or objects.

Grounded theory requires data that are or can be transformed into text. Therefore the first two types of data are most commonly used. It is important to recognize the difference between *elicited* data, which are specifically requested and collected by researchers for the purpose of answering the research question, and *spontaneously (or naturally) occurring* data. Most data used for grounded theory analysis are elicited for the purpose of the project by talking to people during interviews or focus groups. However, it is also possible to conduct a grounded theory analysis based on recorded conversations, counselling sessions or other naturally occurring data. A grounded theory analysis of printed materials such as government policy documents, diaries or inspection reports may yield new insights.

How to collect suitable data?

Interviews Interviews are a suitable method of collecting elicited data for grounded theory analysis for a number of reasons. First, they build upon everyday experience of conversations and generally people are pleased to have the opportunity to talk with an attentive person in a face-to-face situation. Participating in interviews requires the ability to talk and understand the questions. Language and comprehension difficulties may exclude people who have learning difficulties/disabilities (Finlay and Lyons, 2001, 2002) or low educational attainment and people who do not understand the language or accent of the interviewer. Typically, face-to-face interviews are popular with researchers because they tend to generate a higher response rate than other methods and there is likely to be less missing data than in questionnaires but they can be expensive and time consuming to conduct. The principles of semi-structured interviews described by Jonathan A. Smith and Virginia Eatough (see Chapter 3 in this volume) are relevant for grounded theory studies.

In Western cultures, the interview format is familiar from television shows, professional consultations and other encounters. In the study with older Chinese people, we found that by describing Phase 2 data collection as 'conversations' rather than interviews, we achieved better recruitment and improved data. Initially older Chinese people perceived 'interviews' to be threatening and were reluctant to divulge their views for fear of being wrong and challenging the interviewer.

Group discussions Group interviews are rather like other types of interviews in that the researcher directs the questioning and responses are made to the interviewer. They are not the same as focus group interviews because participants are not encouraged to engage with each other by challenging, debating and arguing about issues. They are commonly used in group settings, like schools, and are a cost effective way to collect data from many participants.

Focus groups In focus groups, the purpose is to encourage interaction between the participants so that a range of views may be elicited and discussion is generated. Decisions must be made at the outset whether focus group participants should be similar or not and whether they should be strangers or already known to each other. These are likely to relate to the research question, topic area and sampling strategy and should take account of cultural norms and gender and power relationships. For example, in some cultures women may feel uncomfortable discussing sexual health problems in mixed gender groups. Focus groups are generally run by a facilitator, whose role is to introduce topics, encourage participation and address participant confidentiality, comfort and safety issues, while an observer has the role of recording the nature and type of participation by group members. The number of participants may vary from six to twelve depending upon the topic and group. There needs to be a balance between the desire to have a range of views represented and the difficulties of managing a large group and making sense of the resultant audio-recording. It may be preferable to have smaller groups if topics are likely to be very personal or elicit strong emotions, such as with bereaved people. For more on focus group interviewing, see Cronin (2001) and Millward (2006).

In the study of older Chinese people, we conducted focus groups with participants who were already known to each other as members of Chinese community groups. This had the advantage of providing access to older Chinese people (a normally 'hidden' population) and, as they were familiar with the community settings and other members, they appeared to be relaxed and generally willing to participate and talk freely. However, their experience of other group sessions had been in the context of health education talks and, despite careful explanations of the purpose of the research (both written and verbal), some participants expected to be told about cancer services rather than volunteering their views. In Phase 2, we selected the vignette method of prompts for interviewing, which involves presenting participants with a fictional or real-life 'case' or scenario relevant to the research topic/question, as it allows people to discuss sensitive topics such as cancer and dying in relation to a third person; it also facilitates comparison as well as revealing how choices and preferences are expressed. In practice, many participants preferred to tell their own stories and describe experiences of cancer in friends and family members.

Timing of data collection

In a grounded theory study, data collection and analysis are concurrent activities. Typically, an initial period of data collection is followed by preliminary open coding (explained below), from which the research focus may be refined and research questions modified. This in turn requires changes to data collection protocols and sampling. Grounded theory research involves reciprocal periods of data collection, analysis, reflection, theory development and theory testing in spiral patterns of activity which are unlike formal linear experimental designs. These are both hard to capture in written accounts of the method such as this chapter and in submissions for ethical review boards that are typically more familiar with more structured linear approaches.

Sampling

Grounded theory, along with other types of qualitative research, does not rely on notions of statistical representativeness to make claims about the generalizability and authenticity of the findings. Samples are generally selected purposively because it is believed that they can contribute to the topic under investigation. This is different from 'convenience' samples which consist of people who were most readily available and willing to participate. Purposive samples should be selected on the basis of criteria which must be explicitly stated when reporting the results. At the outset, it is important to define the characteristics of the sample that are assumed to provide data of relevance to the research topic. During the process of data collection, as the research question becomes refined, the sampling strategy may be modified to include others who may contribute different perspectives or experiences. During the process of analysis and theoretical testing, a process referred to as **'theoretical sampling'** may be used explicitly to seek 'negative' cases that challenge or illuminate emerging constructs. To draw a statistical analogy, it is helpful to recruit 'outliers' to test the emerging theory. Theoretical sampling is defined as a process of ongoing data collection for the purpose of generating theory, where previous analysis influences decisions about subsequent data to be collected. It is *theoretical* because it is guided by and contributes to the emerging model. Theoretical sampling is an essential characteristic of a complete grounded theory study.

For example, in the study of older Chinese people, we sought to recruit older (defined as over 50 years of age) Chinese people resident in two areas of the UK, one city with a large 'China town' and one area without, as we believed that these social differences could reflect cultural identification and support. While we started by accessing those people who used Chinese community groups, we extended data collection in the interview phase to those who chose not to use these groups. The research team also debated whether to include second generation 'born in Britain' Chinese people because they were more likely to be more fully integrated into Western culture and to be English-speaking. We purposively sought a heterogeneous sample of older Chinese people who varied in terms of gender, places of origin (e.g., Hong Kong, mainland China and Malaysia) and socio-economic status.

Stance of researcher to participants and data

It is important to consider the status afforded to the responses of participants and the implications which are drawn from talk, and the purposes of the analysis of talk from differing perspectives. I will start by differentiating between two major conceptual approaches in qualitative methods of analysis:

- Those approaches which are concerned with inferring *meaning* from data and draw inferences about what people think, feel and do. These can be characterized as 'experiential' approaches. They include methods of analysis such as thematic analysis, framework analysis, grounded theory analysis, IPA and narrative analysis.
- Those approaches which are concerned with how talk is *used* in social situations and that do not make inferences about how people feel or think. These can be characterized as 'discursive' approaches. They include methods such as discourse analysis, conversation analysis and analysis of institutional interaction.

The conventional status afforded to interview data, for example, when using grounded theory analysis is that responses are construed as evidence of what people think and feel and how they *understand* their world. These insights are assumed to have stability over time and are inferred as being characteristic of that individual. Grounded theorists feel able to draw conclusions about the state of mind of individuals on the basis of their talk. They are interested in exploring the influence of previous experiences and personal understanding on the emotional and cognitive reactions displayed in talk. Thus, from this perspective, talk is seen as representing the contents of people's minds and providing direct access to thoughts and emotions. Descriptions are taken to represent a 'real' account of experiences and are seen as indicative of feelings *at the time* of the experience although it is clear that the interview presents a retrospective account of experiences. The social situation of the interview is regarded as largely unproblematic. In comparison, discursive approaches regard interview responses as evidence about how people *use* language to construct that particular situation at that particular time (although these approaches can be wary of interview data and prefer naturally occurring data) (see Chapter 7 in this volume). Discursive approaches make no assumptions about consistency of responses in other situations, no inferences about how people think or feel and explain talk as representing a repertoire of ways that people have of dealing with questions in social situations, such as in research interviews. In the study of older Chinese people, we accepted the utterances of participants as indicative of their knowledge, attitudes and beliefs about cancer and end-of-life issues.

Data preparation: Transformation of data

To transcribe or not? Types of transcription

Prior to undertaking any type of qualitative analysis, 'raw' spoken data need to be transformed into a textual format. Typically, this involves the **transcription** of audio recordings into written text. This is the first stage of the analysis and critical decisions need to be made at this point about the style of transcription to be used (O'Connell and Kowal, 1995). In grounded theory analysis, it is usual to transcribe both the speech of the researcher and the participant but not usual or necessary to transcribe prosodic, paralinguistic or extralinguistic elements (as some discourse analysts and all conversation analysts would do, for example). Novice researchers may wish to undertake at least a few transcriptions themselves because this allows them to develop an intimate familiarity with the data and to identify some potential analytic lines of inquiry. If the majority of transcriptions are done by clerical workers, it is necessary to listen to all the audio tapes and carefully check through the transcriptions for errors and omissions. Rennie (2000) maintains that there should be continuity in data collection and analysis. He argues that the person undertaking the interviews will already have an understanding of the text and analysis of elements of the text will be influenced by knowledge of the whole interview and its social context. In the study of older Chinese people, interviews were first transcribed into Chinese and then translated into English. Careful checking of the transcripts was done using the original audio tapes and the research team discussed problematic words in the translation. Box 5.4 provides an excerpt of an interview to demonstrate the type of transcription conducted.

Box 5.4 AN EXCERPT OF AN INTERVIEW AND POSSIBLE OPEN CODES

Transcript	Open codes
(conducted in Mandarin, translated into English)	
Ms Sing:	
This . . . this congee, I think when patients are weak it is easier to be absorbed.	'nature of food'
Interviewer:	
Yes, easier.	
Ms Sing:	
Right, easier to be absorbed. So for patients, medicine is important but food therapy is also important. You should let her eat whatever her condition allows her to eat. I think we have lots of food therapy in Chinese culture; this is one of the strengths of our Chinese culture. Also, I said earlier I mentioned to have a community centre and the problem nowadays, people take too much medicine. These medicines are chemicals and they stay in your tummy and you don't know what they would do to you.	'beliefs about digestion' 'food therapy' 'Chinese culture' 'too much medicine' medicine – problems
So if you have this community centre the doctors or nurses can give you a check up regularly and monitor	'check-up on medicine use'

(Continued)

your medicines. If you have taken the medicines for a long period they would see if you really need them at all. Or you might need to change to another type of medicine that might cause fewer side effects.	medicine problems

Interviewer:

Right, right, that is important.

Ms Sing:

Right, but there are many old people who do not understand what drugs they are taking and they just swallow them in confusion.	medicine – old people

Notes:

- Last names are used as a mark of respect with older Chinese people and we have used a pseudonym here.
- Congee is a type of rice porridge.

An alternative position in grounded theory is that analysis should be directly conducted from the spoken word rather than from transcripts because it allows access to the prosodic and paralinguistic features of the data. For example, irony is difficult to 'capture' in written transcripts because the tone of voice or an accompanying giggle may indicate the intention of the speaker that is not directly evident from the words alone. There are also disagreements about the use of punctuation in transcriptions and how the text is presented. Coffey and Atkinson (1996) argue that parsing text into clauses retains more of the emotional resonance of the spoken words. This type of transcription gives the written text a poetic appearance. In conclusion, transformation of spoken language into written text should be regarded as the first stage in the interpretative process.

Use of computer software to assist analysis

Grounded theory analysis requires researchers to manage large volumes of textual data. It is therefore essential to establish consistent and reliable systems to handle data, whether data are to be stored and processed electronically or in paper form. This ensures that, during analysis, data can be retrieved when required and also provides an audit trail (part of the process of establishing the quality of an analysis). To this end, novice researchers should consider the use of qualitative data analysis software if they have a reasonably large dataset and/or if more than one person is going to be involved in the process of analysis. There are many different software packages, with some specially designed to facilitate grounded theory analysis. They have the advantage of facilitating the manipulation, indexing and retrieval of data but do not alter the need for an intensive engagement with the data during the intellectual process of coding and interpretation. The disadvantage of some packages is that they are labour intensive to learn and also in terms of their input and coding requirements and may inadvertently serve to structure data analysis in prescribed ways (e.g., as hierarchical or linear models).

Data analysis

As highlighted earlier, there are numerous versions of grounded theory analysis and many lively debates about what constitutes the 'correct' procedures. The account offered here draws heavily on the procedures described by Bartlett and Payne (1997) which are derived from the position taken by Strauss and Corbin (1990, 1998). They are summarized in Box 5.5 and offer a possible way to conduct data analysis. Novice researchers should use the analytic procedures which are most congruent with their philosophical and epistemological stance. However, there are key features of analysis which are typical of grounded theory and they will be emphasized in the following account.

Box 5.5 PROCEDURES FOR A GROUNDED THEORY ANALYSIS (BASED ON BARTLETT AND PAYNE, 1997)

Activity	Comments
Collect data	Any source of textual data may be used but semi-structured interviews or observations are the most common.
Transcribe data	Full transcriptions of interviewer and interviewee talk.
Develop initial categories – open coding	Categories are developed from the data by open coding of the transcripts. 'Open coding' means identifying and labelling meaningful units of text which might be a word, phrase, sentence or larger section of text.
Saturate categories	'Saturation' means gathering further examples of meaningful units as one proceeds through the transcripts until no new instances of a particular category emerge.
Defining categories	Once the categories have been saturated, formal definitions in terms of the properties and dimensions of each category may be generated.
Theoretical sampling	From the categories which have emerged from the first sample of data, choose theoretically relevant samples to help test and develop categories further.
Axial coding – the development and testing of relationships between categories	During axial coding, possible relationships between categories are noted, hypothesized and actually tested against data obtained in ongoing theoretical sampling.

(Continued)	
Theoretical integration	A core category (or, in some cases, more than one main category) is identified and related to all the other sub categories to determine its explanatory power and finally links with existing theory are established and developed.
Grounding the theory	The emergent theory is grounded by returning to the data and validating it against actual segments of text. A search for deviant cases may be used to test the emergent theory.
Filling in gaps	Finally, any missing detail is filled in by the further collection of relevant data.

Initial coding and the constant comparison technique

The initial **coding** of text is done after careful and repeated readings of the material. Meaningful units are identified, highlighted and labelled. These units may be words, phrases or longer segments of text. The labels are referred to as **categories**. Strauss and Corbin (1990, 1998) describe this as **open coding** and suggest asking repeated questions of the data at this stage. Glaser (1992) describes this as **substantive coding** and recommends that labels are closely dependent upon the data, perhaps even using the words of participants if appropriate (*in vivo* categories). There are dilemmas for researchers in how conceptually concrete or abstract to make their initial codes. There is a danger that a very concrete approach to initial coding results in numerous codes for small units of text which are very close to the data but do little more than repeat the text (Rennie, 2000). Alternatively, the rigorous questioning proposed by Strauss and Corbin (1990, 1998) may mean that analysis is very protracted and that conceptual categories are introduced early in the analysis thereby shaping the analysis according to the theoretical influences of the researcher rather than staying true to the data. Whichever approach is taken, the aim of initial coding is to capture the detail, variation and complexity of the source data (Henwood and Pidgeon, 1994).

As more data are accumulated, further instances of the same and new meaningful units are coded in each transcript. This results in numerous categories and subcategories. Unlike content analysis, the same data may be attributed to more than one category. It is normal for categories to be initially descriptive and to become more analytical during the process of analysis. The researcher will become aware that certain categories occur frequently in the data and that coding of new data yields fewer and eventually no new examples. This is described as **saturation**. It serves as an indication when initial coding and data collection can cease. Glaser and Strauss's (1967: 1) original version of grounded theory emphasized the use of 'a general method of comparative analysis'. This is commonly described as the **constant comparison** technique in which, as segments of text are identified, they are examined against previous categories for similarities and differences. This process means that coding may need to be revised and categories relabelled, merged or split to take account of new insights. This may require previously coded transcripts to be revisited and recoded. This is characterized by Henwood and Pidgeon (1994) as a 'flip–flop' between data and conceptualization.

Novice researchers need to develop a systematic way to index categories and track the segments of text which provide the instances of these categories. This was traditionally done by physically cutting and pasting chunks of transcript but it is now more usually managed electronically with a word-processing program or with specially designed qualitative data analysis software. Once categories appear to be saturated, concise and meaningful **definitions** of the properties and dimensions of each category should be written. In Box 5.6, an example is given of how a section of transcript which had been open coded (see Box 5.4) was further revised in the light of other data to produce more conceptually refined codes.

Box 5.6 AN EXAMPLE OF THE CONSTANT COMPARISON PROCESS

Excerpt	Open codes	Revised codes
Right, easier to be absorbed. So for patients, medicine is important but food therapy is also important. You should let her eat whatever her condition allows her to eat. I think we have lots of food therapy in Chinese culture. This is one of the strengths of our Chinese culture. Also, I said earlier I mentioned to have a community centre and the problem nowadays, people take too much medicine. These medicines are chemicals and they stay in your tummy and you don't know what they would do to you.	'beliefs about digestion' 'food therapy' 'too much medicine' 'medicine – problems'	food as an essential therapeutic tool ambivalence towards Western medicine

---

Theoretical sampling and axial coding

During the intermediate period of analysis, further data collection is undertaken. It is usual at this stage to move into theoretical sampling of further participants who are selected because they are assumed to illuminate or test the emerging theory. Strauss and Corbin (1990, 1998) describe a process of **axial coding** in which the numerous categories generated during their method of initial coding are refined and reduced. The analytic work required during axial coding involves examination of each category to discover linkages, relationships, redundancy and new patterns. They advocate the use of a coding paradigm which is designed to sensitize the researcher to higher order features such as 'process'. This may require the reformulation of some of the categories as greater insight is achieved and conceptual abstraction moves the categories further from a descriptive account of the data. This is called **theoretical coding**. Strauss and Corbin incorporate hypothesis testing (e.g., by repeatedly proposing statements that account for the findings and examining if they can be substantiated from the data) into the method of producing a grounded theory, while Glaser emphasizes this more in the final phase. Glaser's (1978, 1992) version appears to focus more closely on coding emerging from the data, with more abstract analysis occurring in the later stages.

Data synthesis

Throughout the whole process of analysis, researchers are encouraged to write **memos** (see Box 5.7 for an example). These are ways to capture the thought processes of the researcher. In research teams they are also useful ways to share insights and justify how analytic decisions are made. Memo writing functions as an audit trail which may be helpful in tracking analytic processes. Memo writing is regarded as essential and many specialist qualitative analysis software programs have the facility to display memos alongside categories. During later stages of theory development, there is an active interplay between memo writing, data analysis and data questioning. The researcher works proactively with the data and with the initial and subsequent categories to achieve steadily more analytic insights. This may also involve further refinement of the research question.

BOX 5.7   AN EXAMPLE OF AN ANALYTIC MEMO

The role of food in health and illness

When talking about the use of foods in illness, the participants seemed to divide their discussion into foods that were believed to prevent cancer and foods to be avoided and the special anti-cancer 'therapeutic' foods. It is evident in the data that older Chinese people in our sample believe that the body in illness has lost its normal balance and generally this is attributed to the presence of toxins. So the role of foods in illness seems to be about getting rid of the toxins and to replenish the body with the lost elements required in balancing the body and thereby strengthening it.

Development of new theory

In the final stage of analysis, careful scrutiny of the categories will result in the identification of a **core category** which has major explanatory power.

The aim of this stage is to organize and integrate the remaining categories in conceptually meaningful ways (see Box 5.8 for an example). Practically, it may be helpful to work with visual images of categories so they can be arranged and rearranged to develop an understanding of patterns which emerge to form theory. Strauss and Corbin (1990, 1998) describe this process as selective coding, while Glaser (1992) refers to it as theoretical coding. During this process, links are made with existing theory which may further develop the **emergent theory**. This is described as **theoretical sensitivity**. Grounded theories tend to be specific to the context from which they are derived but should have explanatory potential and be more than merely descriptive accounts of the data. There are differences in Strauss's and Glaser's views on what constitutes a good theory. Strauss and Corbin (1990, 1998) emphasize the need for a complex, detailed account while Glaser (1992) emphasizes parsimony and its potential modifiability in presenting theory. In my view, a grounded theory should offer a coherent account to explain the topic under investigation. This may be clustered around a core category or a number of linked themes but should not comprise a diverse collection of interesting but largely unrelated themes. This may mean that researchers need to be selective in their emphasis.

Box 5.8   AN EXAMPLE SHOWING LINKS BETWEEN EXISTING THEORY AND CODING

Existing theory and policy related to cancer diagnostic information

Current communication practices in cancer care emphasize the full and open discussion of diagnosis and prognosis with the patient at a pace and style compatible with their wishes (National Institute for Clinical Excellence, 2004). However, actual communication practices are probably more 'conditional' than fully 'open' (Field and Copp, 1999). Current trends in the UK have highlighted the autonomy of the patient in health care decision-making (Fallowfield, 2001). There are assumptions in the literature that Chinese people favour disclosure of a cancer diagnosis to family members rather than the patient (Rowlands, 2005). Our research indicated there were various preferences about the disclosure of a cancer diagnosis. Some of the participants expressed a wish to be told of the diagnosis while a minority would not want to be told. There were quite a few participants who were non-committal. While great importance was attached to family life and obligation, there was also a sense in which people still wanted to be fully informed themselves. Overall, there was a preference that disclosure should be given to both the patient and family members together.

(Continued)

Links to data and coding

Main category: preferences for disclosure

Participants were asked about their own preferences for disclosure of cancer and nearly two thirds of them said they would want to be told of the diagnosis. The following are examples of subcategories in the initial open coding:

Needing to make arrangements

'And some people are frightened by the thought of death, but then on the other hand if death is unavoidable through your cancer then it would be nice for the sufferer to be able to put things in order.' (Woman, interview 27)

To prepare mentally

'If it was myself, I would want to know. Then I would mentally prepare myself.' (Woman, interview 16)

To know the cause of death

'So you would know what you died of.' (Man, interview 23)

Testing of emerging theory

Having developed new theory, the researcher needs to return to the data to validate it against segments of text. In this process, there is a continuation of the rigorous constant comparison process described previously. It may also be appropriate to collect small amounts of new data specifically to test aspects of the theory, perhaps by returning to the same participants or new people selected purposively. In addition, a search for deviant cases will help assess the limits of the theory (Willig, 2001). According to Glaser and Strauss (1967: 6), 'generating a theory from data means that most hypotheses and concepts not only come from the data, but are systematically worked out in relation to the data during the course of the research.' Early formulations of the grounded theory method emphasized the need to derive hypotheses from the new theory which may lead to further qualitative or quantitative research.

How to assess the quality of a grounded theory analysis?

There are a number of criteria for judging the quality of qualitative research generally (e.g., Elliott et al., 1999; Henwood and Pidgeon, 1992; Silverman, 1993;

Yardley, 2000; see also Chapter 2 in this volume). None are perfect and some have been the focus of lively debate (see Reicher, 2000). Much will depend upon the version of grounded theory espoused by the researcher and his/her epistemological position. However, some suggestions are offered below.

Goodness of fit

In the original version, Glaser and Strauss (1967) emphasized the require-ments of 'goodness of fit' and 'work'. By **'goodness of fit'**, they meant that cat-egories must be applicable to the data and not 'forced' and the term 'work' referred to the emergent theory which must explain the behaviours under investigation. Glaser's subsequent critique of Strauss was largely about the 'forcing' of analysis caused by the use of a coding paradigm, which he thought no longer allowed theory to emerge or to be 'discovered'. In addition, grounded theory should be accessible. According to Glaser and Strauss (1967: 3), 'The theory must also be readily understandable to sociologists of any view-point, to students and to significant laymen.' Of course, for grounded theory analysis conducted within psychology, we should replace 'sociologists' with 'psychologists'.

Many of the analytic procedures of grounded theory are designed to ensure robustness. According to Rennie (2000), in Glaser's version there is a distinc-tion between verification and validation. Validation of the theory involves procedures within the method while verification comes from hypotheses derived from the theory and subsequently tested using quantitative methods. In comparison, Strauss and Corbin (1990) argue for the inclusion of hypothesis testing within the analytic method.

External validation

A number of strategies may be used which seek to confirm the quality of the analysis with reference to the views of others. Triangulation has been proposed to support the claims made (Foss and Ellefsen, 2002). This refers to exploring the same phenomenon from different vantage points, on the assumption that similar findings from each perspective indicate that the research has presented a valid picture. Triangulation may take a number of forms such as method-ological triangulation, theoretical triangulation or respondent validation but it should not be regarded as a panacea. Respondent validation involves returning the emerging theory to participants to obtain their views on its credibility. In my view, this often just generates more data from differing perspectives rather than establishing the validity of one particular perspective. Likewise, triangu-lation suggests that it is possible to obtain validation of theory by collecting data from more than one source, either using different techniques of data col-lection or by combining different theoretical positions. Heath and Cowley (2004) caution against combining Glaserian and Straussian versions of grounded theory in a single study. A team approach to analysis may offer support to novice researchers but there is a danger that in trying to establish consensus, individual insights are lost. Rennie (2000) is critical of all these approaches to validation because he considers them to be inherently positivist, providing a spurious 'objectivity'. They rely on the notion of a single reality against which the emerging theory can be assessed.

In the study of older Chinese people, initial open coding was conducted independently by team members on the first five focus group transcripts and, from that, consensus was reached on categories. The actual coding of transcripts was then undertaken by the researcher who collected the data. Repeated discussions of problematic categories and revisions occurred throughout the analysis.

Reflexivity

Reflexivity allows the researcher to acknowledge their role in the creation of the analytical account. Procedures central to the grounded theory method such as constant comparison and the writing of memos promote a critical awareness of the role of the researcher and their cognitive processes. The recognition of one's theoretical and disciplinary background should be attempted before undertaking data collection to ensure that the research agenda is open to new insights from the participants. Likewise, the techniques of open coding which draw on participants' own words for category labels help to prevent premature closure of the developing theory. Grounded theorists do not claim that it is possible to 'bracket' presuppositions as in phenomenology; instead researchers are generally acknowledged to be co-producers of the data, for example during interviews and during interpretation of the data and development of theory.

Writing–up and presentation

As Michele Crossley emphasizes in her discussion of narrative analysis in this volume (see Chapter 9), the literary ability to construct an argument is needed in writing up qualitative research. Generally the presentation of results is much less formulaic than in experimental reports but the methods used and the processes undertaken during the analysis need to be made explicit to readers. Coffey and Atkinson (1996) suggest some novel ways to present the analysis, such as in poetic stanzas. In presenting a grounded theory, it is important to explain the process of analysis (as in any methodological account) and demonstrate how the core category and subcategories are derived from the data (Elliott et al., 1999). The new theory is then presented with sufficient detail of the constituents of the core category to be understandable, together with the relationship of the core category to other categories. Graphical representations of conceptual categories and their linkages may be helpful for readers. In addition the research report should provide excerpts of data such as text, images, field notes or transcriptions upon which the analysis is based. Novice researchers should be explicit in how they have selected the supporting excerpts to defend against the criticism that they have just found a few 'juicy quotations'. Excerpts should be clearly labelled with identifiers that allow readers to know that more than a single participant has been cited in support of a claim. In writing up qualitative research, a compromise is required between providing sufficient data for readers to draw alternative conclusions and enabling them to see how the interpretations have been arrived at, and an overly long account. Willig (2001) provides a helpful account of how to write up grounded theory research and a useful exemplar of a written-up grounded theory study is presented in Appendix 2 in the present volume.

Summary

This chapter has presented and discussed the origins, principles and practicalities of grounded theory analysis, drawing upon one study to exemplify the analytic process. Undertaking a grounded theory analysis can be challenging, exciting, frustrating and enjoyable. In an ideal world, it is important to be well prepared, well equipped and adequately funded and to design your research carefully, setting goals and targets using a realistic time frame. Of course, you need also to be flexible in accommodating the unexpected, be open to new experiences, discoveries and ways of seeing the world. Finally good research is rigorously conducted and accurately recorded. Grounded theory requires intellectual engagement, innovation, theoretical sensitivity, reflexivity and the ability to write. It is hoped that this chapter will inspire and guide your research.

Further reading

Mason's (2002) *Qualitative Researching* is an excellent starting point for new researchers with guidance about addressing the difficult questions underpinning qualitative research methods. This book is aimed at students undertaking higher degrees and offers advice on both fundamental principles and practical procedures. Murray and Chamberlain's (1999) edited volume, *Qualitative Health Psychology: Theories and Methods* considers the application of particular qualitative methods (including grounded theory) and provides concrete examples of how they are used in health related projects. Charmaz's (2006) *Constructing Grounded Theory: A Practical Guide Through Qualitative Analysis* is an engagingly written book which presents one version of grounded theory procedures in a concise and explicit style. This book would be of value to both novices and experts.

6

DOING GROUNDED THEORY

Sheila Hawker and Christine Kerr

This chapter presents a grounded theory analysis of data on two ex-soldiers' experiences of leaving the army. It describes how researchers become immersed in the data through thorough familiarization with the context and the content of the interviews. In this exercise, the two transcripts were interrogated through the use of open codes and categories which facilitated the identification of patterns, relationships, similarities and differences both within and across the two accounts. As concepts emerged, categories were grouped together and the two transcripts were subjected to further interrogation. A working hypothesis was generated and outlined, which is ready to be tested by additional interviews. Suggestions about future participants are made and the process of theoretical sampling is described. Finally the strengths and weaknesses of using a grounded theory approach in this context are considered.

Key terms

axial coding	memos
categories	open coding
coding	saturation
constant comparison	selective coding
core category	software packages
emerging theory	theoretical sampling
goodness of fit	theoretical sensitivity
iterative process	

Introduction

Grounded theory is a systematic method of data analysis and theory development. **Constant comparison** of data is the key component of this method. Textual data in the form of interview transcripts, often accompanied by field notes and observations, are systematically examined in order to uncover the subjective realities of participants through thorough scrutiny of their accounts. The aim of grounded theory is to identify the social processes which produce the phenomenon being studied. Put simply, cases that have the same outcomes are examined to see which conditions they have in common, thereby revealing potential causes. Cases that are similar on many variables but have different outcomes are also compared to see where the main causal differences might lie.

For the purposes of the analytic exercise presented in this chapter, the grounded theory method was simplified and is presented here as a series of stages (see Figure 6.1). However, it must be stressed that grounded theory

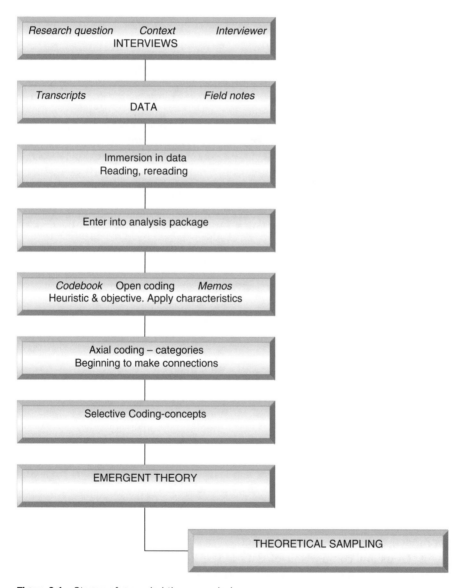

Figure 6.1 Stages of grounded theory analysis

analysis is an iterative and recursive process; while each stage informs the next, all stages are revisited as the research project progresses. As theory emerges, the researcher will return to the data and select new participants to test it (a process referred to as 'theoretical sampling'). Chapter 5 in this volume presents a more detailed account of the principles and practicalities of grounded theory analysis; here we shall focus on how these were applied to two transcripts of interviews conducted as part of a qualitative study on ex-soldiers' experiences of leaving the army and their post-army lives.

Most researchers utilize specialist **software packages** when analysing qualitative data. There are clear advantages to this in terms of managing data, recording codes and concepts, the construction of a code book, searching and sifting codes and grouping them into **categories**. The qualitative software analysis package NVivo was used for this exercise (Gibbs, 2002). However, before any data were entered into the analysis package, the two authors spent time reading and rereading the two transcripts in order to familiarize themselves with these data. In a real study, there would be continuity in data collection and analysis; we would either have conducted these interviews personally or at least have had access to the recordings and field notes in order to familiarize ourselves with both the content and the context of the data (Rennie, 2000). Similarly while only a general description of the focus of the project was available to us for this exercise (see the Preface to Appendix 1), a researcher would also normally be familiar with the specified project's particular research question(s) before approaching the data analysis.

Whether or not a literature review should be carried out in advance when applying grounded theory is debatable but in this case neither of the authors was familiar with the academic literature on ex-service personnel. To this extent, we were truly 'naïve' researchers. The two interviews used here are semi-structured and this type of interview is often better suited to later stages of grounded theory analysis. It is more usual to start with less structured interviews to explore the subject before the analysis is further refined.

A researcher must be reflexive about her/his own role in data collection and analysis. It is notable here that the interviewer himself is an ex-serviceman, which is reflected in his choice of words during the interviews – for example, 'Civvie Street' – and the participants were aware of his service background. This factor should be noted as it may have intimated or encouraged shared understandings between the interviewer and his participants, thereby influencing the content of the interviews. So although **coding** the transcripts may at first appear to be the main activity in a grounded theory analysis, it should be recognized that analysis begins from the very start of the project. Familiarization with the research question, the context of the interviews, the interview data and reflection upon researcher influence are all an integral part of a grounded theory analysis.

As explained above, under normal circumstances, a researcher would have more contextual data than we had available here. The researchers would also have had more time and space to explore these data. If this were a real study, we would probably have spent weeks analysing the first batch of data as coding generally only becomes more rapid and efficient as a study progresses. It is difficult to outline the **iterative process** of grounded theory in a straightforward and accessible way within the confines of a short chapter. To combat this problem, we will focus on only one small part of our coding and analysis and explain it in-depth.

As readers are probably quite distanced from the data under discussion, we suggest that, before proceeding, they thoroughly familiarize themselves with the two transcripts, think about what they notice while reading them and consider what words they could use as 'shorthand' to represent any ideas they may have. This experimentation is an important part of the exercise because explaining the practicalities of grounded theory analysis without being familiar with the data is a little like explaining how to swim without being in the water.

Characteristics of the sample

It is important to record the characteristics of the sample as it grows. This allows the analyst to examine responses from different groups of people and to note and record similarities and differences; it also informs further recruitment of participants. It must be emphasized that this categorization is not aimed at finding a representative sample or as a form of content analysis. The purpose is to delve into the breadth of experiences around the phenomenon being investigated. By recording these details, any strong bias in the sample is also highlighted. The advantage of an analysis software package is that these attributes can readily be assigned to each transcript so that data can be sifted and sorted under the various headings. Using the information we have about the ex-soldiers, Brian and David, we have drafted a preliminary chart for this exercise (see Table 6.1). Additional variables would normally be added as a study progresses so, as well as informing future sampling, recording information in this way will aid familiarization with the data and the eventual writing-up of the study.

Open coding

When thoroughly familiar with the early data, it is time to begin the **open coding** of the first interview transcript. This process of coding is well described in Chapter 5. The purpose of coding is to continue systematically the process of 'noticing'. The application of code words to sections of data – be they single words, part or whole sentences or complete paragraphs – constitutes the naming of phenomena which facilitates collecting, sorting and thinking about

Table 6.1 Attributes of the sample

Variable	David	Brian
Gender	Male	Male
Age	Not known	Not known
Marital status	Married	Married
Children	Has children	Has children
Length of service	Not known	Not known
How long since leaving the army	Not known	'several years'
Rank on entry	Not known	Not known
Rank on exit	Sergeant	Sergeant
Job in army	Driver	Not known
Current employment	School caretaker	'training'
Reason for joining army	"to get away because I didn't have a trade"	Not known
Reason for leaving army	'Options for change'	Health

things in the data. Each code acts as a label to highlight items that have been noticed in the accounts. Some codes will be objective or concrete and serve to echo what is contained in the text, while other codes will be more abstract or heuristic, reflecting the analyst's ideas as each line of the data is studied for information relating to the research question. The actual names of the codes are decided by the individual researcher who, in order to remain consistent between coding sessions and to facilitate comparisons with others coding the same piece of data, records the meanings of the code words she/he has assigned. Some codes will be *in vivo*, consisting of words or phrases used by the interviewees themselves, thereby reflecting the reality of the participants. For instance, two *in vivo* codes we coded for the exercise were 'used up' (David, line 119) and 'locked the gate' (David, line 98). These are expressions taken directly from the transcripts. The complete list of code words and the meanings assigned to them constitute a code book for the project, another task greatly simplified by the use of a software package.

When we began to code Brian's and David's accounts for the first time, we utilized a great many codes and assigned meanings which varied from the very objective 'age' ('the age of the participant at interview') to the more heuristic 'the army as carer' ('holistic care of soldiers as part of the army package – examples housing, health'). We noted that there were many similarities between the two accounts: both participants are male, married and have children (codes included 'gender', 'marital status' and 'children'); both participants appeared to value what being in the army afforded them (codes included 'duty', 'self esteem', 'education' and 'social life'); both men expressed a sense of loss when they left (codes included 'abandonment', 'loss' and 'locked out'); both expressed some resentment at the way the army had treated them at the time of their leaving (codes included 'bitterness', 'on your own', 'used up' and 'best years') but both Brian and David had maintained some association with the army (codes included 'links', 'transition', 'social life' and 'ex-soldier'). In a normal study, all of the issues we identified would be interrogated further by contrasting, comparing, sifting and sorting all of the codes we applied to the text. For the purposes of this exercise, we are going to focus upon just one cluster of codes relating to the issue of army standards and the way these are reported to impact upon civilian life.

The study from which this exercise originates was concerned with the renegotiation of identity after leaving the army. With this focus in mind, we coded the text excerpt below with the following codes: 'terminology', 'us and them', 'army education' and 'standards'. It would appear that Brian viewed service personnel and civilians very differently and believed his army training had instilled more commitment, a sense of duty and higher standards than those of many civilians. Interestingly, the terminology he used ('we', 'they') could suggest that he still viewed himself as part of the army rather than as a civilian.

4	**Brian:**	I think I've learned in the forces and the thing is you learn these
5		things in the army without realizing it a lot of the time, so that when you
6		come out and start comparing yourself to the people working alongside you, you find
7		that you've got a much greater sense of urgency. You tend
8		to pay more attention to detail, you don't bother about the time so much,
9		you don't clock on or clock off. If the job takes twice as long as it should,
10		you just work on as necessary. We seem to be much more flexible, much
11		more adaptable to situations, and it's all stuff I've learned in the forces and
12		the experience I've had where you need to be adaptable, where the
13		situation might change. You've already learned to adapt to new situations
14		– and that comes through all the time. When I look around I see that all of
15		the time, lack of attention to detail, how they just skimp over things, and
16		no attitude. You know, we do our best all of the time.

When we compared David's account with Brian's, we could see there were similarities. Like Brian, David intimated that, as an ex-soldier, he had higher standards than civilians and was prepared to spend extra time and do a job efficiently. Consequently, the codes attached to the text excerpt below were similar to those used for Brian's excerpt, including 'standards', 'discipline', 'terminology' and 'us and them'.

240	**David:**	. . . when I used to come back at night, I used
241		to park all the wagons up so all the bumpers were level. Funny as it
242		may seem, they had them parked all over the car park. It made it harder
243		to get out. They couldn't see the fact that by lining them all up it was
244		easy to get them out. Um, it was other little things like your paperwork.
245		Keep your paperwork in order – it makes it easy. I think that side of
246		life used to hinder me because all I would do was spend an extra ten
247		minutes. All they wanted to do was in, out and go.

However, we noted that the terminology used by the two participants differed slightly. Although David also talked of 'they' when he referred to civilians, he used the term 'I' rather than 'we' when he made comparisons with the way he performed at work. This could suggest that he was more distanced from the army than Brian and we would add a memo to this effect here. The use of **memos** is a key element of grounded theory. Memos are recorded throughout the analysis in parallel with data collection, familiarization, note-taking and coding. Essentially a memo is a note or reminder to oneself about an idea, a code or property, an observation about a relationship between codes or a thought about future possible questions or participants. Making memos at all stages of the research project, from the design to the final analysis, informs the gradual build-up of theory and aids **theoretical sensitivity** which guides the researcher to examine the data from different angles rather than simply focusing upon that which is immediately obvious. In this case, our memo would have speculated about why David might have been more distanced from the army than Brian. Had Brian been in the army for longer than David? Had David been out of the army for longer than Brian?

Table 6.2 shows some of the open or free codes that were generated around the issue of army and civilian standards and shows how they were collapsed into groups or categories containing codes with similar qualities as the analysis proceeded. The categories tend to be more abstract than the open codes and again the meanings assigned to them by the researchers are recorded.

At this stage, the categories are arbitrary and the open codes can be grouped into more than one category. Again it must be emphasized that codes and categories will change and adapt throughout the analysis as ideas and linkages

Table 6.2   Code groupings

Code words	Categories	Axial coding	Emergent theory
Education Socialization Duty Discipline Standards	Army standards		
Self-esteem Status Terminology Difference	Self-identity		
Ex-soldier Links		Army added value	'Once a soldier, never again a civilian'
Preparation Adjustment Job search Ex-soldier Outside Links	Period of transition		
Problems in Civvie Street Links Terminology	Us and them		

emerge. It is important to keep track of these processes and record thoughts and emergent ideas in memos. Systematic tracking of the process of analysis is an integral part of the theoretical sensitivity which grounded theory researchers must have if insights and ideas are to be developed into a theory that is truly grounded in the data. We cannot over-emphasize the importance of this. Remember that the key criterion for evaluating any grounded theory is '**goodness of fit**' – that is, the extent to which the theory accords with the data that generated it – and so a researcher needs to be able to identify exactly how any aspect of their theory arose from the data. A complete record of the analytic process is therefore essential.

So open coding is not a linear process; it involves the creation of puzzle pieces which are fitted together, only to be disassembled and reassembled into different pictures. Our account of the analysis now moves into the next stage where we continued to look for types, sequences, processes, patterns and relationships within and across accounts.

Axial coding

Axial coding refers to the way in which categories are now further refined through examination, comparison and thinking about them in relation to each other. At this stage, developed categories are now reassembled into major categories or axial codes, which reflect the working hypotheses or propositions that the analyst has induced through the systematic examination and questioning of the data.

Returning to the exercise, the categories in Table 6.2 – 'army standards', 'self identity', 'period of transition' and 'us and them' – were considered again and related back to each participant. The transcripts suggested that both ex-soldiers believed that in some way the army had made them different from civilians in terms of their work practices. In fact they went further and suggested that they were more committed, more efficient and better organized than many civilian workers. They claimed that their ways were superior and that this can cause problems for them in civilian life because other workers did not work in the same way. So now these grouped codes or categories can be related together under the new major category 'army added value'. We now need to ask what constitutes this 'added value'. These accounts suggested that an eye for detail, organization, commitment and discipline were some of the contributing factors.

Major categories can be tested against the data in order to confirm or refute them. To test the emergent axial code 'army added value', we returned to the transcripts to look for more examples and any counter examples of this phenomenon and code them accordingly (see lines 49–60 in David's transcript and lines 70–78 and 259–262 in Brian's transcript for further examples). However it was also clear that in some instances the participants' army training and army standards had not been viewed as having provided value and had caused problems for the two men when other (civilian) workers either resented or were not comfortable with their ways of working. See below for an example:

```
230    Brian:  . . . A lot of my work, I train people
231    up . . . my work is training and I've had to adapt my training style to be more
232    civilian friendly than in the military because it was . . . people used to say,
233    'Well, we come to you and you don't teach us – you shout at us', which
234    was – all I was doing was projecting my voice so that people would hear
235    me at the back but I've had to adapt it in such a way that people are more
236    happy with it and it's slightly less structured than what it was when I was
237    in the forces – a bit more casual.
```

The study is trying to understand the process of renegotiating identity on leaving the army. From the transcripts, we understood that army socialization meant that ex-soldiers may be left with skills and a demeanour which could be somewhat redundant in civilian life or were not valued in the same way as they were in the army. However, it would seem from these two accounts that ex-service personnel may still be likely to value these ways and be reluctant to discard them.

Now we can add more factors and density to the analysis. Further insight is gained and more questions are raised through examining the codes and categories, thinking about the axial coding and asking further questions of the data. How do ex-servicemen deal with these conflicts? Do they try to change? The extract above indicates that Brian had to adapt and change his demeanour in order to become more acceptable to civilians. It was also clear from his account that he spent much of his working life in the company of other ex-service personnel. Has this made the transition easier for him? Has it been easier for him than for David? Both men were reluctant to leave the army. Does this make a difference to the interpretation?

Selective coding

Selective coding is the final stage of analysis and the aim is to draw together the codes and categories to create an overarching theory or explanation that can be applied to all accounts and will also explain conflicting data. When the researchers reach the stage where one category is mentioned with high frequency and is well connected to other categories, it is safe to adopt this as the **core category**. This core category then acts as the thread or the story line of the research and integrates all aspects of the **emerging theory**. The ideas that have been presented as significant by the participants will be clearly represented within this explanatory core concept.

Considering the limited data that were available to us in this exercise, it was obviously impossible for us to come to any conclusions, report findings or safely adopt a core category for this study. However, for the purposes of the exercise, we are proposing that 'once a soldier, never again a civilian' could be considered as a 'working hypothesis' that has the potential to develop into an emerging theory. From the data, it seemed apparent that, although these participants had left the army and were now technically civilians, they had been socialized into army ways of being and thinking and could not completely revert back to civilian life. They considered themselves to be different from civilians; no longer soldiers, they were now ex-soldiers rather than civilians. As stated earlier, we have focused upon and drawn out just one cluster of codes so this is necessarily a very early and tentative speculation and should be treated as such.

What next?

In order to test this working hypothesis or proposition, we need to apply it to further data. This is the stage of theoretical sampling. Participants are now selected according to their ability to shed further light on our research problem and see how useful our developing theory is for explaining the similarities and differences in these additional accounts.

The potential core category of 'once a soldier, never again a civilian' should now be tested with other ex-army personnel to see whether they feel the same as Brian and David. Interviews with further participants would allow us to examine whether the transition to civilian life was any different for them in any way. Do other ex-soldiers compare themselves favourably to civilians in terms of work practices? It would be important to find out whether participants of different gender, army rank or those with longer or shorter periods of service than the first two participants expressed similar views to them. Does length of service make a difference in terms of ease of transition to civilian life? Do all ex-service personnel miss the social life that Brian and David reported as part of army life? How have they coped with that? Have they all maintained some link with the army? What we would be seeking at this stage are confirming but especially disconfirming cases in order to test the limits of the theory being developed.

The emergent theory should be tested against new data until 'saturation' is reached. By this, we do not mean that certain issues or themes are being raised repeatedly. Saturation is reached when the theory that has emerged can fully explain all variations of the data. When saturation will happen cannot be predicted as each grounded theory study is unique in terms of the process, the recognition of emergent theory and the number of participants required for this to happen.

Strengths and weaknesses of the approach

Grounded theory is data driven; it allows researchers the freedom to develop their theory through thorough and systematic examination of the empirical material. The method aids the understanding of complex behaviours and their meanings through the exploration of the social processes which produce them. This makes grounded theory particularly useful in situations where little is known about a topic or where a new approach to a familiar area is required (Holloway, 1997). Importantly, grounded theory has its own source of rigour. There is a continuing search for evidence which can disconfirm the emerging theory. It is driven by the data in such a way that the final shape of the theory is likely to provide a good 'fit' to the situation in a way that also makes sense to the participants involved in the study (Glaser, 1992).

However grounded theory is not the most straightforward method of qualitative enquiry and should not be chosen lightly. As the data are fragmented through coding and categorizing, the researcher can run the risk of losing sight of the totality as expressed by the participants. It is a method that requires procedures to be repeated and recorded systematically yet also demands imagination and insight (Silverman, 1993; Strauss and Corbin, 1990). Most importantly, the iterative nature of grounded theory makes it a time consuming method without a clearly predictable end point. In the competitive world of academic research, writing successful research proposals and completing projects on time are of paramount importance. Grounded theory can present problems in terms of providing advance details of a sample, calculating costs, gaining ethical approval and predicting the length of a project.

Summary

This exercise has necessarily been limited by the data and information available to us as well as by the confines of space and time. What we have tried to demonstrate is the way ideas emerge through immersion in both the content and the context of the data, through coding and categorizing and through repeated testing. The key to grounded theory is constant comparison. Data are compared with data until theory emerges and it is this emergent theory that informs the selection and recruitment of subsequent participants. Grounded theory is a method of systematic enquiry. We emphasize the importance of recording all ideas, codes, meanings, categories and discrepancies to ensure rigour and validity through a clear 'decision trail' which begins at the outset of the study and ends with the final theory.

7

DISCOURSE ANALYSIS

Adrian Coyle

This chapter provides an account of discourse analysis which attends not only to the practicalities of the approach but also to the assumptions which underpin it. Attention is paid to the diversity of approaches to discourse analysis, the types of research questions that it answers and the types of data to which it can be applied. The process of subjecting data to discourse analysis is illustrated through an analytic engagement with an excerpt of data generated by a focus group.

Key terms

action orientation	Foucauldian discourse analysis
coding	functions
critical discursive psychology	positioning
discourses	social constructionist
discursive psychology	texts
epistemology	variability

Introduction

Since it was formally introduced to British social psychology in the late 1980s, discourse analysis has made tremendous strides in terms of its theoretical and conceptual development and its influence on the discipline – and not only on social psychology. Discourse analytic work has also appeared in journals in health psychology, counselling psychology and developmental psychology among others. However, despite its popularity, discourse analysis is an approach to inquiry that can be difficult to 'pin down'. This should not surprise us as it owes a particular debt to post-structuralism, which holds that meaning is not static and fixed but is fluid, provisional and context-dependent. It seems that this applies not only to how discourse analysis treats qualitative data but also to any attempt to capture the meaning of discourse analysis itself. The term 'discourse analysis' has been applied to diverse analytic approaches that are often based upon different assumptions and have different aims. This makes it difficult to provide an account of the commonalities of discourse analysis except in the broadest terms and any representation of the field will inevitably satisfy some and irritate others.

Jonathan Potter and Margaret Wetherell's classic 1987 text *Discourse and Social Psychology: Beyond Attitudes and Behaviour*, which introduced discourse analysis to British psychology, urged a radical reformulation of the issues that social psychology has traditionally addressed. Social psychologists have long worked with linguistic and textual material in the form of spoken responses within interview settings and written responses to questionnaire items. The question then arises as to what status should be accorded to this material. It is generally assumed that language is a neutral, transparent medium, describing events or revealing underlying psychological processes in a more or less direct, unproblematic way. The possibility of self-presentational and other biases occurring within this material may be acknowledged but it is assumed that these can be eradicated or at least minimized by refining methods of generating and collecting data. Discourse analysis offers a very different understanding of the nature and function of linguistic and textual data.

Assumptions, approaches and applications

Within a discursive approach to psychology, language is represented not as reflecting psychological and social reality but as *constructing* it. There are no objective truths existing 'out there' that can be accessed if only the appropriate scientific methods are employed. Instead, language in the form of **discourses** is seen as constituting the building blocks of 'social reality' (note that it is common practice to use inverted commas to draw attention to the constructed nature of taken-for-granted 'things'). The analysis of discourse emphasizes how social reality is linguistically constructed and aims to gain 'a better understanding of social life and social interaction from our study of social texts' (Potter and Wetherell, 1987: 7).

Discourse analysis can therefore be classed as a **social constructionist** approach to research (although exactly what this means varies across discourse analytic approaches). Social constructionism represents its **epistemology** – its core assumptions about the bases or possibilities for knowledge (for more on epistemologies, see Chapter 2 in this volume). In broad terms, the social constructionist perspective adopts a critical stance towards the taken-for-granted ways in which we understand the world and ourselves, such as the assumption that the categories we use to interpret the world correspond to 'real', 'objective' entities (Burr, 2003). These ways of understanding are seen as having been built up through social processes, especially through linguistic interactions, and so are culturally and historically specific (see Box 7.1 for an example).

Box 7.1   THE SOCIAL CONSTRUCTION OF SEXUALITY CATEGORIES

The categories 'gay man', 'lesbian' and 'homosexual' are now a taken-for-granted part of how we talk about sexualities. It is easy to forget that defining people in terms of their preference for sexual partners of the same gender as themselves only began in the eighteenth century. Prior to this, there were terms that referred to sexual activity involving people of the same gender but these terms did not denote a particular kind of person. Furthermore, the ways in which these behaviours were socially organized, regulated and responded to varied across cultures. The term 'homosexual' was not coined until the mid-nineteenth century with the increasing medicalization of sexuality. Terms such as 'gay man' and 'lesbian' were only adopted in the 1960s and 1970s in line with the political concerns of the gay liberation and women's movements (for detailed analyses of the social construction of 'the homosexual' up to that point, see Plummer, 1981). And with the postmodern trend within 'queer theory', concepts of 'the gay man' and 'the lesbian' have been subjected to critical scrutiny (Sedgwick, 1990; Simpson, 1996). So, from this one example, it can be seen that there is nothing fixed or inevitable about what may appear to be common sense ways of representing the world: they are socially constructed.

The emphasis on language as a constructive tool is one of the core assumptions of discourse analysis. The language user is viewed as selecting from the range of linguistic resources available to them and using these resources to construct a version of events, although not necessarily in an intentional way. The person may not be able to articulate the constructive process in which they are engaged but this does not mean that it does not exist. It simply highlights the extent to which the constructive use of language is a fundamental, taken-for-granted aspect of social life.

Discourse analysis does not use people's language as a means of gaining access to their psychological and social worlds. As Burman and Parker (1993a: 1) have contended, 'Psychological phenomena have a public and collective reality, and we are mistaken if we think they have their origin in the private space of the individual'. Instead, discourse analysis focuses on this 'public and collective reality' as constructed through language use. It examines how people use language to construct versions of their worlds and what is gained from these constructions.

It can be difficult to specify exactly what discourses are because, although they are generally represented as broad patterns of language use within spoken or written material, a variety of meanings have been ascribed to the term. It may be useful to consider various definitions of 'discourse' and of related concepts in order to divine some basic commonalities. Parker (1992: 5) emphasized the constructive potential of discourses and defined a discourse as 'a system of statements which constructs an object'. In their classic text, Potter and Wetherell (1987) preferred the term 'interpretative repertoires' rather than 'discourses' because the idea of 'repertoire' implies flexibility in the ways in which the linguistic components of the repertoire can be put together. They regard these interpretative repertoires as linguistic phenomena which have coherence in terms of their content and style and which may be organized around one or more central metaphors. In a similar vein, Burr (2003: 202) defined a discourse as 'a systematic, coherent set of images, metaphors and so on that construct an object in a particular way'. This definitional survey is hardly exhaustive but, amalgamating these and other related ideas, discourses can be defined as sets of linguistic material that have a degree of coherence in their content and organization and which perform constructive functions in broadly defined social contexts. Different discourses can be invoked to construct any object, person, event or situation in a variety of ways.

Discourses are identified through the examination of **texts**. All spoken and written material (and indeed the products of every other sort of signifying practice too) can be conceptualized as a text and subjected to discourse analysis, in the same way that within traditional scientific paradigms, almost anything can be construed as data and analysed. Indeed, the post-structuralist philosopher, Jacques Derrida (1976: 58), held that 'Il n'y a pas de hors-texte' ('There is no outside-text'/'There is nothing outside the text'), meaning that everything is part of the context of a signifying system. This raises the question of whether discourse analysts hold that there is a real world outside texts/discourse: we shall return to this issue shortly.

Discourse analysis assumes that linguistic material has an **action orientation**, that language is used to perform particular social functions such as justifying, questioning and accusing, and it achieves this through a variety of rhetorical strategies. Key tasks that discourse analysts within this action-oriented approach set themselves are to identify what functions are being performed by the linguistic material that is being analysed and to consider how these functions are performed and what resources are available to perform these functions. This entails a close and careful inspection of the text. In this process, some discourse analysts are concerned with the fine grain of talk. These writers tend to adopt and adapt the approaches of conversation analysis in their work (see Atkinson and Heritage, 1984), recursively moving between a micro-level focus on textual detail and a consideration of the rhetorical functions to which the text is oriented. Generally, though, discourse analysis is more concerned with the social organization of talk rather than with its linguistic organization. This approach involves looking at what discourses are shared across texts and what constructions of the world the material can be seen as advocating, rather than focusing on the details of how utterances relate to the conversational sequences to which they belong and the interactional work accomplished by these utterances and sequences.

Exploring this issue of different approaches further and returning to a point made at the start of the chapter, it is worth noting that there are two main approaches to the study of discourse within UK psychology. The approach known as **discursive psychology** views language as a form of social action, addresses the social functions of talk and considers how these functions are achieved. It is particularly attentive to the ways by which 'factual accounts' and 'descriptions', which might be interpreted by other research approaches as straightforward 'objective' representations of internal or external psychological and/or social realities, are made to appear as such. More recently, its focus has encompassed linguistic interaction in everyday settings (e.g., see Wiggins, 2004) and institutional contexts (e.g., see Hepburn and Wiggins, 2005). Discursive psychology is most closely associated with the work of writers such as Jonathan Potter and Derek Edwards (e.g., Edwards and Potter, 1992; Potter, 1996). Work conducted within this tradition adopts a thoroughly social constructionist position: writers do not necessarily deny that a material reality exists but they do not see it as reflected in our language use and they query the possibility of obtaining direct knowledge of material reality.

This approach has been represented as politically limited by other practitioners who are more concerned with issues such as identity and selfhood, ideology, power relations and social change. This perspective has been termed **Foucauldian discourse analysis** as it owes a particular debt to the work of the philosopher, Michel Foucault. Writers within Foucauldian discourse analysis see the world as having a structural reality, which they usually describe in terms of power relations; these are viewed as underpinning how we understand and talk about the world (Burr, 2003). The Foucauldian approach holds that discourses 'facilitate and limit, enable and constrain what can be said, by whom, where and when' (Willig, 2001: 107). Hence, dominant discourses privilege versions of social reality that accord with and reinforce existing social structures and the networks of power relations associated with them. Analysts study the availability of discursive resources within a culture and the implications that this carries for those living within that culture. This form of discourse analysis is most closely associated with the work of Ian Parker, Erica Burman and Wendy Hollway (e.g., Burman, 1992, 1995; Burman and Parker, 1993b; Hollway, 1989; Parker, 1992; Parker et al., 1995).

As we can see, although Foucauldian discourse analysts agree with the discursive psychology emphasis on the linguistic construction of social reality, one major difference is that they advocate a need to hold on to some idea of language representing things that have an existence independent of language. Parker (1992) has suggested that 'things' should be represented as having different statuses as objects. Some objects are said to exist independently of thought and language, namely those that are needed for thought to occur (such as our brains and bodies) and around which thinking can be organized (such as the physical and organizational properties of the environment). Yet, we do not have direct knowledge of these objects because thinking is a constructive and interpretative process. Other objects are constructed through language but are treated in language as if they had an enduring reality.

One feature of discourse analytic research that is associated with Foucauldian discourse analysis is **positioning**, which comes from the work of Bronwyn Davies and Rom Harré (1990). This represents one discursive interpretation of the social psychological concept of identity. When an individual is constructed through discourse, he/she is accorded a particular subject position within that discourse, which brings with it a set of images, metaphors and obligations concerning the kind of response that can be made. For example, within a biomedical discourse, people who are ill are placed in the subject position of 'the patient', with its obligation to act as a passive recipient of care from those who are placed in the subject position of 'medical experts'. In their linguistic response to that positioning, the individual can accept it (and fulfil the obligations of their position) or they can resist it. Of course, the person can also position themselves within a discourse and their audience can accept or reject this positioning. Any individual may assume some positions fairly consistently within their talk while other positions are more temporary, giving rise to variability. As Davies and Harré (1999: 35) have commented, the question of 'who one is . . . is always an open question with a shifting answer depending upon the positions made available within one's own and others' discursive practices'. Some exponents of Foucauldian discourse analysis have dealt with self and subjectivity by drawing upon particular versions of psychoanalytic theory to introduce into their analyses a notion of the person as motivated and as having agency – as acting upon their environment (Frosh et al., 2003; Parker, 1997). The necessity of invoking psychoanalytic theory to develop analyses of self and subjectivity is, however, open to debate.

In addition to the two approaches outlined so far, a third approach has emerged which has been termed **critical discursive psychology** and which attempts to synthesize discursive psychology and Foucauldian discourse analysis. The tenets of this approach are expounded in Margaret Wetherell's 1998 paper, although it can also be seen in action in her work on masculinities with Nigel Edley (e.g., Edley and Wetherell, 1999). The discourse analytic report in Appendix 2 in this volume also adopts a critical discursive psychology approach.

Moving on to consider the issue of research questions, although discourse analysis has been used to investigate a wide variety of research topics, it is only appropriate for the exploration of particular types of research questions. Many research questions from elsewhere in psychology are based on a logic of factors and outcomes, whereas discourse analytic research questions focus on construction, rhetoric, ideology and action (see Box 7.2). With these critical and analytic foci, it is not surprising that discourse analysis has been taken up with enthusiasm by those who wish to give psychology a radical, political edge. Some analysts choose to focus on discourses which reproduce social relations of dominance and oppression and/or which include oppressive aspects that are often glossed over. Discourse analysis can be used to indicate that alternative discourses could be constructed in their place. Yet it is important to acknowledge that the supplanting of oppressive discourses is a complex and lengthy process and there is no way of predicting with confidence what the social implications of discursive change might be.

Nevertheless, the critical and analytic focus counteracts the accusation sometimes levelled at discourse analysis that it is far removed from 'real life' concerns and threatens psychologists' aspirations to influence practices and policies outside the research domain (Abraham and Hampson, 1996). Given that 'Language (organized into *discourses*) . . . has an immense power to shape the way that people . . . experience and behave in the world' (Burman and Parker, 1993a: 1, original emphasis), discourse analysis *does* have considerable practical potential. Indeed, Carla Willig (1999) produced an edited volume entitled *Applied Discourse Analysis*, which demonstrated how discourse analysis can inform social and psychological interventions on issues such as smoking, sex education and psychiatric medication.

Box 7.2   DISCOURSE ANALYTIC RESEARCH QUESTIONS

Potter (2003) identifies four foci in discourse analytic research questions:

- How specific actions and practices are linguistically done in particular settings. For example, Barnes et al. (2004) explored the question of how people claim citizenship and to what ends by analysing letters of complaint written to council officials concerning the use of rural space by travellers.
- How particular accounts of things are constructed and made to seem factual and objective or how seemingly factual accounts are challenged. For example, Wallwork and Dixon (2004) examined how fox hunting was constructed as a national issue in Britain in pro-hunting newspaper and magazine articles.
- Psychological practice: this involves re-framing psychological concepts in discursive terms. For example, Harper (1994) examined the resources used by mental health professionals to construct and identify 'paranoia'.
- Exploitation, prejudice and ideology: this involves examining how racism, sexism, homophobia and other oppressions are expressed, justified or rendered invisible. For example, see Wetherell and Potter's (1992) extensive study of racist language and practice in New Zealand and Forbat's (2005) examination of themes of care and abuse in talk about informal care relationships.

Sampling discourse

In order to conduct an analysis of discourse, texts are required in which discourses may be discerned. These texts may take many forms. The preferred form of text within discursive psychology is a naturally occurring one, although transcripts of interviews (preferably focus group interviews) conducted on the research topic or excerpts from writing on the topic are also acceptable within other approaches. Accurate transcription is a lengthy process, which is made even more laborious if the transcriber wishes to include every 'um' and 'uh' uttered by the speakers and to measure pauses in speech production. This sort of detailed approach is less often seen in discourse analysis than in conversation analysis, although Robin Wooffitt (2001: 328) has rightly observed that 'it is a good methodological practice always to produce as detailed a transcription as possible'.

Within traditional approaches to sampling in psychological research, the emphasis is placed upon securing as large and representative a sample as possible. Within discourse analysis, if interview material is used as a source of data, there is no necessity to sample discourse from a large number of people. If newspaper reports of a particular event are to be used, it is not necessary to collect all reports from all newspapers on that event. The analysis stage of qualitative data is almost always more laborious and time-consuming than the analysis of structured data so the researcher must beware of ending up with an unmanageable amount of unstructured data to sift through. What is important is to gather sufficient text to discern the variety of discursive forms that are commonly used when speaking or writing about the research topic. This may be possible from an analysis of relatively few interview transcripts or newspaper reports, especially where common discursive forms are under consideration. In this case, larger samples of data add to the analytic task without adding significantly to the analytic outcome. Where an analysis is purely exploratory and the analyst has little idea in advance of what the analytic focus might be, larger samples of data are required.

Techniques of discourse analysis

While it is relatively easy to expound the central theoretical tenets of discourse analysis, specifying exactly how one goes about doing discourse analysis is a different matter because there is no rigid set of formal procedures. It has been contended that the key to analysing discourse is scholarship and the development of an analytic mentality rather than adherence to a rigorous methodology (Billig, 1988). The emphasis is placed upon the careful reading and interpretation of texts, with interpretations being backed by reference to linguistic evidence in the texts. The first step is said to be the suspension of belief in what is normally taken for granted in language use (Potter and Wetherell,

1987). This involves seeing linguistic practices not as simply reflecting underlying psychological and social realities but as constructing and legitimating a version of events. The development of such an outlook is no easy matter because it runs counter to how we usually treat people's language. Anyone who is undertaking discourse analysis for the first time has to be prepared to make repeated mistakes in this respect because it is usual for novices to offer interpretations that assume that the language being analysed is reflecting some reality in a straightforward way. Attentive supervision by a more experienced discourse analyst is necessary to identify these lapses until eventually the novice develops an interpretative framework that is sufficiently and consistently social constructionist.

Despite the reluctance of some discourse analysts to be prescriptive about techniques and procedures, one cannot help feeling that a systematic methodological approach would be beneficial to those entering the field for the first time until they develop the confidence needed for analytic creativity. In an attempt to provide some pointers, Potter and Wetherell (1987) have suggested a loose ten-stage approach, with two stages devoted to the analytic process, and Willig (2001) has outlined a six-stage approach to Foucauldian discourse analysis. Potter and Wetherell's (1987) analytic process begins with what is termed **coding**. By this is meant the process of examining the text closely. With a large data set, it may be worth using appropriate software to help organize and code the data, such as NVivo (Richards, 2000). If the research focus has been specified in advance, instances of the research focus are identified at this point. It is worth being as inclusive as possible, identifying implicit and borderline instances of the research focus. This makes it possible to discern less obvious but nonetheless fruitful lines of inquiry. The coding stage overlaps with Willig's (2001) 'discursive constructions' stage, where the analyst identifies the different ways in which the discursive object (the focus of the research questions) is constructed in the data. The coding process is more complex if the research focus has not been determined in advance. In this case, it is necessary to read and reread the text, looking for recurrent discursive patterns shared by the accounts under analysis. This represents Willig's (2001) second analytic stage, which she terms 'discourses' and which involves identifying wider discourses within which the discursive constructions are located. Willig (2001: 110) provides a useful example of what this might entail, suggesting that, in an interview about her husband's cancer, a woman may draw upon a biomedical discourse when discussing diagnosis and treatment, a psychological discourse when she tries to make sense of how the disease developed and a romantic discourse when talking about how she and her husband have fought the illness together. In this analytic stage, hypotheses about which discourses are being invoked in the text are formulated and reformulated. This can be very frustrating as hypotheses are developed, revised or discarded as the linguistic evidence needed to support them proves not to be forthcoming. It is important that the analyst should remain open to alternative readings of the text and to the need to reject hypotheses that are not supported by the text.

A useful strategy for the next stage of analysis in the schemes of both Potter and Wetherell (1987) and Willig (2001) involves reading the text mindful of what its **functions** might be. Any text is held to have an action orientation and is designed to fulfil certain functions, so the question is what functions is this text fulfilling and how is it fulfilling them? The formulation of hypotheses about the purposes and consequences of language is central to discourse analysis. However, identifying the functions of language is often not a straightforward process because these functions may not be explicit. For example, when someone asks you to do something, they may phrase it not as an order or command ('Make scrambled eggs on potato cakes for breakfast') but as a question to which the expected answer is 'Yes' ('Did you say something about making scrambled eggs on potato cakes for breakfast?').

In seeking to identify discursive functions, it may be helpful to examine a text mindful of what version of events it may be designed to counteract. Any version of events is but one of a number of possible versions and therefore must be constructed as more persuasive than these alternative versions if it is to prevail. This process is formalized in some settings, such as in a court where the prosecution and the defence present different versions of events that seek to persuade the jury, with one account attempting to win out over the competing account. Sometimes alternative versions will be explicitly mentioned and counteracted in a text but on other occasions they will be implicit. If analysts are sensitized to what these alternative versions might be, they may be well placed to analyse how the text addresses the function of legitimating the version constructed therein.

In analysing function, it is useful to become acquainted with the ways in which various features of discourse are described in the discourse analytic and conversation analytic literatures. These discursive features frequently perform specific rhetorical functions. Therefore, if analysts are able to identify these features, they can examine the text mindful of the functions that these features typically perform. For example, the use of terms such as 'always', 'never', 'nobody' and 'everyone' may represent what have been called 'extreme case formulations' (Pomerantz, 1986). These take whatever position is being advocated in the text to its extreme and thereby help to make this position more persuasive. For those interested in becoming acquainted with these technical features of discourse, Potter (1996) has outlined a wide range but the best strategy is to examine studies which have used discourse analytic and conversation analytic approaches.

According to Potter and Wetherell (1987), one means of elucidating the functions of discourse is through the study of **variability** in any discourse. The fact that discourse varies appears to be a commonsense statement. If we were analysing discourse from different people about a particular object, we would expect variations related to whether individuals evaluated the object positively or negatively. However, variation also occurs *within* an individual's discourse, dependent upon the purposes of the discourse. Indeed, this was a key feature of Harper's (1994) study of mental health professionals' talk about diagnosing 'paranoia' (see Box 7.2). It has been claimed that, in their search for individual consistency, mainstream approaches to psychology have sought to minimize or explain away intra-individual variation (Potter and Wetherell, 1987). Discourse analysis, in contrast, actively seeks it out. As variability arises from the different functions that the discourse may be fulfilling, the nature of the variation can provide clues to what these functions are. The process of discourse analysis therefore involves the search for both consistency (in the identification of discourses) and variability (in the analysis of discursive functions).

In her outline of Foucauldian discourse analysis, Willig (2001) identifies three stages after the consideration of action orientations, beginning with an examination of the subject positions offered by the discourses that have been discerned within a text. Of course, a consideration of subject positions may be part of a consideration of a text's action orientations because a text can function to assign or resist particular subject positions. A more distinctively Foucauldian discourse analytic concern appears in Willig's penultimate stage of 'practice'. This involves exploring how discursive constructions and the subject positions associated with them open up or close off possibilities for action. Different discourses and subject positions are seen as carrying different possibilities for what might be said or done. So, for example, Willig (1995) found that unprotected sex is bound up with a marital discourse; within this discourse, marriage and equivalent relationships (such as 'long-term relationships') are constructed as incompatible with using condoms. The same phenomenon can be discerned in the work of Flowers et al. (1997) on unprotected sex among gay men (although this was not a discourse analytic study), where participants constructed unprotected sex in terms of a romantic relationship discourse of sharing and intimacy. Thus these sorts of relationship discourses legitimate the practice of unprotected sex, which reproduces the relationship discourses that legitimate it. The final stage in Willig's (2001) outline of Foucauldian discourse analysis is termed 'subjectivity' and considers the implications that follow from taking up various subject positions for people's subjective experiences – for their thinking and feeling. However, a thorough social constructionist perspective views 'thinking' and 'feeling' as ideas generated within cultures to mediate people's dealings with each other and to enable them to engage in social life. Some discourse analysts would therefore contest the premises of this analytic stage of 'subjectivity'. The application of some of Willig's stages to the data set in Appendix 1 can be observed in Chapter 8 in this volume.

Before leaving this consideration of analytic strategies in discourse analysis, we should note one major analytic limitation, which is the difficulty discourse analysis has in dealing effectively with some data that are not spoken or written. While photos and other visual images *can* be treated as text and examined, it is more difficult to incorporate gestures, facial expressions and analogous non-verbal data within an analysis in a way that accords these data equivalent status to verbal data. There may in the past have been insufficient motivation to develop strategies for analysing such data, given the difficulties of conveying these data and their nuances in printed journal articles or books. The development of online journals and advances in digital technology mean that it is now possible to include sections of relevant footage from interviews or real life situations in analyses. It is to be hoped that this provides a spur to develop sufficiently sophisticated ways of analysing such data that, where appropriate, the interpretation of spoken data is routinely elaborated by insights gained from the analysis of non-verbal data.

Working with data

In this section, the practicalities of conducting discourse analytic work are explored. Here I take as an example a study in which I was involved, with Chris Walton (the author of Chapter 8), in collecting and analysing the data. As part of a larger study of the social construction of new genetic technologies,[1] we wanted to explore how members of the public constructed a technology known as Pre-implantation Genetic Diagnosis (PGD) and a phenomenon associated with it, commonly termed 'saviour siblings'; how the public negotiated the permissibility or non-permissibility of this technology; and how they made sense of associated issues. Thus, in terms of the types of research questions outlined by Potter (2003), our research questions fall into the category of those that examine how particular accounts of things are constructed (see Box 7.2).

PGD was developed in the 1980s in response to requests from people who were at risk of passing on a serious genetic condition to their children. In this technology, in vitro fertilization is used to create embryos, a cell from each embryo is tested for the specific genetic abnormality and healthy embryos are transferred to the uterus. In a public consultation paper on genetics and reproductive decision-making, the UK Human Genetics Commission (2004: 13) stated that 'The use of PGD is not uncontroversial'. Their construction of possible areas of controversy included the use of PGD to identify embryos that had a particular tissue type and that could be selected as a 'saviour sibling'. The idea is that these embryos could be implanted in the uterus to produce a baby that would provide matching tissue to enable the treatment of an existing sibling affected by a serious or life-threatening (but not necessarily inherited) disorder. This tissue takes the form of blood from the umbilical cord or bone marrow. Of course, the embryo selection process in this case would also aim to identify embryos that will not develop the condition that affects the sibling (if that condition had been inherited). In literature on the ethics of the saviour sibling process, its acceptability has been contested on the grounds that it leads to the creation of a child who is not valued in their own right but rather to serve the interests of their sibling: they become a means rather than an end (Spriggs, 2004).

To explore the responses of members of the general public to these issues, we conducted eight focus group interviews in six locations in England, Scotland and Wales with 80 members of public who had no particular involvement or investment in genomics-related issues. When we subjected the focus group transcripts to discourse analysis (after having coded them using NVivo), we found that the data specifically addressing PGD were embedded within data across the groups which grappled with major philosophical questions and which constructed a complex moral universe. These questions related to issues such as the existence of an 'order of things' and the place of illness and death within this order, the drawbacks of modern discourses about the satisfaction of desire and the role of motivation in determining the acceptability of particular actions. This process represented the preliminary 'coding' and, to some extent, 'discourses' stages of analysis outlined earlier.

Here I present the analysis of one passage which featured some of the key themes from our data on PGD and saviour siblings. The passage is reproduced below (transcribed in a very basic way – the only notation used is three dots which signify a short pause).

538	**Gabi:** I think a lot . . . a lot of the stuff on that, what I read in the paper about, you
539	know, being able to grow organs to . . . to save children or, you know, parents
540	that can't have kids mothers that can't give birth and . . . and finding some ways
541	to take their DNA and . . . and give them children, I think I was all quite happy
542	with that until they started with this preferential genetic profiling or something
543	where you can, you know, pick what colour your baby's hair is going to be
544	and, you know, how many toes they'll have and, you know, what colour eyes
545	and taking certain parts and I think that's when I thought 'You've taken
546	something really good and made it, you know, monstrous'.
547	**Jocelyn:** It also seems a bit ruthless to have another child only if it has a particular thing
548	that's needed to save the first one.
549	**Connor:** What's the psychological impact on that kid when he's 18, 19, 20?
550	**Sebastian:** Your morality you would say no but as a parent you would say, 'I have to . . . I
551	have to save the child'.
552	**Jocelyn:** Yes.
553	**Archie:** Absolutely. The courts have actually . . . the courts are going to give permission
554	for that very thing to happen. And, yes, I can see where you're coming from,
555	that the child who is going to be conceived . . . I mean, they're not going to be
556	taking organs from him or anything as . . . as gross as that. But, yes, they're
557	going to take cells, as I understand it. It was, yes, from the placenta which will
558	then be used to . . . to nourish or to . . . to provide a marrow transplant for his older

559		brother. And, okay, the younger kid might read about this in the paper in 20
560		years time and think, 'Jesus, they didn't really want me, they just, you know . . . '
561	**Jocelyn:**	. . . used the bit.
562	**Archie:**	But on the other hand maybe he'll think, 'Well . . . '
563	**Connor:**	'I saved my brother'.
564	**Archie:**	. . . 'I saved my older brother's life'.
565	**Jocelyn:**	Yes. Yes.
566	**Archie:**	At the end of the day it's an individual case and I think it's very hard to
567		generalize with these issues.
568	**Joel:**	Living . . . living siblings do that just now. Helping save each other, if there's a
569		genetic match.
570	**Archie:**	Yes.
571	**Joel:**	But, I mean, that's the thin end of the wedge, isn't it?

In two places in this extract, we see speakers construct versions of the technicalities of PGD and the saviour sibling process. In lines 541–545, Gabi constructs herself as 'quite happy' with what she had read about advances in genetic technologies until 'they started with this preferential genetic profiling'. Her account of what falls under this category features something that may or may not relate to the saviour sibling process ('taking certain parts') but her version of PGD relates to selection for what might be regarded as minor or trivial traits such as hair or eye colour, thereby invoking a 'designer babies' discourse or interpretative repertoire. This discourse or repertoire was routinely used in press coverage of PGD possibilities at the time. It constructed the process as permitting parents to choose to implant embryos that had particular desirable characteristics to produce 'high quality', specially tailored, 'designer' babies. In her construction of her thinking, the milestone nature of the time when she encountered the possibility of selecting embryos for what might be seen as trivial traits is conveyed by her reported thought 'You've taken something really good and made it, you know, monstrous'. The contrast between 'really good' (then) and 'monstrous' (now) creates a sense of taint, with the intensity of the terms constructing the change as substantial and with 'monstrous' invoking Frankensteinian associations.

What we have here is an example of the 'slippery slope' argument – a rhetorical feature that was discerned across the data on all new genetic technologies in the study. This argument constructs an innovation or proposed innovation as the first step on a path that will lead to (sometimes unspecified) catastrophic later developments. Gabi's 'slippery slope' argument is slightly different from the standard version because she constructs this betrayal of a beneficial technology as having *already* happened. The betraying agent is unspecified but presumably includes professional bodies involved in PGD which have allowed this to occur.

In lines 555–559, Archie constructs a version of the saviour sibling process that does not accord with the 'official' version in that he sees cells being taken 'from the placenta' and being used 'to nourish or to . . . to provide a marrow transplant'. This was typical of the versions of PGD and the saviour sibling process that were produced in the other focus groups, with some departing much further from the 'official' version than this. If we were to apply a deficit model of public understanding (which assumes that public scepticism towards science and technology is due to the public's inadequate knowledge about science – see Wynne, 2006, for a review), we could interpret these data as indicating a lack of 'accurate' public knowledge. However, this would be to ignore the sense-making that was actually going on here and in other focus groups, where speakers draw upon parts of medical and moral social discourse about genetics and construct complex versions of PGD and the saviour sibling process from these resources.

Moving on to consider how speakers negotiated the permissibility of these technologies, Jocelyn's and Connor's responses (lines 547–548; line 549) represent common evaluative positions on saviour siblings that were taken up across the focus groups – the contention that its permissibility can be assessed through a consideration of the motives and desires of the parents (so the parents become the object of moral inquiry) and a consideration of the potential psychological implications for the child conceived as a saviour sibling. The latter issue recurs in lines 559–565, where the potential psychological implications are first specified through speech attributed to the child who has fulfilled the role of saviour sibling – a sense of not having been wanted for their own sake but for what they could provide. The hypothetical reported speech functions to make this contention appear more 'real'; rather than being discussed in abstract terms, the implications are conveyed through the musings of an imagined saviour sibling in twenty years time (an analysis of action orientation can apply to the mode of speech rather than just to the words). Note that Archie does not finish the imagined speech in line 560 but tails off into a short pause, leaving Jocelyn to complete his sentence in line 561. This could be tentatively interpreted as Archie implying that the effect of having been conceived as a saviour sibling on that imaginary person's sense of value could be too horrific for them to name. However, an alternative and a more positive psychological implication is suggested by Archie and Connor in lines 562–564, again advanced in co-constructed hypothetical reported speech, and assented to by Jocelyn in line 565 – that the person might feel that he/she saved their sibling's life. Considering both positioning and action orientation, the fact that Archie advances two contrasting possibilities could be seen as positioning him as a balanced contributor to the discussion rather than as a partisan advocate of a single viewpoint. This may serve to build advance credibility for any future contributions that he might make.

Returning to lines 550–551, Sebastian could be seen as creating a contrast between a moral position ('Your morality you would say no') and a position that is implicitly constructed as immoral because the 'but' in line 550 makes it contrast with the explicitly moral position ('but as a parent you would say "I have to . . . I have to save the child"'). However, his construction of the subject position of the parent and his use of imagined reported speech creates a moral order in itself – one that, through the reported speech, is given more immediacy than the contrasting position. Here the subjectivity of the parent is constructed as different from the subjectivity of the general public and these subjectivities are taken as the bases for assessing the permissibility of the technology – a version assented to by both Jocelyn and Archie in lines 552–553. There is therefore an implicit relativity being constructed around assessments of the permissibility of PGD and saviour siblings.

Moving to the end of the data excerpt, there is no resolution offered for the dilemmas that the speakers raise. The extract shifts between various levels of argument, none of them well developed and none of them resolved in an agreed position. Towards the end of the extract, in lines 566–567, Archie says 'At the end of the day it's an individual case and I think it's very hard to generalize with these issues'. He acknowledges that their discussion cannot be resolved in any general way and brings the acceptability of this technology down to an individual, case-by-case level. Joel, in lines 568–569, plays down the contentious aspect of PGD by constructing an equivalence between it and an existing, implicitly accepted technology, namely where someone might donate something from their body (such as bone marrow) to a sibling in need where there is a sufficient genetic match. This happened in other focus groups too where various analogies were invoked which constructed the saviour sibling process as not unique and which may have been oriented towards offering reassurance about any potential risks. However, in the final line, Joel produces a cliché invoking the 'slippery slope' argument ('that's the thin end of the wedge, isn't it?') that seems to open up debate again.

What I have tried to do in this brief analysis is to provide some flavour of the ways in which one particular genetic technology was constructed in our data set and thereby to demonstrate how some of the techniques of discourse analysis outlined previously (especially the identification of the functions performed by language) might be used in practice. To see how other techniques are applied, readers should consult analyses in discourse analytic journal articles. The analysis of a single extract like this may appear as part of a discourse analytic paper. Some papers present many short data extracts to illustrate a range of interpretations; other papers present longer data extracts and analyse these in detail, with the interpretations contributing to a progressively unfolding analytic narrative; and some papers combine both approaches. For an example of how a discourse analytic paper might be written up, see Report 3 in Appendix 2 in this volume.

Evaluating discourse analytic work

The discourse analyst is sometimes accused of 'putting words into the mouths' of those whose discourse is being analysed and of unnecessarily complicating apparently straightforward speech acts. Yet, post-structuralist writers, with their contention that meaning is not fixed or stable, have noted how language use may have consequences that the speaker did not intend. For example, in their analysis of talk about community care policies, Potter and Collie (1989) pointed out how the notion of 'community care' invokes a reassuring community discourse, centred around images of neighbourliness, close ties and social support. This poses problems for those who wish to criticize community care, as, in naming it, they end up invoking these positive associations and thereby undermining their arguments. As individuals may not be aware that their language creates such effects, the method sometimes advocated for evaluating qualitative analyses which involves asking those who produced the data to comment on the analyses is inappropriate for discourse analysis. In relation to our analysis here, some of the focus group participants might protest 'But I never meant that', yet this does not invalidate the analysis. The analyst is engaged in elaborating the perhaps unintended consequences of the language that was used, tracing the ripples that discourses create in the pool of meaning into which they are tossed.

This does not mean that analysts are free to posit whatever interpretations they please. For discourse analysis to be taken seriously, there must exist criteria which allow the quality of an analysis to be evaluated. Discussions about the evaluation of psychological research generally focus on success in hypothesis testing and concerns about reliability and validity. It is inappropriate to evaluate discourse analytic work within such a framework because discourse analysis is positioned outside this tradition. Criteria such as reliability and validity are based on the assumption of scientific objectivity, which in turn assumes that the researcher and the researched are independent of each other. With discourse analysis, this cannot be the case. Analysts who demonstrate the contingent, socially constructed, rhetorical nature of the discourse of others cannot make an exception for their own discourse. Like the person whose talk or writing they analyse, analysts construct a purposeful account of their texts, drawing upon their available and acknowledged linguistic resources and ideological frameworks. In the analysis offered in this chapter, factors such as my training as a psychologist, my familiarity with existing work relevant to the research topic and my 'personal' views and investments that are directly relevant to PGD (and that are, of course, socially constructed rather than personal) all influenced the ideological framework which I brought to bear on the analysis. Acknowledging this should not be seen as undermining the analysis because no one can adopt a perspectiveless, utterly 'objective' stance on the world. Instead, it should be seen as part of a process of making research more accountable, more transparent and easier to evaluate.

This reflexivity bridges the chasm that more traditional research approaches create between the researcher and the researched and makes it impossible to assess an analysis of discourse using traditional evaluative criteria. Yardley (2000) has suggested four alternative criteria for the evaluation of qualitative research, namely sensitivity to context, commitment and rigour, transparency and coherence and impact and importance (for more on these, see Chapter 2). With some modifications and caveats, these criteria can assist in the evaluation of discourse analytic work. However, the method of reporting discourse analytic studies potentially provides the most useful means of evaluating them. Alongside interpretations, the analyst should try to present as much of the relevant text as possible, demonstrating how analytic conclusions were reached with reference to the text. Readers can then judge for themselves whether the interpretations are warranted. They can offer alternative readings of the text so that, through debate, coherent and persuasive interpretations can be achieved. The only problem with this is that the submission guidelines of most academic journals make it difficult to present large amounts of raw data in research reports. However, with the advent of the internet, it should become standard practice for discourse analytic (and other qualitative) researchers to include in their articles the address of a website where they have made their raw data available for inspection.

Summary

This chapter has outlined the principles and practicalities of discourse analysis, illustrating the analytic process through an engagement with a data extract. Although it is hoped that some indication has been provided of how discourse analysis might be undertaken, it is also hoped that readers have gained a clear sense of how discourse analysis cannot be treated merely as an analytic technique. Researchers who choose to use discourse analysis also choose to employ a range of assumptions about the social world (although the precise nature of these assumptions will vary according to the type of discourse analysis used) and should ensure that their contextualization of their study (e.g., in a literature review), research questions, analyses and discussion of the implications of the research accord with these assumptions. In conclusion, it is fair to say that, while discourse analysis is perhaps not a research approach for the faint-hearted, nonetheless for those who can work with text in a sustained, detailed way and who relish the prospect of critically interrogating the 'taken-for-granted' of social life, it can prove most rewarding. Readers who wish to practise their discourse analytic skills could take advantage of the contention that a discourse analytic report can be seen as a text which attempts to construct a particular version of social reality and which can itself be subjected to discourse analysis. This means that the analysis of the data extract that I presented in this chapter could be treated as a text and discourse analysed, as could the entire chapter!

Further reading

Potter and Wetherell's (1987) very readable and broad-ranging text *Discourse and Social Psychology: Beyond Attitudes and Behaviour* remains the obvious starting point for anyone interested in discourse analysis. Potter's (1996) *Representing Reality: Discourse, Rhetoric and Social Construction* offers a clear and comprehensive account of the history, epistemology and practicalities of discursive approaches, with many clarifying examples. For an outline of the principles of the other major discourse analytic tradition in the UK, see Parker's (1992) *Discourse Dynamics: Critical Analysis for Social and Individual Psychology*. Wetherell et al.'s (2001a, 2001b) companion volumes *Discourse Theory and Practice* and *Discourse as Data* are invaluable to novice analysts as they focus on the process of analysis within different traditions and present a wide range of examples. Willig's (1999) *Applied Discourse Analysis: Social and Psychological Interventions* provides examples of how different versions of discourse analysis can inform interventions on a range of practical issues, thereby demonstrating how questions about the utility of discourse analytic work can be answered.

Note

1   This study was funded by the Economic and Social Research Council (ESRC Award Number: L145251005).

8

DOING DISCOURSE ANALYSIS

Chris Walton

This chapter presents one researcher's account of how an analytic group applied the principles of Foucauldian discourse analysis to transcripts of two interviews with ex-soldiers which offered accounts of being in and leaving the army and post-army life. The chapter begins by identifying the discursive objects that were focused on in the analysis and then provides an account of how the various stages of the analytic process were negotiated and what they produced. Consideration is given to alternative research questions that could have been asked of the data and the different transcription formats that may be used in discourse analytic research. Comparisons are offered with other forms of discourse analysis and questions are raised about some aspects of Foucauldian discourse analysis.

Key terms

action orientation	practice
discourses	reflexivity
discursive objects	subjectivities
discursive resources	subject positions
extreme case formulation	three-part list
positioning	

Introduction

After conducting discourse analysis with accounts of leaving the army, the group of researchers of which I was part concluded that 'doing discourse analysis' seemed less to do with following the steps of a particular method than with developing a confidence in our use of analytic concepts and the reporting of our analysis in terms that were consistent with the theories and epistemological positions of discourse analysis. In other words, doing discourse analysis seemed to us to be about achieving a familiarity with and a fluency in the use of the analytic concepts relevant to the various forms of discourse analysis.

Finally, doing discourse analysis seemed to have as much to do with the appropriate use of these concepts in the presentation of our findings as it did with the analytic work that we had undertaken.

The early statement of such profound reflexive concerns might unnerve a reader seeking a step-by-step account of 'how to do discourse analysis' based upon our experiences. However, such a reader can be assured that, in accordance with the framework offered in the preceding chapter, this chapter *will* provide a step-by-step account of our analytic endeavours. The above reflexive concerns are foregrounded only to establish one of the key features of our experience, that **reflexivity** was central to the performance of discourse analysis. Thus, whilst this chapter will provide an account of the step-by-step workings of our analysis, it will, in parallel, also provide an account of our reflexive concerns about the work that we were doing at each step. Also, I need to point out that, though I am offering here an account of the analyses and reflections of an analytic group, this is very much my account of the analytic process; other analysts may have represented the analytic process in a different way and emphasized different considerations.

The following analysis focuses on 12 researchers' work on two transcripts of interviews with ex-soldiers (see Appendix 1 in this volume) over a period of two days (approximately 16 hours working time in total). In keeping with the focus of the research within which the data were generated, we chose to pursue a form of analysis the findings of which might be applied to the real life problems faced by ex-soldiers in their transition to civilian life. To this end, we chose to pursue a Foucauldian discourse analysis (FDA) (Willig, 2001), given that this approach provides for discussion of subjectivity and of the possibilities for practice. That said, in common with Willig (2001), we recognized that, in working towards engaging with practice and subjectivity, we would necessarily be working through levels of analysis that are common to other forms of discourse analysis. For example, identifying the various ways in which particular discursive objects are constructed is common to all forms of discourse analysis, while a focus on the action orientation of talk is a primary feature of the discursive psychology approach (Edwards and Potter, 1992) and the identification of 'discourses' is common to the critical discursive psychology approach (Wetherell, 1998) and to other forms of discourse analysis (see Burman and Parker 1993b and Chapter 7 in this volume). Consequently, the descriptions of the various stages of our analysis remain relevant to readers contemplating pursuing forms of discourse analysis other than a Foucauldian approach. However, whether we ever actually managed to produce a Foucauldian discourse analysis of the interview transcripts is debatable and, indeed, this concern will be oriented to at the end of this chapter.

The research questions

Before we read the transcripts of the two interviews with ex-soldiers that constituted the data for our analysis, as a group we tried to outline what our analytic interests were as follows. We tried to formulate our research questions in a way that would guide our readings and our analysis. Given that the study from which the interviews were drawn was concerned with ex-soldiers' experiences of renegotiating identity after leaving the army, the research questions as we understood them from an FDA standpoint were as follows:

- How did David and Brian construct the experience of leaving the army?
- How did they construct their identities before and after leaving the army?

These questions, we felt, provided us with three **discursive objects** of which we ought to be mindful during our initial readings. Those discursive objects were 'the experience of leaving the army', the 'army identity' and the 'post-army identity'. A focus on these discursive objects would, we hoped, allow us to move through the steps of a Foucauldian discourse analysis.

Box 8.1 ALTERNATIVE RESEARCH QUESTIONS

Researchers with different analytic concerns might have formulated very different research questions. For example, researchers with an explicit interest in gender might have formulated such research questions as:

- How do men construct the experience of leaving the army?
- How does the experience of leaving the army affect masculine identities?

Similarly, researchers with an interest in organizations might have formulated such research questions as:

- How does the individual construct the culture of an organization?
- How does the constructed culture of an organization affect the individual's experience of leaving that organization?

One of the observations that emerged from our initial readings – reported here because of the implications that it had for our final analysis and therefore for the presentation of that analysis in this chapter – concerned the different tenor of the two interviews: Brian and David seemed to talk about their experience of leaving the army in different ways. On the basis of these initial impressions, we decided to treat Brian's and David's interviews as case studies. Consequently, the analysis presented here will, at each stage, move between the two interviews. Whilst this approach was an effective strategy for working with just two texts, the group agreed that it would not work so well for a larger data set, where an analysis of consistent general similarities and differences across the data set would be the more likely aim: see the example of discourse analysis in Report 3 in Appendix 2. It should also be noted that, at each stage, the analysis presented here is only partial; this chapter is intended only to provide an illustrative rather than exhaustive analysis of the interviews.

Box 8.2 LEVELS OF TRANSCRIPTION AND TYPES OF ANALYSIS

The issue of the level of transcription was already resolved for us, since the interviews were given to us already transcribed. Similarly, transcription is not an issue for researchers subjecting textual materials, such as magazine or newspaper articles, to discourse analysis. However, for researchers setting out to do discourse analysis on interactional data, such as interviews, focus groups and naturalistic recordings, the issue of the level of transcription is an important one. The fundamental basis upon which a researcher might choose a more or less detailed level of transcription is whether they are interested in the organization and structure of talk or only in the content of talk: the level of transcription is primarily determined by the level at which the analysis will operate.

For example, conversation analysts, for whom the structure and organization of talk are important, typically employ the transcription notation system developed by Gail Jefferson (Atkinson and Heritage, 1984). This notation system allows the analyst to include and consequently analyse such things as rising and falling levels of pitch and the precise location of the starts and ends of speakers' turns, all of which might serve some function in determining the meaning of an utterance; with a more detailed notation system, the analyst can orient not only to what was said but how and when it was said. If, however, an analyst intends to adopt a more Foucauldian discourse analytic approach, they will be less concerned with *micro-textual* details of talk, such as pauses and overlaps, and more concerned with identifying *macro-textual* features such as discourses, which would remain identifiable in a less detailed transcript. Whatever level of detail you adopt in your transcription, extreme care should be taken to reproduce the data as accurately as possible.

Transcribing interactions using the Jefferson notation system is, however, highly time consuming; estimates for the number of hours required to transcribe one hour of recorded data vary between 10 and 20 hours. Consequently, practical considerations such as the volume of data collected and the amount of time available to the researcher will also determine the level of transcription adopted.

Discursive constructions

Having identified the discursive objects and having divided the analytic group in two, with each subgroup examining one transcript, the first step in the analysis was to identify how each of the three discursive objects was constructed.

Even this first step seemed to require a move into the new and unusual. We were not really interested in Brian and David as individuals or in the reality of their experiences. Instead, we were trying only to focus on the words and phrases that they drew upon when they talked about or constructed their identities, both army and post-army identities. Their constructions of the experience of leaving the army and the functions that they serve will be dealt with in the section on 'Action orientation'. Our task was to identify these **discursive resources** and to try to develop a sense of how they fitted together.

Given the introduction of the term 'identity', before we engage with the data it is worth noting how identity is conceptualized within discourse analytic approaches and how this compares with more traditional social psychological theories of identity. For example, in social identity theory (Tajfel and Turner, 1986), an individual's identity, the way he/she might think, feel and act, is supposed to be based upon and made relevant by his/her relatively stable membership of any number of social groups. An individual's identity might be supposed from what we might know about him/her – for example his/her sex, age, ethnicity or sexuality. In contrast, within discourse analytic approaches, identity is highly dynamic; it is both a social construction and social accomplishment managed and achieved through speakers' orientations to interactional concerns. Within this analysis, identity will be oriented to as both a topic within talk (the social construction) and an effect of talk (the social accomplishment). Identities, within discourse analytic approaches, are evident in and constituted by the discursive resources that speakers draw upon, for example in the categories of which speakers claim membership and through the subject positions offered by the discourses upon which they draw.

The army identity

David   David drew upon a wide range of discursive constructions when talking about his army identity. Most obviously, his army identity was constructed in terms of being 'a member of a team' (repeated in lines 17–18). Team membership carried with it moral implications such as 'being honest to your mates' (repeated in lines 66–68) and was potentially extendable such that it could include not only 'your mates' but the army as a whole: 'I was a driver and, without us drivers, no-one would get their goods' (lines 28–29). David's army identity was also constructed through the use of particular categories, such as 'driver' (line 28), 'Sergeant' (line 93) and 'soldier' (line 321). These categories are located within the logistical and hierarchical structures of the army and confer certain rights and responsibilities.

Other less explicit discursive constructions of David's army identity include the emphasizing of independent capabilities and the importance of orderliness: 'I can make my breakfast, I can make my dinner, I can sew, I can iron, I can wash' (lines 208–209), 'I like things in lines. I like things in neat packages' (lines 238–239) and 'Keep your paperwork in order' (line 245).

Brian Brian's army identity was rarely explicitly the topic of talk; rather it was implicit in his constructions of differences between his own working practices and those of his civilian colleagues. Out of these contrasts, there seemed to emerge a clear construction of a typical army identity with which Brian self-identified. This was most clearly evidenced by his use of first person plural pronouns: 'We seem to be much more flexible' (line 10) and 'we do our best all of the time' (line 16). As novice analysts, we were immensely excited at recognizing the last-mentioned quotation as containing an **extreme case formulation** (Pomerantz, 1986) – a rhetorical feature that increases the persuasiveness of an account – in this case, highlighting the contrast between the working practices of military or ex-military and civilian personnel.

As with David, we noted in Brian's talk that the hierarchical rank structure of the army seemed to be central to individual identity and to a valuing of individual identity, particularly through its role in constituting relational social identities: 'You've got an identity there and you feel good about yourself' (lines 287–288), 'you had a much more definite identity which other people could relate to' (lines 323–324) and 'I think that's because I had a definite label [sergeant]' (line 339). Appearance and the wearing of a uniform were, again, integral discursive constructions of an army identity: 'in the military you can tell just by looking at someone where they are in the pecking order [ ] and so you can temper what you say to them and how you say it to them (lines 184–186).[1]

The post-army identity

David The centrality of team membership to David's army identity was, we found, reflected in the discursive constructions of his post-army identity. David, who at the time of the interview held the post of school caretaker, reported that 'you're not a team member within the school because you're not a teacher' (lines 48–49). The absence of team membership in civilian life seemed to be central to David's post-army identity. Indeed, David explicitly constructed 'civilians' as having 'different ideas of being in teams' (line 58) and that this was another source of disaffection: 'That's the difficult part, I find' (line 60). This construction of the differing concepts of teams between the army and civilian life and its implications for David's identity seemed to be summed up in the segment of reported speech in lines 42–43, ' "Well, that's it. David, you did a good job, we miss him, fine, get someone else in." ' In contrast to his army identity, David's post-army identity was constructed in terms of an absence of 'real' team membership and his being under-valued in those 'teams' to which others might ascribe him membership.

Other notable discursive constructions of David's post-army identity included the emphasis that he placed on appearance and the contrasting effects that it had in army and civilian contexts: 'Now I walk out the door in my overalls and I think, "Well, yeah, that's it". You try to give an appearance of someone who's been trained and disciplined but it's not the same, it's not the same. You don't have the same effect as anywhere else' (lines 321–324). This quotation seemed to us to work up the importance that is assigned to appearance in the army, specifically the wearing of a uniform, and the relational effects of that uniform, which are a consequence of the semiotics of uniforms within military contexts (uniforms convey important meanings such as the location of the wearer within the rank structure). Put simply, in David's account of his post-army identity, there was a constructed absence of the constitution of social identities through appearance.

Brian   Again Brian's account differed from David's simply because he constructed his post-army identity as not dissimilar to his army identity, at least in terms of its implications for his sense of self-worth: 'And since I've been out, it's almost the same I think – not much has changed there really' (lines 288–289). This is not to say that Brian constructed his post-army identity as identical to his army identity. Indeed, features of his army identity were invoked as potential sources of tension and conflict within civilian contexts: 'I came across as aggressive, abrupt, arrogant . . . but I was just sort of being what I was doing really and in the military environment that was . . . it wouldn't even have been picked up on' (lines 220–223). We recognized that this quotation contained a **three-part list** (Jefferson, 1990), another rhetorical device that works up the persuasiveness of an account. However, Brian did not construct such tensions as intractable nor as requiring a wholesale reworking of his army identity. Instead, it seemed to us that Brian's post-army identity was constructed as a marginally 'civilianized' version of his army identity: 'I've had to adapt my training style to be more civilian friendly' (lines 231–232). It was this invocation of adaptability and flexibility, which Brian did construct as part of his army identity, that really seemed to us to mark Brian's interview out as different from David's.

Discourses

This stage of the analysis required us to try to organize and categorize the various discursive constructions drawn upon in relation to each of the discursive objects, namely the army identity, the post-army identity and the experience of leaving the army. This process of categorization would result in the identification of the **discourses** that we believed to be at play within the transcripts. The deployment of the concept of 'a discourse' or 'discourses' is the primary distinction between conversation analysis and discursive psychology (Edwards and Potter, 1992), whose analyses remain *micro-textual* (closely linked to and not straying beyond the text) and other forms of discourse analysis, such as Foucauldian discourse analysis (Willig, 2001), which aim to identify *macro-textual* patterns in language use and, in doing so, may move beyond the text subjected to analysis. In our efforts to do this, we tried to be attentive to similarities and differences between the discursive constructions.

The first discourse that we settled upon was the *collectivistic* discourse. This discourse seemed to be prominent in David's accounts of his army identity and his post-army identity. Within it we felt that we could locate all David's constructions of the importance and value of team work and team membership within the army and the constructed contrasts with civilian life. Further, we felt the collectivistic discourse, with its emphasis on collective aims, could encapsulate David's constructed lack of purpose on leaving the army.

The second discourse that we settled upon was an *individualistic* discourse. Though David and, to a lesser extent, Brian drew upon a collectivistic discourse in the construction of their army identity, they both drew upon discursive constructions that emphasised individual capabilities, agency, dedication, adaptability, performance and, perhaps most significantly, the importance of individual status and recognition through the hierarchical rank structure of the army. Just as the collectivistic discourse was pre-eminent in David's interview, so it seemed to us, the individualistic discourse was pre-eminent in Brian's.

Whilst the collectivistic and individualistic discourses seemed to allow us to categorize most of the discursive constructions of David's and Brian's army and post-army identities, there were also a number of constructions that did not fit neatly into either. Again, when we reminded ourselves that there could be any number of discourses at play within the interviews, we realized that this need not be a problem. The use of the category 'civilians' by David, Brian and the interviewer, Arnie, and the construction of civilians as a group with shared characteristics seemed also to be part of a very particular *military* discourse, *military* because the concept of the military rests on its distinction and the distinction of its personnel from 'civilian' and 'civilians'. Finally, we decided that such discursive constructions as 'civilianized' could be located with in an *assimilationist* discourse.

As a group, we were more comfortable with some of our categorizations than we were with others. We agreed that, perhaps given more time and a larger data set, our organization of the discursive constructions and the discourses that we settled upon might have been different. Similarly, we acknowledged that another group of readers might have identified different discursive constructions and categorized them differently. However, these were the constructions that we had identified and categorized and these were the discourses that we had found to be most persuasive in our group discussions and deliberations. In a world of infinite readings, we reasoned that persuasiveness and closeness to the data counted for a great deal.

As we were doing the analysis, we recognized that, by categorizing certain discursive constructions as belonging to a collectivistic discourse and others as belonging to an individualistic discourse, we were drawing upon terms and concepts that had existing meanings within social psychology. As concepts, collectivism and individualism have typically been applied at a cultural level, as dimensions along which cultural differences might be understood (Triandis, 1996). Collectivism and individualism applied at the individual level, as dimensions of personality, have been conceptualized as allocentrism and idiocentrism (Triandis et al., 1985). Our analysis and our argument that Brian and David both drew upon discourses of collectivism and individualism could, therefore, be read as an account of what allocentrism and idiocentrism might look like in practice. However, the important distinction is that, within a discourse analytic approach, the evident use of these discourses would not be assumed to be a consequence of some underlying personality tendency – a position that is bolstered by the fact that both David and, to a lesser extent, Brian drew upon both the collectivistic and individualistic discourses. Within the non-discursive, personality-based approach of Triandis et al. (1985) and based on the evidence presented in this analysis, Brian and David would have to be viewed as being simultaneously idiocentric and allocentric.

Action orientation

This stage of the analysis and the next stage, positioning, were the cause of some of our greatest analytic headaches and dilemmas. We finally managed to resolve our concerns and dilemmas when we realized why the two stages were conceptualized as distinct. Following long discussions, we decided that the distinction lay in the level at which *function* was theorized. A consideration of **action orientation**, in the manner prescribed by discursive psychology (Edwards and Potter, 1992), stays close to the details of talk, the *micro-textual* level. In doing so, it follows conversation analytic traditions in trying to identify the local, interactional functions or action orientations of particular discursive constructions or structures. **Positioning** is concerned with the functions served by subject positions (Davies and Harré, 1999; Hollway, 1989), where subject positions are understood to be afforded by discourses and to locate speakers within 'the structure of rights and duties for those who use that repertoire' (Davies and Harré, 1999: 35). Consequently, positioning and subject positions would follow from the discourses that we had identified within the interviews.

Given that Arnie had used broadly similar questions in each interview and given the analytic focus on the discursive object of the experience of leaving the army, we decided to focus on David's and Brian's responses to Arnie's invitation to recount their experience of and feelings about the transition from army to civilian life (lines 76–78 in David's interview and lines 54–58 in Brian's interview). Again, it should be remembered that the analysis presented below is not exhaustive and is intended only to illustrate this particular stage of a Foucauldian discourse analysis.

David In lines from 89 to 114, David constructed leaving the army as having immediate relational, physical, social and affective effects. The immediate relational effects of leaving the army were worked up through the use of reported speech and the titles that it contains: 'someone's saying "ID card – thank you, Mr Jones". And that hit you, you know. Someone's actually calling you "Mister".

No-one's calling me "Sergeant" any more' (lines 91–93). David's relational identity constituted through the army's rank structure was constructed as immediately and casually extinguished through the simple use of titles. The consequences of this were subsequently constructed in a three-part list of responses: 'That was funny. That was a shock. That's when you knew' (lines 93–94).

This list also seemed to us to construct a process of 'realization', from the initial acknowledgement of oddness of the use of 'Mister' as a form of address ('funny'), to an affective response to the use of 'Mister' ('shocked') and finally to a cognitive understanding of the implications of the use of 'Mister' ('you knew'). Again, this list and the process that it constructed worked up the persuasiveness of David's account of the personal impact and importance of leaving the army.

The immediate physical and social effects were constructed in terms of the negation of David's rights of access to physical spaces and resources: 'it's like they're throwing you outside and locked the gate' (lines 97–98) and 'you can't pick up the phone and get hold of the old housing people any more' (lines 101–102). This exclusion from spaces and services was also constructed as provoking affective responses: 'That was painful' (line 99) and 'it's a funny feeling' (line 103). These various constructions of the effects and affects of leaving the army all seemed to us to work up the sense of leaving the army as a transition from interdependence to independence, from inclusion to exclusion and from group membership to individual isolation.

Brian Where David focused on the historical event of leaving the army, Brian focused only on one aspect of the transition from army to civilian life, that of finding a job: 'obviously I was totally preoccupied in trying to find a job' (lines 60–61). By having focused on his constructed need to find employment, Brian could be interpreted as delimiting the effects of leaving the army; the only effect of leaving the army is that it forced a change of job. Such a move may be interpreted as having the action orientation of directing the discussion away from, glossing over or even denying the existence of any other more personal effects that the transition might have had.

Lines 60 to 99 could be seen as having the action orientation of managing and attributing responsibility for the problems that Brian constructed himself as having encountered in finding work and in working in 'Civvie Street'. The issue of finding work was dealt with in lines 60 to 70. This section seemed to have two defining characteristics: normalization and extrematization. *Normalization* was apparent in the three-part list of activities that comprises lines 62–64: 'I was sending loads and loads of applications off and I was getting loads and loads of interviews and I was going to the interviews and getting down to the last two or three people'. *Extrematization* was apparent in the repeated phrase 'loads and loads' in these lines. Combined, these two features functioned to work up the sense that, by his agency – the repeated 'I was' positions Brian unquestionably as the agent in this sequence – Brian came close to getting a good many jobs. They are also interpretable as oriented to, and potentially inoculating against, the possibility that Brian's failure to secure these jobs could be attributed to him.

Positioning

According to positioning theory, one of the things that discourses do is provide **subject positions** for those discourse users. Discourses do not only constitute the objects of talk but they also constitute subjects, that is, those who are doing the talking. In constituting subjects, a discourse is also theorized as providing a location for those subjects within the structure of rights and duties for those who use that discourse. As the concept of subject positions within a Foucauldian discourse analytic framework follows from the concept of discourses, our analysis of Brian and David's positioning would, more than any prior stage of the analysis, be based on our identifications and interpretations of the discourses at play in the interviews. As such, the persuasiveness of our analysis of the subject positions afforded to speakers and the functions they served would depend upon our individual and collective competence as members of a particular culture in understanding the identified discourses. For some members of the analytic group, this was a profoundly unsettling step, seeming to represent a move away from the concreteness of the texts and to place too great a reliance on our subjective perceptions and our cultural competence. The uncertainty of this step in the analysis was ameliorated somewhat by the fact that we were able to check our interpretations and their persuasiveness with the other members of the group.

Following the previous identification of the prominence of the collectivistic discourse within David's talk and of the individualistic discourse within Brian's talk, we decided to try to theorize the kind of subject positions that they respectively afforded David and Brian and what possibilities might be opened up or closed down. Having identified the collectivistic and individualistic discourses as predominant within David's and Brian's interviews respectively, it made sense to focus on the occasions of their use. What did the emphasizing of collectivism do for David? What did the emphasizing of individualism do for Brian?

By drawing upon the discourse of collectivism, David occupied a subject position from which he could contrast his experiences of army and post-army life and construct a sense of dissatisfaction with civilian life. In turn, this contrast provides the basis for the assimilation discourse, the process of becoming 'civilianized', a process that he constructed himself as not yet having completed. Furthermore, the subject position constituted by the collectivistic discourse allowed for the constructed sense of purposelessness that David ascribed to civilian life; in the absence of collective aims and occupying a subject position constituted by a discourse of collectivism, there could be no individual purpose. In contrast, by drawing upon a discourse of individualism, Brian occupied a subject position that allowed for a constructed sense of continuity between his army and post-army identities. Consequently, in Brian's interview, there was a marked absence of the construction of the experience of leaving the army as a negative event. Indeed, the discourse of individualism constituted a subject position from which Brian could unproblematically construct himself as valued more in his civilian work context than he was in the military context.

Practice and subjectivities

One feature of Foucauldian discourse analysis that struck us forcibly was the amount of time that it takes (although I know from my own subsequent experience with other forms of discourse analysis that they too are lengthy processes). Hence, we were not able to engage fully with the stages of practice and subjectivity within the time frame that we had allowed for the analysis. Consequently, the discussion of how the analysis might have developed through these two stages is speculative.

Willig (2001: 111) describes the focus on **practice** within Foucauldian discourse analysis as following from the idea that 'discursive constructions and the subject positions contained within them open up or close down opportunities for action. By constructing particular versions of the world, and by positioning subjects within them in particular ways, discourses limit what can be said and done'. This idea presented us with a theoretical conundrum that, as novice analysts, we were not entirely able to resolve. This conundrum centred on the status that could be accorded to 'practice' or 'what can be done'. Our concern arose from our understanding that, within discursive approaches, talk and texts are not assumed to reflect 'practice' or 'what can be done' unproblematically; talk of 'practice' or 'what can or cannot be done' is just that and its functions are limited to the interactional context within which it occurs. What we seemed to be striving for was some way of linking the discourses within the interviews and the constructions of action and practice that they supported to the world beyond. We did, after some discussion, recognize or remember that talk is action and that what Brian and David did within the interviews could be theorized as practice and therefore was constrained and constituted by the discourses that they drew upon. However, this line of argument would again limit our discussion of practice to Brian's and David's interviews. Ultimately, we decided that, though we could appreciate how discourses as culturally available resources could be identified as serving particular functions within texts and as opening up or closing down various possibilities, we were not sufficiently confident, on account of our limited data, analysis and experience, to extrapolate what possibilities for practice were opened up or closed down by the discourses that we had identified.

Similar concerns and dilemmas arose when we considered the final stage of a Foucauldian discourse analysis: **subjectivities**. Willig (2001: 111) argues that 'discourses make available certain ways-of-seeing the world and certain ways-of-being in the world' and that a focus on subjectivities involves a concern 'with what can be felt, thought and experienced from within various subject positions'. Theorizing the possibilities of feeling, thought and experience that might follow from discourses of collectivism and individualism seemed to us very similar to and riven with the same epistemological dilemmas as theorizing the possibilities for practice. Certainly, the discourse of collectivism could be interpreted as providing for David's *feelings* of abandonment, exclusion, isolation and even bereavement. Yet what status should we, as discourse analysts, ascribe to those feelings, given that they are present only in talk and we do not necessarily assume that talk reflects an underlying reality of thoughts and feelings? That David reports experiencing these feelings is explicit in the text and their action orientation has been engaged with above. The question that we faced was could the potential for *really experiencing* such feelings be a consequence of the forced abandonment of the use of a collectivistic discourse in the construction of self-identity? The answer to this question depended, we decided, primarily upon whether we, as analysts, adopted a strongly social constructionist or a critical realist epistemological position. At best we were only able to conclude that there was some scope to view the content of the interviews as demonstrative, only in a very partial way, of the constitution of David's and Brian's subjectivities.

Reflections

As ought to be apparent from the preceding speculations about how our analysis might proceed to the levels of practice and subjectivity, one of our main concerns was how far from the data we could or should move. As novice analysts, perhaps we lacked the theoretical sophistication and confidence to support building links between our idiographic analysis of just two interviews on the topic of leaving the army with the practicalities of leaving the army and the experiences faced by the many ex-service men and women that are *out there*.

A second concern was one of responsibility to Brian and David and, indeed, to anyone whose texts may be subjected to discourse analysis. By focusing on the way that they constructed their accounts, by identifying the discourses that they drew upon and that structured their experiences, were we in some way not taking the reality of those experiences seriously enough? In focusing on the language that they drew upon, were we diverting attention away from the materiality of their experiences? Also we were concerned that, in doing discourse analysis, in representing their accounts in such an obscure and potentially unrecognizable way, were we failing to meet some kind of implicit agreement as social researchers to report their experiences in a way that they would recognize and agree with?

Third, though we endeavoured to create dialogues between our discursive analysis and existing social psychological literature on such matters as identity, collectivism, individualism, allocentrism and idiocentrism, we remained uncertain as to how to do this effectively and in ways that would be consistent either with a social constructionist or critical realist position. We were convinced that such dialogues are possible and necessary, if discourse analytic work is to enter effectively into mainstream social psychology. However, we felt that our uncertainty about how to create such dialogues was a consequence of our failure, as a group, to determine clearly the epistemological position from which we were operating.

The resolution of such concerns, we were forced to conclude, might only come with greater knowledge of the history and philosophy underlying the various discourse analytic approaches, further experience of the method and greater confidence born of external validation or challenge. Whether we had succeeded in doing Foucauldian discourse analysis and whether we could count ourselves as discourse analysts would depend upon our having at least the confidence to write and publish this analysis or some other piece of discourse analytic work and invite the scrutiny of our peers, which is exactly what we have done in this chapter.

Summary

This chapter has offered an account of Foucauldian discourse analytic practice, applying the various stages of analysis to a discrete data set. The account has constructed certain stages as more challenging than others, with difficulties attributed to the constraints of the analytic context but also to the apparent requirements of some stages to move beyond what some analysts regarded as a credible evidence base and also to make inferences about the 'real world'. I hope that researchers who are inexperienced in discourse analysis will find this account useful in identifying one way through the discourse analytic process and raising some important matters for further consideration. However, I wish to emphasize that, in developing skill in discourse analysis, there is really no alternative to 'getting your hands dirty' trying to apply the principles of discourse analysis to text and obtaining feedback from experienced analysts. Also, as with Chapter 7, I would remind readers that this chapter, like any text, is itself open to discourse analysis, so you may wish to use this text as data for your first steps into discourse analysis or to refine your existing analytic skills.

Note

1   In the quotations, empty square brackets indicate where material has been omitted from a quotation. Three dots indicate a pause (untimed) in the speaker's talk.

9

NARRATIVE ANALYSIS

Michele Crossley

This chapter outlines the theoretical basis of a narrative psychological approach, describing its relationship to other social constructionist approaches within psychology. Highlighting narrative psychology's dominant concern with issues of identity construction and self-exploration, it examines some of the central concepts underpinning this approach. The chapter also highlights some of the potential data sources that might be of relevance to a narrative psychological approach and outlines a preliminary methodology for the exploration of personal narratives. It then proceeds to outline some general analytic steps. The chapter concludes with reflections and reservations regarding the possibility of reducing narrative psychological analysis to specific methodological steps, emphasizing that narrative analysis is more akin to a creative art than a scientific procedure.

Key terms

coherent story
imagery
interpersonal dialogue
narrative tone
phenomenology

reading
realist epistemology
self and identity
stories
themes

Introduction

Social constructionist approaches and the study of self/identity

Social constructionist approaches to the study of self and identity, sometimes called 'language-based' approaches, have gained momentum over the last 20 years or so as a major challenge to some of the implicit assumptions embedded within more 'traditional' approaches found within social and personality psychology such as behaviourist, humanistic and psychoanalytic/psychodynamic approaches (see Potter and Wetherell, 1987). Perhaps the most commonly-known social constructionist approaches within psychology include discourse analysis (Edwards and Potter, 1992; Parker, 1992; Potter and Wetherell, 1987; see also Chapter 7 in this volume), feminist psychological approaches (see Henriques et al., 1998; Wilkinson, 1997), post-structuralist/postmodernist approaches (see Gergen, 1991) and rhetorically based approaches (see Billig, 1991; Shotter, 1993, 1997).

The aforementioned social constructionist approaches, although obviously distinct from each other, are commonly united in their critique of the 'realist' assumptions of traditional psychological studies of self and identity in which it is allegedly assumed that 'the self' exists as an entity that can be discovered and described in much the same way as can any object in the natural or physical world. Such 'realist' assumptions are considered problematic because the alternative conceptualization of the self promoted by social constructionism is one which sees it as inextricably dependent on the language and linguistic practices that we use in our everyday lives to make sense of ourselves and other people. In making use of such language, we are constantly and perpetually interpreting and changing the meaning of ourselves and other people's actions in accordance with our practical and moral tasks. Hence, the 'realist' assumption that we can 'describe' some sort of 'pre-existent' self, in isolation from such everyday interactional and interpretative contingencies, is regarded as radically misguided.

The social constructionist commitment to 'deconstructing' the self stems from an appreciation of the inextricable connection between linguistic structures and concepts of self. This leads to an understanding of the 'self' as a phenomenon characterized by interpretation, variability, relativity, flux and difference. From this perspective, it is impossible to make universal claims about the nature of human selves and personal experiences because such selves and experiences differ in relation to historical, cultural and practical contexts. It is from this theoretical recognition of a lack of unity and constancy that post-modernists declare the 'death of the subject' (see Heartfield, 2002). If there is no 'one' essential nature or self to describe, then the concept of 'a' self, of 'having' or 'possessing' a self, must be abandoned. Discourse and rhetorical analysts, in recognition of the variable and functional nature of talk about selves, similarly reject the traditional assumption of 'a' central and unitary concept of self (e.g., see Chapter 7 in this volume).

Problems with social constructionist approaches: 'Losing the subject'

As has previously been pointed out by researchers such as Parker, although the turn towards the discursive structuring and deconstructing of self and experience is important, one of the main problems with many social constructionist approaches is that they repeatedly beg the question: 'what is going on inside human beings when they use discourse?' (Parker, 1992: 83). Parker argues that the capacity to be reflexive (to think about oneself, to reflect inwardly) is at the core of human agency and understanding and it is this capacity to be reflexive which is 'the point of connection between the individual and the social' (Parker, 1992: 105). Unfortunately, it is this ability to be reflexive that many social constructionist approaches tend to omit from their accounts of human subjectivity.

This links to a more general critique of the discursive approach to the understanding of human psychological and social life highlighted by Augoustinos and Walker (1995: 276). This is the argument that the 'individual purposive-agent' appears absent in such accounts which deliberately avoid the suggestion that human beings have any fundamental or internal 'sense' of themselves as a self. Self is studied only in terms of individual, discursive acts which perform various social activities such as presenting a certain image of the self, excusing and blaming. This results in a conception of self in which 'subjective experience . . . is made so context-dependent, so fluid and flexible, that there seems to be little beyond a personal psychology which is a moment-to-moment situated experience' (Augoustinos and Walker, 1995: 276). Language and context are emphasized to such an extent that the self is 'engulfed, if not annihilated' (Dunne, 1995: 140). It is in this sense that both postmodern and discourse analytic approaches have been characterized as a 'retreat from the investigation of core questions' (Abraham and Hampson, 1996: 226). Hence, there is a need within contemporary psychology for a theoretical and methodological approach which appreciates the linguistic and discursive structuring of 'self' and 'experience' but also maintains a sense of the essentially personal, coherent and 'real' nature of individual subjectivity. Narrative psychology enables the achievement of this objective.

Epistemologically, narrative psychology is similar to Smith's (1996) interpretative phenomenological analysis (IPA) approach (see Chapter 3 in this volume). Smith et al. (1997) have argued that it is important to distinguish between IPA and social constructionist approaches such as discourse analysis (as represented by Potter and Wetherell, 1987). It is important to address the reasons for this distinction because they are equally applicable to the distinction between narrative approaches and discourse analytic approaches.

Smith et al. (1997) argue that, although IPA (like narrative psychology) shares with discourse analysis a commitment to the importance of language and qualitative analysis, the two approaches differ in terms of the status they afford to subjectivity and experience of the self and body. Discourse analysis is generally sceptical of mapping people's 'accounts' onto underlying subjective experiences. It prefers to treat people's verbal or written accounts as behaviours in their own right which should be analysed in accordance with the functions and activities they are performing in particular situations. By contrast, IPA (again like narrative psychology) *is* concerned with subjectivity and experience, with coming to grips with how a person thinks or feels about what is happening to him/her. It does this by assuming a 'chain of connection' between what a person says or writes and how they think, feel and reflect about themselves, their bodies, other people and the world more generally. Hence, IPA is based on 'realist' assumptions similar to those found within traditional social psychological approaches such as social cognition (Smith et al., 1997). In other words, it operates with a '**realist epistemology**' which assumes that there is a knowable domain of facts about human experience and consciousness that can be discovered through the application of certain methods (Augoustinos and Walker, 1995). This epistemological position, this assumption of a chain of connection between language and the experiencing 'self', is questioned in discourse analysis which brackets assumptions about the 'reality' of the latter and can therefore tell us very little about how the person subjectively thinks or feels about the phenomena under investigation (see also Abraham and Hampson, 1996; Smith, 1996). This 'realist epistemology' also underpins a narrative psychological approach.

Narrative psychology and the study of self/identity

Central to a narrative psychological approach are questions of self and identity – 'What is a self?', 'Who am I?' C.S. Lewis once commented, 'There is one thing, and only one in the whole universe which we know more about than that we could learn from external observation. That one thing is ourselves. We have, so to speak, inside information, we are in the know' (Lewis, 1952: 3). But how true is this? To what extent are we 'in the know' about ourselves? How do we go about 'discovering' and 'constructing' our concepts and understandings of self and others?

Underpinning narrative psychology's understanding of self are concepts deriving from the theoretical perspective of **phenomenology** (see Crossley, 2000a). Central concepts include a phenomenological understanding of human 'lived' time (Polkinghorne, 1988), self as an interactional process (Crossley, 1996) and the intrinsic connection between temporality, interaction and morality (Taylor, 1989). From a narrative psychology perspective, concepts of self and morality are inextricably intertwined insofar as we are selves only in that certain issues matter for us. As Taylor (1989) argues, what I am as a self, my identity, is essentially defined by the way things have significance for me. To ask what I am in abstraction from self-interpretation makes no sense. Moreover, my self-interpretation can only be defined in relation to other people, an 'interchange of speakers'. I cannot be a self on my own but only in relation to certain 'interlocutors' who are crucial to my language of self-understanding. In this sense, the self is constituted through 'webs of interlocution' in a 'defining community' (Taylor, 1989: 39; see also Crossley, 1996). This connection between our sense of morality and sense of self means that one of our basic aspirations to satisfy is the need to feel connected with what we see as 'good' or of crucial importance to us and our community. We have certain fundamental values which lead us to basic questions such as 'What kind of life is worth living?', 'What constitutes a rich, meaningful life, as against an empty, meaningless one?' (Taylor, 1989: 42). Hence, connections between notions of 'the good', understandings of the self, the kinds of stories and narratives through which we make sense of our lives, and conceptions of society, evolve together in 'loose packages'. This brings us to another essential concept within narrative psychology – the 'story'.

The central role of language and stories

Stories play a central role in the process of identity construction. As Crites (1986: 152) wrote, 'A self without a story contracts into the thinness of its personal pronoun'. Moreover, as Mair (1989: 2) stated, 'Stories are the womb of personhood. Stories make and break us. Stories sustain us in times of trouble and encourage us towards ends we would not otherwise envision. The more we shrink and harden our ways of telling, the more starved and constipated we become'.

It is not incidental that I felt the need to develop a narrative psychological approach when addressing traumatizing research topics such as HIV infection and childhood sexual abuse (Crossley, 2000a). When such events happen, people often find themselves experiencing breakdown and disintegration and are forced to make sense of events through the utilization of 'stories' or 'narratives'. The same applies when people are undergoing important transitions in their lives. As Broyard (1992: 21) argued, 'always in emergencies we invent narratives . . . we describe what is happening as if to confine the catastrophe'.

Research questions and potential sources of data

It is important at this point to highlight a distinction between the terminology used in narrative psychology and discourse analysis. Discourse analysts often refer to people's 'accounts'. Is the narrative psychologist's focus on the 'narrative' or 'story' the same thing as the discourse analyst's 'account'? On the most basic level, a 'narrative' differs from an 'account' in terms of length. The narrative constituting the focus of the narrative psychologist's inquiry will tend to be a great deal longer than the discourse analyst's 'account'. A discourse analyst can perform an analysis on almost any piece of text, no matter how short or long. This is obviously not the case for narrative psychology which is explicitly interested in issues relating to the exploration of **self and identity**. Adequate reflection upon these matters can take some time, potentially generating considerable data.

This points to a larger issue concerning the epistemological status of the 'narrative' versus the 'account'. As has already been made clear, narrative psychology assumes a 'realist' conception of its subject matter. Although narrative psychology, like discourse analysis, is interested in the discursive *function* of certain linguistic practices, this is not its sole interest. Unlike discourse analysts, narrative psychology has a strong focus on the actual *content* of the narrative. A narrative analysis will be an analysis *of something*, of some specific event or trauma that features significantly in a person's life and is the driving force for them having produced their narrative (see Box 9.1 for examples of narrative analyses).

Box 9.1 EXAMPLES OF NARRATIVE PSYCHOLOGICAL ANALYSES

- Exploring fictional and autobiographical narratives of gay men's sexual practices and their relationship to contemporary culture (Crossley, 2004).
- An autobiographical examination of one man's adaptation to living and dying with oral cancer (Crossley, 2003 – see Report 4 in Appendix 2 in this volume).
- A historical study of psychiatric patients' 'voices' and how they have changed over time (Crossley and Crossley, 2001).
- An autobiographical study of illness (cancer) and the challenges involved in adapting to a 'life of uncertainty' (Frank, 1995).
- An interview-based study of men living with a long-term HIV diagnosis (Davies, 1997).

For instance, it may be an analysis of an episode of mental or physical illness or child sexual abuse or abortion or pregnancy. One of its major interests is in the existential significance such events have for people's lives. This is obviously very different from a discourse analytic approach which would regard such issues as lying beyond its focus of inquiry.

This has implications for what actually constitutes data from a narrative psychological point of view. Narrative psychologists are interested in exploring issues of identity and self construction. Potential data sources are therefore quite wide and might include semi-structured interviews, diaries, autobiographies, biographies, fiction and internet chat rooms concerned with specific issues (e.g., people living with HIV/AIDS). This list is obviously not exhaustive and any student interested in pursuing a narrative psychological approach would be encouraged to think imaginatively about potential sources of data. A useful preliminary step, however, is to conduct one's own personal narrative analysis.

A method for exploring personal narratives

In contemporary life, the two most common means used to identify personal narratives and stories are psychotherapy and autobiography. Beyond these two approaches are other methods that can be used to enhance self-understanding and identify your personal narrative. These include 'private' explorations such as keeping a diary, recording your dreams and engaging in dialogue with your many 'selves' or 'inner voices'. While these methods may be very useful, however, the autobiographical method of exploration created by McAdams (1993) is particularly interesting because it provides a useful way of eliciting material for autobiographical research. In addition, it emphasizes the importance of **interpersonal dialogue** in the exploration of self and identity. This is important in terms of the interactive concept of self and identity presupposed within narrative psychology.

The first step is to identify someone who will serve as an interviewer for you to conduct your autobiographical interview (see Crossley, 2000a). McAdams (1993) provides a semi-structured interview protocol to follow. This is detailed below. The interview should be recorded and transcribed. The transcription will provide the data from which a narrative analysis can be conducted.

Autobiographical interview protocol

Question 1: Life chapters   Begin by thinking of your life as if it were a book. Each part of your life constitutes a chapter in the book. Certainly, the book is unfinished at this point; nevertheless it still contains a few interesting and well-defined chapters. Choose as many or as few as you like but McAdams suggests dividing it up into at least two or three chapters and, at most, about seven or eight. Think of this as a general table of contents for your book. Give each chapter a name and describe the overall contents of each chapter. Discuss briefly what makes for a transition from one chapter to the next. The first part of this interview can go on for a long time but try to keep it relatively brief – say, 30–45 minutes. You do not (and cannot) tell the 'whole story' – just a sense of the story's outline, the major chapters in your life.

Question 2: Key events   Ask about eight key events. A key event is a specific happening, a critical incident, a significant episode in your past. It is helpful to think of such an event as constituting a specific moment in your life that stands out for some reason. For example, a particular conversation you had with your mother when you were 12 years old or a particular decision made one afternoon last summer might qualify as a key event in your life story. These are particular moments in a particular time and place, complete with particular characters, actions, thoughts and feelings. For each event, describe in detail what happened, where you were, who was involved, what you did and what you were thinking and feeling in the event. Try to convey the impact that this key event had in your life story and what this event says about who you are or were as a person. Did this event change you in any way? If so, in what way? Be very specific. People are most articulate and insightful when talking about particular, concrete episodes in their lives. You should, therefore, focus considerable time and energy on each recalled event, providing as much detail as possible.

The eight key events to be dealt with in this way are as follows:

1   Peak experience: a high point in your life story; the most wonderful moment of your life.
2   Nadir experience: a low point in your life story; the worst moment in your life.
3   Turning point: an episode where you underwent a significant change in your under-standing of yourself. You do not need to have understood it as a turning point at the time when it happened but only now, in retrospect.
4   Earliest memory: one of your earliest memories complete with details of setting, scene, characters, feelings and thoughts. It does not have to be especially important; the main point is that it is an early memory.
5   An important childhood memory: any memory, positive or negative, from your childhood that stands out.
6   An important adolescent memory: any memory, positive or negative, from your teenage years that stands out today.
7   An important adult memory: a memory, positive or negative, that stands out from age 21 onwards.
8   Other important memory: one particular event, positive or negative, from your recent or distant past that stands out.

Question 3: Significant people   Every person's life is populated by a few significant people who have a major impact on the narrative – for example, parents, children, siblings, spouses, lovers, friends, teachers, coworkers and mentors. Describe *four* of the most important people in your life story. Specify the relationship you had or have with each person and the specific way in which he/she has had an impact on your life story. After this, describe whether or not you have any particular heroes or heroines in your life.

Question 4: Future script   You have talked about the past and present – what of the future? What might be your plan or script for what is to happen next in your life? Describe your overall plan, outline or dream for the future. Most of us have plans or dreams which provide our lives with goals, interests, hopes, aspirations and wishes. These plans may change over time, reflecting growth and changing experiences. Describe your present dream, plan or outline. How, if at all, does your plan enable you to (a) be creative in the future (b) make a contribution to others?

Question 5: Stresses and problems   All life stories include significant conflicts, unresolved issues, problems to be solved and periods of great stress. Consider some of these. Describe *two* areas in your life in which you are experiencing at least one of the following: significant stresses, a major conflict, a difficult problem or a challenge that must be addressed. For each of the two areas, describe the nature of the stress, problem or conflict in some detail, outlining the source of the concern, a brief history of its development and your plan, if you have one, for dealing with it in the future.

Question 6: Personal ideology   This question is all about your fundamental beliefs and values:

1   Do you believe in the existence of some kind of God or deity or a force that reigns over or in some way organizes and influences the universe? Explain.

2 Describe in a nutshell your religious beliefs, if any.
3 In what ways, if any, are your beliefs different from most people you know?
4 How have your religious beliefs changed over time? Have you experienced any rapid changes in your personal beliefs? Explain.
5 Do you have a particular political orientation? Explain.
6 What is the most important value in human living? Explain.
7 What else can you tell me that would help me to understand your most fundamental beliefs and values about life and the world?

Question 7: Life theme Looking back over your entire life story as a book with chapters, episodes and characters, can you discern a central theme, message or idea that runs throughout the 'text'? What is the major theme of your life?

Analysing narrative

The assumption within narrative psychological analysis is that we are interested in learning something about our own and others' personal narratives and, in turn, about the light those narratives throw upon psychological and social realities. Understanding the content and complexity of meanings in which narratives are produced is therefore crucial. This is no easy task. Meaning is not just 'transparently' available within an interview, a transcript or an autobiographical script. It has to be achieved through a process of interpretation and engagement with the text. A number of specific analytic steps need to be taken when conducting an analysis of one's own personal narrative. These are identified in Box 9.2. More on each of these steps is provided below (for more detail, see Crossley, 2000a).

Box 9.2   SIX ANALYTIC STEPS IN NARRATIVE ANALYSIS

1) Reading and familiarizing
2) Identifying important concepts to look for (specifically tone, imagery and themes)
3) Identifying 'narrative tone'
4) Identifying narrative themes and images
5) Weaving all of this together into a coherent story
6) Writing-up as a research report

Step 1: Reading and familiarizing

The very first step in the analysis consists of repeatedly **reading** through the whole transcript (or alternative data source) about five or six times in order to familiarize yourself with the material and to obtain a very general gist of emerging and significant themes.

Step 2: Identifying important concepts to look for

The second step is to develop a grasp of the principal elements of the 'personal narrative' that you need to identify. According to McAdams (1993), there are three of these: (a) narrative tone, (b) imagery and (c) themes. Each of these is discussed in more detail below.

(a) Narrative tone   **Narrative tone** is perhaps the most pervasive feature of a personal narrative in adulthood and is conveyed both in the *content* of the story and also the *form* or *manner* in which it is told. For example, the tone can be predominantly optimistic or pessimistic. An optimistic story can be optimistic because good things happen or because, even though bad things happen, one remains hopeful that things will improve. Similarly, a pessimistic story can be pessimistic because of a series of bad events or because good things are perceived in a negative light (see McAdams, 1993). Drawing on a range of studies from developmental psychology, McAdams (1993) argues that the most formative influence on narrative tone derives from the achievement of secure or insecure attachment relationships during the early childhood years. It may be interesting to explore this hypothesis in relation to your own case.

(b) Imagery   Every personal narrative contains and expresses a characteristic set of images. In order to understand our own narratives, we must explore the unique way in which we employ **imagery** to make sense of who we are. Pay careful attention to the kind of language used in describing and characterizing your life chapters and key events. It may provide a clue to personally meaningful images, symbols and metaphors. Like our identities, imagery is both discovered and made. We make our own images but the nature of that making is strongly dependent on the raw materials (such as language and stories) made available in our culture. When you have identified the characteristic set of imagery employed in your own case, try and explore the *genesis* of that imagery. How has it developed? Is it related to your family background – some psychologists argue that an adult's personal imagery is largely established in the complex family dynamics of the first three or four years of life – or can it be located more widely within the dominant discourses (incorporating morals, values and belief systems) of the society in which you live?

(c) Themes   What are the dominant **themes** in your personal narrative? Underlying the many events reported in your account, can you see any pattern with regard to what has motivated you or what has been particularly important to you? McAdams (1993), again drawing on numerous psychological theories, argues that power (the desire for agency and independence) and love (the desire for connection and dependence) constitute two of the most important themes of stories because they correspond to two of the central (and often conflicting) motivations in human life (for a critique of McAdams, see McLeod, 1997). In interpreting your autobiographical account, you should look carefully at what it tells you about your own motivational themes. To what extent are you driven by power or love? More importantly, in what particular

ways do the needs for power and love express themselves in your story? These needs often become especially apparent during times when we experience our identities as 'in crisis' – for example, during adolescence, when experiencing illness or when experiencing bereavement. We notice inconsistencies between who we once were and who we are now. This disparity may be so striking that we summon up questions never asked before, such as 'Who is the real me?', 'Who am I'? We may begin to take seriously the possibility of alternative lives never before seriously entertained. Such 'episodes' in our lives provide clues to what drives, motivates and is important to us in our lives.

Step 3: Identifying 'narrative tone'

In order to identify narrative tone, you need to look at both what you have reported in relation to your own past experiences and also the way in which you have done so.

Step 4: Identifying 'imagery' and 'themes'

It is useful to look for both imagery and themes together. This is because they overlap and the use of certain images and imagery tends to point towards and be indicative of particular themes. I have found that the easiest way to identify imagery and themes is to work through the transcript in a systematic fashion, starting first with the 'life chapters' question and then proceeding separately through each of the interview questions. Imagery and themes should be identified in relation to each question. At this stage of the analysis, you are still really only trying to get a very general overview of the data. The aim is to draw up a kind of 'rough map' of the picture emerging from the interview.

Step 5: Weaving all of this together into a coherent story

Having constructed a rough, 'working map' of the various images and themes emerging from your interpretation of the interview data, your next step is to weave all of this together into a **coherent story**.

Step 6: Writing up as a research report

At this stage, you should be in a position to move from your identification, analysis and construction of a coherent account of your personal narrative to the actual process of writing this up. It may be that this write-up will take the form of a research report to be submitted as part of coursework assessment. To some extent, in this kind of qualitative analysis, the division between analysis and writing-up is arbitrary because analysis continues during the actual process of writing (Smith, 1996). How do you transform your narrative analysis into a research report? There are a number of different sections to be included in a research report. These sections should be constructed in the following order: (i) Introduction; (ii) Method; (iii) Results; (iv) Analysis/Discussion (where the findings from the Results section are discussed in the context of wider theoretical debates relevant to the study); (v) Reflection; (vi) References. However, it is possible to be creative in the development of alternative forms of reporting narrative research (see for example Report 4 in Appendix 2).

Reflections on the analytic process

Although a very general identification of analytic steps may be useful, I am increasingly coming to the viewpoint that narrative types of analysis cannot, and perhaps more importantly, *should not* be reduced to step-by-step guidelines in the same way that is possible (and desirable) with more quantitative types of approaches. To attempt to do so, I believe, does narrative psychology a disservice by trying to fit it into a model with which it is simply inconsistent. The essence of a narrative type of approach, as far as I am concerned, is an ability to understand and appreciate the personal and cultural meanings conveyed within oral or written texts and to explicate the socio-cultural resources utilized in this process. This is all about interpretation and the ability to put together a coherent and convincing argument in a quality narrative format. An absolute imperative is the ability to write creatively and imaginatively and to be able to build up a convincing and engaging story. This sounds easy but it is, in fact, a rather difficult process. I would argue that it is more of an art rather than a science insofar as it is a process that is impossible to deconstruct into logical, step-by-step stages. I think that is why many traditionally trained psychologists, with a training heavily influenced by scientific and reductionist modes of thought, have difficulty with such approaches. I strongly believe, however, that it is important to hold on to the principle that this kind of approach is not amenable to such deconstruction and to allow more space within psychology for innovative, imaginative students and researchers to push forward the boundaries by providing analyses which do not simply conform to predetermined methodological schemas.

Methodological considerations

This plea for innovative modes of analysis does, however, bring forth issues of validity. As in other qualitative and discursively oriented approaches, narrative approaches assume that the material used in any kind of analysis is deeply influenced by the researcher. This is in contrast to more 'scientific' types of approach which aim to achieve a state of objectivity and neutrality in which the analytic material exists and can be interpreted independent of the researcher. Rather than collecting 'neutral' data, the narrative psychological researcher frames the question, picks the participants (which may include him/herself) and interacts with them to produce data that are then used for analysis. Further processes of selection and interpretation shape the conclusions and presentation of the analysis. It is therefore hypocritical to attempt to 'withdraw from the picture and treat the material or the findings of the research as an objective record of "reality"' (Yardley, 1997: 35–36).

One of the important issues here is the question of 'representativeness' and 'generality'. Quantitative approaches often assume that the sample on which their data and analysis are based should be sufficiently typical of a particular population in order that any conclusions drawn from the sample can be generalized to the population as a whole. However, narrative psychological research, again along with other qualitative approaches, does not work with the same concept of representativeness. The aim of these kinds of approaches, by contrast, is to produce detailed 'information rich' data, which are impossible to separate from context if their full meaning is to be appreciated and understood. Accordingly, these approaches often use a case study approach, the aim of which is to create a 'detailed and profound insight into a particular, perhaps unique, account or experience rather than a set of broad generalisations about commonalities between different people. The rationale of this approach is to fully exploit one of the principal merits of qualitative methods, the analysis of meaning in depth and in context' (Yardley, 1997: 36). The aim is therefore to produce in-depth analyses and insight into individual case histories which appreciate the complexities and ambiguities of the interrelationships between individuals and society.

These considerations regarding selection, interpretation and representativeness also have implications for the way in which qualitative researchers go about justifying or, in other words, validating their analyses. If we relinquish any conception of 'objective' truth, of a truth existing in isolation from our own selective and interpretative practices, then on what basis do we claim that our analysis is 'correct'? How do make claims for the authority of our account? In narrative research, the concept of validity generally means being 'well grounded and supportable' (Polkinghorne, 1988: 175). Hence, in order to support his/her analytic findings, the researcher has to build up arguments and present evidence from the data set in front of him/her. The argument does not produce certainty; rather, it produces *likelihood*. Most researchers therefore justify their account by 'asserting only a limited local authority based on a combination of thorough and conscientious exploration and reporting, intellectual excellence, consensus of opinion and productive utility' (Yardley, 1997: 40). For example, an interpretation may be justified on the grounds that it is 'comprehensive and coherent, consistent with the data and theoretically sophisticated, and meaningful to both participants and peers' (*ibid.*), otherwise known as being 'plausible or 'persuasive'. All of these considerations are important in establishing the validity of narrative psychological research. Once more, I would reiterate the absolute imperative of a researcher being able to write creatively and concisely in order to pull this process off.

Summary

This chapter has outlined the theoretical basis of narrative psychology, highlighted some of the dominant issues constituting the focus of analysis and briefly outlined some methodological and analytic steps for conducting a narrative type analysis. In sum narrative psychological analysis:

- focuses on processes of identity construction and exploration.
- is concerned with both the 'what' and the 'how' of processes of self-construction.
- focuses on how people use personal and cultural resources in order to make sense of traumatic and transitional life events.
- explores narrative more as a creative art than a scientific procedure reducible to specific methodological steps.

I cannot emphasize the last point enough. Narrative psychology is suited to the student or researcher who feels the need to push beyond boundaries, to explore without the restrictive mandate of following specific methodological steps. The methodology outlined in this chapter is produced merely as a preliminary step to encourage the student or researcher to think about his/her own life and the process of autobiographical exploration. To produce a narrative psychology of any consequence, the student or researcher is encouraged to use the preliminary steps as a loose scaffold and then to kick them down and move beyond them!

Further reading

For more on the theoretical basis of narrative psychology, see Carr (1986), Crossley (1996), Crossley (2000a, b and c), Polkinghorne (1988), Smith and Sparkes (2006) and Taylor (1989). In terms of related narrative psychological approaches, see Frank (1995), Kleinmann (1988), McAdams (1993) and Sarbin (1986). For specific examples of narrative analytic studies, see Box 9.1 in this chapter, Report 4 in Appendix 2 and McAdams et al. (2001).

10

DOING NARRATIVE ANALYSIS

Neil Harbison

This chapter examines one group's attempt to conduct narrative analysis using a transcript of an interview with an ex-soldier, reflecting upon his experiences of leaving the army and of post-army life. Disagreements about whether to adhere to or deviate from the loose analytic steps described by Crossley (see Chapter 9 in this volume) led the group to split into two subgroups and to develop very different analyses of the interview and very different standards for evaluating our progress. We presented our results in a way that highlighted these differences and unresolved tensions – differences and tensions which may be intrinsic to the task of 'qualitative psychology' itself.

Key terms

historical narratives
interactional dynamics
performative analysis

tone, themes and imagery
validate

Introduction

What happens when researchers new to narrative analysis come together to conduct a narrative analysis of fascinating interview transcripts? I would not presume that the events within the narrative analysis group reported in this chapter are representative, generalizable or even typical of narrative inquiry as a whole. However, I hope that my own retrospective narrative of how we worked on the interview data within a narrative framework says something about the different ways that analysis might proceed, and provokes some useful thoughts among others who are beginning to experiment with narrative analysis.

Our analytic process – and its end result – speaks to long-running tensions among qualitative psychology's orientations to methodological traditions. Here are some questions to bear in mind as you read about our experiences. First, can methodologies be learned from books and teachers (as statistical methodologies might be) or are they embodied skills (akin to playing the violin)? Second, should methodologies play the role of developing an analytic inquiry or the role of defining what counts as 'valid' conclusions of interpretation? Third, if narrative analysis continues to acquire legitimacy as a psychological methodology but all people are assumed to communicate in narratives quite spontaneously, who is to say what counts as an expert analysis and on what basis? Fourth, is 'narrative methodology' – as described by Crossley (2000a; see also Chapter 9 in this volume), for example – a complete methodology or a step along the way to one? Finally, will the method be improved by adherence to its norms or deviation from them? As we pored over the transcripts of interviews with ex-soldiers about their experiences of leaving the army that formed the data for our narrative analysis (see Appendix 1), we came to adopt different stances in regard to all of these vexing dilemmas, which led our group to split into two subgroups. However, we ultimately produced a form of analysis that foregrounded these dilemmas and which represented the different forms of interpretation we had pursued.

At various times, this was an outcome that none of us was certain of achieving but it was a process to which we were all ultimately pleased to have contributed. I was keen to include something in this chapter concerning the emotions that we experienced in doing this work. I am particularly grateful to three group members who wrote reflections about the group and our analysis immediately after we had completed it. Independently, I also wrote down what I could remember of our time together. These notes (which formed narratives in their own right), along with the records of our analysis, have hopefully allowed me to construct something of what we did without overly confusing my own perspective with the literal truth. Certainly those people with whom I disagreed most directly during the workshop taught me the most with their written reflections.

Narrative analysis

The researchers who attempted to apply the principles of narrative analysis to the data set worked together over three days (two days of analysis, one for familiarizing ourselves with guidelines provided by Michele Crossley and another for organizing how we would present our analyses). We began as individuals with different levels of familiarity with narrative analysis and different understandings of the necessity of such familiarity for effective participation in the analytic process. Consider the following differing quotations from group members' reflections on the analytic process:

When I came . . . I knew nothing at all about narrative analysis.

When I arrived . . . my main aim was to gain some practical experience of using narrative analysis, to increase my confidence in being able to use the method to collect and analyze my PhD data.

I started my analysis on the train on the way [to the group meeting], reading the downloaded transcripts on the journey and scanning Michele Crossley's [[2000a]] book.

During the first session, we reviewed Crossley's outline of narrative analysis (see Chapter 9 in this volume) and distilled three stages of the analysis. First, an analyst should know the psychological literature and think through how 'personal narratives' link to **historical narratives** of a particular time and place. As Crossley states in Chapter 9, 'The essence of a narrative type of approach, as far as I am concerned, is an ability to understand and appreciate the personal and cultural meanings conveyed within oral or written texts and to explicate the socio-cultural resources utilized in this process.' However, some of us were uncomfortable with the claim that one could know about a past historical period through its 'oral or written texts'; might not that tend to conflate the perspectives of literate, educated or privileged people with the 'truth' about that time and place? For example, in many periods, reliance on texts would confuse men's experience with 'experience' more generally. As men have dominated women in most human societies and as literacy has been a marker of power in all societies that have left recorded history, might not this risk confusing the perspective of the powerful with the objective facts of history (see Box 10.1 for further discussion)?

Box 10.1   DO HISTORIANS HAVE A 'NARRATIVE METHOD'?

Historian Hayden White (1987) argues that the profession of history managed to secure a place in the academy through its use of narrativity to distinguish 'history' from other reports of the past (e.g., the keeping of annals). White cautions us to remember that history does not *occur* in narratives but that there are persistent disciplinary pressures to construct history *as* narrative with a beginning, middle and end and a moral prescription for the future. It is difficult to write history in non-narrative form but it may be a useful way to break with the humanism and individualism of psychology by narrating its history not in terms of individuals and biographies but in terms of objects and their agency (as has been done with the Rorschach test, for example: see Hegarty, 2003).

Next we discussed how to **validate** narrative analysis. A valid narrative is held to be well-grounded in the data, supportable with examples and should be developed by a continuous recursive process of shuttling between categories of analysis and raw data. A group member who had worked with narrative raised the question of the impossible hope of reaching certainty or conclusion in this process and described how her own work had produced different resonances among academic communities and communities of people whose life narratives she had analysed. Finally, we thought about the **interactional dynamics** of the interview, emphasizing how these might affect the stories that people would tell.

For group members who had done previous reading on narrative analysis or who had previously developed some understanding of the method through other channels, our discussion of Crossley's proposals provided some relief that they had grasped the sense of narrative methods. As one group member said:

I was relieved that . . . my understanding of narrative work was on the right track and excited that the method was not over-prescriptive, allowing for some creativity to be used to suit the research topic.

Others were daunted by the open-ended nature of the inquiry:

In the group I was struck by how difficult it would be to reach any resolution about the meaning of the text – or even what might be the best way to proceed if we were to proceed from [Crossley's] guidelines alone.

These comments reflect different comfort levels with the inevitability of interpretation in narrative analysis. Our differences would come to centre on whether we could best produce a narrative analysis of the interview data by conforming to or transgressing the norms that Michele Crossley had provided. A second source of anxiety concerned the data themselves. Crossley (2000a; see also Chapter 9 in this volume) outlines a method for securing narratives that relies on very specific forms of questioning. Interviewees are asked to imagine their life as a novel, to divide this novel into chapters and to narrate each chapter's plot. Clearly the interview transcripts we were given to analyse were not elicited along these lines. As our analysis began with the transcript of the interview with David and our group process became difficult (as I will describe below), our analysis became focused heavily on that one interview but for no solid methodological reason. Finally, many of us were troubled that Crossley had described how to 'write up' narrative analysis but not how to present it orally. Some group members ventured the opinion that standard academic forms of oral presentation were unsuited to narrative analysis, as Crossley defined it. The emphasis on *writing* in Crossley's account is hardly surprising as her approach owes so much to literary understandings of the self. However, as we had decided early on to test out our analyses by presenting them orally to a group of students and researchers at the end of our analytic sessions, the lack of guidelines about oral presentations was a matter of concern.

In brief, our introduction to narrative analysis left us with three sources of anxiety. First, was it possible to produce narrative analysis without privileging certain voices or making unacknowledged political commitments? Would we take up the responsibility of interpreting David's interview responsibly? Second, if a narrative analysis could not capture the truth of experience, by what standards might we judge a 'good' from a 'bad' analysis? Finally, how were we to develop an oral presentation within a methodology that was not obviously suited to that format?

Sutures and stitches in the group process

Given the size of the group and the diversity of views about how to proceed, we broke into two smaller subgroups. We set to work initially on the transcript of the interview conducted by the researcher, Arnie, with David to identify its **tone, themes** and **imagery**. We initially began this as individuals and were later to compile our analyses in the subgroups. I initially found the under-constrained nature of this inquiry confusing. How would we come to agreement about these categories and by appeal to what standards of analysis? Nevertheless, I set about producing lists (see Table 10.1)

When we returned to our subgroups, I realized that I had been working at a much more 'micro' level of analysis than others (and hence had analysed only a short section of the interview). In our subgroup, a fruitful debate began when someone suggested that one of the themes be named 'society'. Another person suggested that 'Civvie Street' – the term that David had spontaneously used in line 156 and thereafter to describe civilian life – would be a better term. After all, the armed forces were a form of 'society' in their own right and they formed an integral part of UK 'society'. David's comments about 'Civvie Street' were directed at events that happened *outside* of military society. The term was not only David's own rather than ours, but was also more precise than the one we had originally imposed. This specific matter of interpretation led us to consider the larger issue of grounding categories of analysis in David's own terms. Another person hit on the idea that the many cases of reported speech in David's transcript were themselves his narratives of social interactions that could usefully link the concept of 'society' to this individual interview. If we were to reconstruct the tone, imagery and themes of David's narratives, where better to start than here?

While this approach deviated from the task we had been set, it did suggest a way of moving past our earlier impasse about how to present a narrative analysis orally. We could re-enact these internal dialogues, beefing up David's account of those conversations that made an impression on him on his journey from army life to Civvie Street. Rather than simply describing the 'significant people' in his narrative of transition, we could let their reported speech drive the form that our **performative analysis** would take. This was a move away from the form of narrative methodology suggested by Crossley. It also

Table 10.1   My initial narrative analysis of David's interview transcript

Tone	Themes	Imagery
Belonging (lines 17–23)	Job as life task (lines 4–13)	'The dog house'
Insecurity (lines 4–13)	Cooperation (lines 17–43)	'Dark murky stuff'
Dissatisfaction (lines 48–60)	Civilians (lines 48–60)	'A load of crap'

reflected a belief that ordinary people's talk is informative and engaging, without the standardized methods of interpretation of qualitative analysis. Within our subgroup, this deviation from the norm prompted both anxiety about doing analysis the 'right' way and excitement about doing something different. As one person noted:

At first I was a little uneasy that perhaps a novel approach to presenting our work might be seen as inappropriate and concerned that our portrayal of David's experiences might be misunderstood by others as belittling him in some way.

In the other subgroup, the analysis traversed more familiar territory. Here, the narrative methods presented by Crossley assuaged anxiety and formed an effective structure for the analysis that was ultimately produced. While I was not part of this group, its members shared enough of their notes for me to know that they identified the tone of the interview as 'depressed', 'angry', 'hostile', 'disappointed', 'bitter', 'negative', despairing', 'resigned' and 'resenting'. They listed a complex set of images categorized into such clusters as 'animal metaphors' (e.g., 'drunk as skunks' (line 109), 'in the dog house' (line 68) and 'whale of a time' (line 336)). Their list of themes was also lengthy (one of these is described below in the context of the actual presentation). This group found it useful to work with flip charts to force their separation of tone, imagery and themes and they took turns in the role of note-taker to make sure that everybody's voice was heard.

Thus, by the time the two groups reassembled at the end of the first day of analysis, we had adopted very different stances toward the norms of narrative inquiry and had become committed to radically different ways of moving forward. In ways that mirrored larger dynamics within qualitative psychology, those of us in the 'performance group' were unable to communicate why a transgression of methodological norms seemed necessary to us. When we described what we were doing, we were told 'you might have got your story from sitting around and having a conversation in a pub'. The more orthodox narrative analysis group remained anxious to use existing narrative methods as fully as possible to push forward their interpretation. At the time, I could only attribute their reservations about the approach of the performance group to methodological conservatism. However, I later learned that some members of the narrative group were much more experienced with the use of performance in data analysis than I was.

During the three analytic sessions of the second day, we effectively worked as two separate groups with little interaction. Within the more orthodox narrative group, the effort focused on recording the link between personal and cultural analysis, establishing the validity of narrative psychological research and describing the interactional dynamics of the interview situation. This group also began working on the transcript of the interview with Brian (see Appendix 1), in which imagery and themes appeared harder to separate than they had been in David's case. In the performance group, we continued to mime the conversations that David described for the building blocks of our constructed script. Our emotions continued to oscillate between anxiety and excitement, as the journal of one group member noted:

> The preparation seemed to veer between agonizing periods where inspiration was completely lacking and bursts of activity where one of us would hit on a good idea, refuelling the enthusiasm of the others.

Remember that the performance group did not have a clear idea of the ultimate format of their presentation. We worked with varying levels of confidence that our collective creativity would communicate to others what we found poignant and engaging about David's fascinating story. We retired to another room to formally write out our script, to draw the picture of 'Civvie Street' that we would ultimately use in Scene 2 and to practise acting out the drama.

At the end of the second day of analysis, the two subgroups presented rough versions of what they had prepared to each other and members of each subgroup began to see the contribution of the other group. Encouragingly, even the member of the narrative group who had criticized our 'pub talk' encouraged us *not* to qualify or to apologize for what we were doing.

Our final analytic session on the third day was spent preparing and refining the presentation. Due to the dramatic nature of what we were doing, the time passed quite quickly as we collaborated on matters of staging, securing props and so on. Flipcharts were notably absent as we were now working with bodies, objects and spaces rather than words. None of us took adequate notes on this part of the analytic process so we will move ahead to the presentation itself, which we delivered later that day to the audience of interested students and researchers which we had assembled.

Box 10.2 DO QUALITATIVE METHODS HAVE TO BE TEXTUAL METHODS?

The lacunae in our text here raise important questions about narrative psychology in particular and qualitative psychology in general. How do the claims that *text* is either the primary medium of communication or an adequate metaphor for human sociality create hierarchies among people who vary in their linguistic competence or access to linguistic resources? Does the 'turn to language' obscure important forms of human communication such as visual aesthetics and sexuality (see Brown, 2001; Hegarty, 2007)? By which methods of qualitative psychology could we transcribe such ordinary meaningful communications as a smile, a kiss or a knowing wink? Academics normatively communicate in written and spoken words. Is it our status as a text-based academic community or the actual characteristics of human sociality that have led to the 'turn to text' in social psychology?

The presentation

Scene 1: Arnie and David

The scene is a standard classroom in a British university. Chairs for about 40 people are laid out in rows facing an overhead projector on the left side of the stage and a large whiteboard and four chairs are positioned on the right side. One of these chairs is occupied by Actor A (David). A mop is leaning against the right wall. A single line of white masking tape runs along the centre of the room dividing the audience and the presentation area in half.

Actor B begins a standard narrative analysis presentation using the overhead projector. The first acetate is entitled 'David's story: an encounter with Civvie Street'. The aims of the analysis are (1) to outline the key steps in doing a narrative analysis, (2) to present our analysis and interpretation of David's interview and (3) to share some reflections about the process.

The second acetate is titled 'Narrative analysis: a step-by-step guide' and lists five steps. These are (1) reading and listening, (2) identifying important concepts to look for (narrative tone, imagery and themes), (3) reflection (namely, the link between personal and cultural analysis, establishing the validity of narrative psychological research and interactional dynamics of the interview situation), (4) weaving all of this together into a coherent story and (5) writing up the research report.

The third acetate allows the speaker to expand on the concept of 'tone'. Several tones that are evident in the interview are described (including 'depressed', 'angry', 'hostile', 'disappointed', 'bitter', 'negative', despairing', 'resigned' and 'resenting'). The fourth acetate focuses on the linking of imagery-laden language (identified by line number of the interview) with specific themes. The most common theme is 'boundaries' which is evidenced by mention of 'door shut' (line 451), 'slide out instead of fall out' (line 419), 'out that gate' (line 95), 'other side of the fence' (line 404), 'drinking G and Ts' (line 191), 'civilianized', 'Civvie Street' (lines 139 and 156) and 'a bit like a Black trying to join the Klu [sic] Klux Klan' (lines 375–376). The fifth acetate lists 'theoretical concepts we considered'. These are (1) bereavement model, (2) identity theories, (3) psychodynamic perspectives, (4) psychological contract, (5) cultural analysis and (6) alienation.

The sixth acetate is entitled (4) 'Weaving all of this together into a coherent story' and (5) 'Writing up the research report'. Actor B is midway through presenting the material when Actor C leaps up unexpectedly from the audience wearing an army shirt, grabs the acetate that is currently on the overhead projector, crumples it up and throws it on the floor. Initially Actor B protests but Actor C shuns him and tells him to leave the stage. The interrupter moves across the line that divides the room, removes his army shirt and replaces it with a civilian shirt. He turns to Actor A who has been seated on the other side of the stage.

Actor C (to A):   'In what ways, if any, do you think your sense of yourself has been influenced by being in the army?'

B and C leave.

Scene 2: Ghost town and Civvie Street

Actor A (David) reverses the whiteboard showing a large hand-drawn picture of a lonely street of terraced houses ending in a gated graveyard. A crescent moon hangs in the sky. The picture is signed 'David.'

Actor A: 'You walk round and you walk down the street and you see ghosts. You know, you walk down streets where you walked down as a serving soldier and you can see all these ghosts, people you've met, you know. Or, come out of this shop and you expect all the lads to come staggering down the road drunk as skunks or something like that and they don't and I still see them today, you know. I can sit down in the town and yeah, the mind goes back to the times and you think "Yeah but there's no-one there any more" and you know . . . you think "Jesus, you never expected it to be like that". You thought that maybe there's some-one you could talk to but there isn't.'

Scene 3: David's voicings

Actors A (David), C and D are on stage.

Actor C: *(beckoning to Actor A)* 'Yeah if you want a job my son, come this way . . . '
Actor D: 'Right, David, Kuwait has been attacked.'
Actor A: *(to the audience)* 'You know, I was ready to go.'
(Pause)
Actor C: 'You shouldn't be coming in here, you know. You've got a job – what are you doing sort of taking other jobs? There's people out there who are unemployed who want this job.'
Actor A: 'Well why aren't they here taking this job?'
(Pause)
Actor C: 'Oh, we've really enjoyed having you.' *(moves to shake Actor A's hand)*
Actor A: *(accepting the handshake and turning aside to the audience)* 'You lying git.'
Actor C: 'ID card – thank you, Mr Jones'
Actor A: 'Oh Jesus, what have I done?'
Actor C: 'Well that's it, he's got nothing else to offer, the novelty's worn off.'
(Pause)
Actor A: 'Right, this is me. This is what you're getting. Take me and I'll be a great team player.'
Actor C: 'Oh, without the caretaker this wouldn't happen and this wouldn't happen. You know where everything is – we don't'
Actor A: *(looking at Actor D)* 'Right, we are going to pick bits of litter up.'
Actor D: 'Ah, it's only the caretaker and his staff – they'll do it.'
Actor C: 'Well, that's it, David, you did a good job, we miss him.'
(Pause)
Actor C: 'Fine get someone else in.'

(Pause)

Actor A: *(to Actor C)* 'Look, I'm buying a house, I've just come out of the army – any chance of coming along and showing me a few pointers?'
    (Actor C turns and walks away)

(Pause)

Actor A: 'Bloody hell, I've got to deal with that now. Jesus, you never expected it to be like that. What the hell am I doing here? Bugger this. This is me for the rest of my life. Why isn't it like it was in the army? Well what's this? Where am I?'

Scene 4: The missus

Actors A (David) and D (David's missus) are seated. Actor A is holding a hand over Actor D's mouth, preventing Actor D from speaking.

Actor A: 'If it wasn't for my wife, I think I'd have done something totally crazy. I don't think I'd be around today to be honest if it wasn't for the missus. She was, she was very supportive, and I, um, I tended to be a little wild for about a couple of months and I got out, which one does. Uh, it nearly broke the marriage up at one stage. But she stuck with us and here we are.'

Scene 5: Arnie and David

Actors A (David) and C (Arnie) are seated.

Actor C (Arnie): 'Well thanks for participating in the interview.'

Interpretation after performance

Judging from immediate reactions, the presentation was a success. An experienced social psychologist present advised us to work together again if we got the chance. Another described the performance as one that had really made her think. The performance also brought the performers to surprising new insights about the data. For example, Actor A wrote:

The performance itself was an incredible thing to be a part of. By this time I had read David's words many times but somehow saying them out loud in front of a large group of people who were not expecting to see what was being presented to them [as they had not been told about the format of the presentation beforehand] really brought David's words to life. I would not try to claim that I was anywhere near experiencing what David had experienced but I did get a stronger sense of his emotions than had been possible from the interview transcript alone.

Emotion resulted from bringing the data 'to life' through performance, a life that is obscured by orthodox forms of presentation. This leads me to reflect on the recurring tensions in our group, in qualitative psychology and in David's traumatic journey to Civvie Street. When we began our analysis, several members of the analytic group were quick to see David's desires for military discipline as a problem that needed to be psychologized. This made me distinctly uncomfortable. I reflected on the first session in my notes as follows:

> In spite of the relativist talk at the table, inferences were quickly made about David's motivational states. For example, there was much discussion of his discipline as a reaction to or compensation for other psychological events.

Both for us and for David, a move away from discipline was a source of anxiety. One response to that anxiety was to stay within the discipline of narrative psychology as offered by the text. Another reaction was to reinvent the interpretative project. Yet, we were all slow to recognize the similarity between our own investments in the anxiety-quelling comforts of methodological directives and David's nostalgia for the comfort that the rigours of army life provide.

Box 10.3 THE DISCIPLINE OF ARMY LIFE AND THE SOCIAL SCIENCES

The resonance between army discipline and the discipline of psychology is not an accidental one. Michel Foucault's (1977) work locates the origins of the social sciences in projects of nineteenth-century government such as studies of army 'discipline' – the regulation of soldiers' bodies. Some of the earliest systematic biometric data were gathered on armies (Hacking, 1990). Armies also provided the context for mass testing of IQ and personality instruments (Kevles, 1968). The history of quantitative psychology and statistics is utterly bound up with military history. So there is more than a coincidental irony in the reluctance of qualitative psychologists to recognize David's desire for order as they themselves are invested in moving beyond the kinds of order that quantitative psychology imposes on scholarship and the interpretation of human experience.

As our presentation highlighted, 'boundaries' are a key theme in this interview transcript. Yet, boundaries could also be said to structure the anxiety about 'proper' interpretation that structured our work together. We tried to create some possibility of a resonance between these two forms of boundaries with a little stagecraft. Within the presentation, the physical space was bounded by masking tape that divided the room into two spaces. On stage, the academic presentation and scenes that occurred in David's military life unfolded on the left-hand side of the tape (from the audience's viewpoint). All events in Civvie Street happened on the right-hand side, where the picture of Civvie Street hung for much of the presentation. The violent interruption of the academic presentation was timed for the moment when the write-up that would never be written up was being discussed. It was also intended to throw into relief the violence inherent in the project of speaking for others' psychologies within an academic discourse that denies its own location.

None of this is to say that we agreed with everything that David said. Scene 4 ('The missus') was staged to emphasize that, while David voiced a reliance on his wife, she was the one person whose speech he never quoted. This scene materialized our earlier concerns about the patriarchal politics of treating men's narratives as neutral texts when they are the only ones available. Both Actors A and C in scene 4 were men and we deliberately cast them in these roles to emphasize the silencing of David's wife. She had not been interviewed and, even if David had repeated her words, they would not have been hers any longer. The physical contact between two men in this scene was also deliberate. Holding someone's head is a very intimate act. We hoped that this would prompt the audience to think about the heteronormativity of the institutions of marriage and the army which David described as supportive.

Box 10.4   SPEAKING BACK TO NARRATIVE PSYCHOLOGY

While qualitative psychology is a relatively new project, anthropologists have relied on participant-observation and ethnography since the nineteenth century. As Mary Louise Pratt (1986) makes clear, ethnography became a genre of writing through which anthropologists deliberately constructed the 'natives' they described as relatively untouched by Western influence and obscured the notion that the anthropologists themselves were agents of colonialism. How do narrative psychologists construct their data as authentic and does this serve to bolster or undermine their positions as legitimate disinterested researchers? What happens when those who were analysed 'speak back' – as formerly colonized people increasingly did to Western anthropologists in the second half of the twentieth century and as lesbian and gay psychologists appear to be doing to narrative psychologists at present (see Barker et al., in press; Crossley, 2004)?

Concluding thoughts

I began this chapter by asking you to recall the five tensions that structure the field of qualitative psychology: the degree to which methods are embodied or disembodied knowledge, the utility of 'methodology' for critical inquiry, the legitimacy of claims to 'expert' narrative analysis, the completeness of current accounts of 'narrative psychology' and the utility of conformity to and deviance from methodological norms in developing those standards. I want to conclude by arguing that these dilemmas are likely to be around for some time and that qualitative psychologists should not be so deafened by the noise they create that they can no longer attend to the meaningful life stories that ordinary people tell. There will, no doubt, be considerable rewards within psychology for those who claim to have developed a new, valid or accessible qualitative method and for those who claim to have radically transgressed against an overly rigid methodological orthodoxy. However, the experience of participation in this group has taught me that there is much to be learned from sticking to a difficult position that creates controversy and anxiety and at the same time it is also necessary for people thinking along radically different lines to keep open minds through open lines of communication. In situations like this, we are more likely to learn from each other than the difficulty of swallowing our pride would lead us to believe.

Of course these dynamics apply not only among researchers but also between researchers and their participants. How does our training as social scientists get in the way of listening to data rather than facilitating that listening? The narratives that lead some people to study the social sciences in Civvie Street, where individuality, originality and creativity are (ostensibly) valued, differ in important ways from those that lead people to army life where order, discipline and routine are (ostensibly) valued. When we meet across an interview transcript, misunderstanding is unlikely to be avoided. However, it would be wrong to assume that the values encouraged in one organization can operate as a neutral standard for people socialized in the other. David's expressed desire for regularity, order and predictability in life need not be psychologized any more than academics' perpetual quest for the new and innovative. With these concerns in mind, I invite readers to become 'significant people' in the unfolding story of what narrative psychology might become.

Summary

This chapter has

- described one group's attempt to produce a narrative analysis
- highlighted the theoretical choices that are made when work is presented through different genres (academic, theatrical, etc.)
- raised questions about the tension between adherence to and pushing beyond the norms for qualitative research in psychology
- invited the reader to consider how academic identities may encourage people to marginalize those that they write about in unreflexive ways.

ANALYSING QUALITATIVE DATA:
COMPARATIVE REFLECTIONS

Evanthia Lyons

This chapter offers comparative reflections on the employment of the four approaches to the analysis of the data presented in the Preface to Section 2, concentrating on the analytic foci, matters of epistemology and the 'value' of the outcomes. The major similarities and differences between the four approaches are highlighted.

Particular attention is paid to how each of the four approaches conceptualizes and deals with the way researchers should use existing psychological knowledge and their personal experiences and speaking positions in the process of conducting qualitative research. It also discusses the goals of psychological enquiry and the question of what are the most appropriate criteria for evaluating research conducted within each approach.

Key terms

abuse/power critique	naïve realist
application	radical constructionist
contextual constructionist	representing the 'Other'
critical realism	rigour and quality of research
description	social critique
explanation	usefulness of research
ideology of application critique	

As I discussed in Chapter 1, when we were developing the concept for this book, Adrian Coyle and I had two main goals. First, we wanted to provide the reader with a sense of how the theoretical and epistemological positions underlying different approaches to qualitative research influence the research process and how (relatively) novice researchers experienced their attempts to apply the ' "experts' " descriptions of the analytic process to a common data set.

We believed this would make explicit the uncertainties and dilemmas that are often faced by qualitative researchers and would also provide examples of how such issues are dealt with in practice. Second, we were keen to provide the reader with a comparative context so that the reasons for and the implications of choosing to employ one approach rather than another would become clear.

This chapter develops that discussion by highlighting some of the differences and similarities between the four analytic approaches that we focus on in this volume: interpretative phenomenological analysis (IPA), grounded theory, discourse analysis and narrative analysis. In particular, the chapter summarizes the epistemological assumptions underlying each approach and discusses the implications of these differences for some central concerns of qualitative research, namely the role of the researcher in the research process, what the appropriate goals of psychological enquiry are and what criteria are most appropriate for evaluating qualitative research. Some of these questions have been raised more or less explicitly in other contributions to this book. I want to extend the discussion by first summarizing and comparing the position each approach takes on these issues and by drawing on the experiences of the researchers who analysed the common data. Also, I will consider the political implications of the choices we make in the research process, especially in relation to how we conceptualize the relationship between ourselves, as the researcher, and the participants.

The chapter starts by summarizing and comparing the epistemological underpinnings of each of the approaches as these assumptions have implications for how each approach deals with these issues. It then turns to the issue of how each approach sees the role of the researcher. Within qualitative research, the researcher is seen as an important part of the process of knowledge production, bringing to it their own understandings, conceptual orientations and a stock of cultural knowledge. Qualitative researchers are therefore expected to reflect on their actions and reactions during all the stages of the research process. These reflections can become part of the data set and play a role in its interpretation. I have focused my discussion on two particular aspects of the researcher's role. First, how should the researcher use their own biographical experiences and existing theoretical knowledge in the analytic and/or interpretative stages of the research? Second, what are the political implications of the relative speaking position of the researcher and the participants?

I then examine the goals of psychological inquiry as stated by each of the four approaches and discuss how far each method strives to produce **description**, prediction and/or **explanation** or to offer a **social critique** of the status quo. Finally, I discuss what criteria are most appropriate for evaluating research carried out within each approach in relation to three aspects: technical proficiency, theory development and **application**.

Comparing the epistemological underpinnings of the four analytic approaches

The main differing epistemological stances that research can take have been described by Adrian Coyle in Chapter 2. The importance of the epistemological underpinnings of the research approach you choose to employ in a project has, we hope, also been illustrated in both the 'theoretical' and 'analytic' chapters in this volume. The epistemological basis of each approach influences the status you give to your data, what your role as a researcher is and what conclusions you can draw from your data.

There are different ways of conceptualizing the epistemological positions underlying different approaches to analysing qualitative data. Henwood and Pidgeon (1994) identified three main strands of psychological enquiry. The first strand is based on an empiricist epistemological position: the main methodological principle is that of a discovery of valid representations by using inductive reasoning and it evaluates qualitative research by using criteria analogous to reliability and validity. The second strand is based on contextualism. The main methodological principle involved is the construction of intersubjective meaning and the usefulness of qualitative research is argued on the basis of generating new theory which is firmly grounded in participants' own meanings in concrete contexts. The third strand is based on constructivism and its main methodological principle is that of interpretative analysis. This strand focuses on 'the reflexive functions of language, which construct representations of "objects" in the world and which have material discursive effects' (Henwood, 1996: 31).

Reicher (2000) distinguishes between experiential approaches and discursive approaches. The former refer to approaches which are concerned with understanding how people experience and make sense of their world, whereas the latter are concerned with how language is used to construct particular versions of reality. Madill et al. (2000) conceptualize the differences in epistemological positions of qualitative research in terms of a continuum where on one end is what they call a **naïve realist** position and on the other is a **radical constructionist** position.

Somewhere in between these two positions is a **contextual constructionist** position. Naïve realism in its simplest form assumes that reality can be discovered by the use of appropriate methods. However, other forms of realism such as **critical realism** recognize that knowledge is not objective and therefore are closer to the contextual constructionist position which assumes that all knowledge is context specific and influenced by the perspective of the perceiver. Radical constructionist epistemologies reject the idea that data reflect reality and focus on how reality is constructed through language.

Any attempt to place the four approaches we focused on in this volume – as they are theoretically described and then put into practice by researchers in the analytic chapters – in any of these classification systems quickly leads to the realization that these classifications are somewhat oversimplified. For example, it can be argued that IPA, grounded theory and narrative analysis fall under the category of experiential epistemologies whereas discourse analysis would be classified under the discursive category. Or if we were to adopt Madill et al.'s (2000) epistemological continuum, grounded theory would be closer to the realist end of the continuum, IPA and narrative analysis would be nearer to the contextual constructionist point and discourse analysis would be near the radical constructionist end of the continuum. However, if we look more closely at the assumptions that these methodologies are based on and how they are applied in practice, we can see that some of them do not fall clearly under one or another category.

For instance, the version of grounded theory discussed by Sheila Payne in Chapter 5 is based on a realist epistemology in that, following Glaser and Strauss (1967), it assumes that participants' perceptions of an event or a social situation directly reflect reality. At the same time, it emphasizes the need to understand the meanings participants attach to particular events and that the resulting theories and knowledge ought to be situated in particular contexts. So, in that respect, the version of grounded theory put forward in Chapter 5 shares some epistemological assumptions with both realist and contextual constructionist approaches.

IPA and narrative analysis are based on a phenomenological approach (see Chapters 3 and 9) or a 'contextual constructionist' epistemology (Madill et al., 2000). The assumption is that language reflects the experiences of and the meanings participants attach to particular events and social situations, although Smith (1993) acknowledges that the process of accessing participants' experiences and meanings is not a simple one: it requires the researcher to *interpret* the data. Discourse analysis is regarded as being based on a radical constructionist epistemology which challenges the taken-for-granted ways we categorize and make sense of the world around us. It sees language as constructing categories and events rather than reflecting 'reality'. However, in Chapter 8, Chris Walton has paid particular attention to Foucauldian discourse analysis which emphasizes not only the constitutive role of language but also that the discourses open to a speaker are shaped by the social structures and power relationships within which he or she is located.

The role of the researcher

Taking into account the researcher's theoretical knowledge and biographical experiences

One of the main implications of the epistemology underlying the methodological approach you choose to employ is the role you, as a researcher, are expected to play in the research process and how you are supposed to use and engage with the theoretical knowledge and biographical experiences you bring into that process. How researchers' theoretical and biographical backgrounds can be drawn into the research is evidenced in the analytic chapters when all the authors discussed their uneasiness at privileging one interpretation over another either because members of a group with different backgrounds put emphasis on other aspects of the data or used different theoretical concepts to make sense of their data.

Within the grounded theory approach as it is presented in this volume, which is based on a realist epistemology, the researcher is expected to generate a theory which accounts as accurately as possible for the data. However, it is important to note that other versions of grounded theory would acknowledge the interpretation and social constructionist aspects of the analytic process (Charmaz, 2006; Rennie, 2000). Irrespective of the researcher's social positioning and/or previous relevant experience and/or the particular views he/she holds, a skilled researcher is expected to be able to discover and present the actors' meanings and understandings of the phenomenon under investigation in a particular context. In analysing the transcripts of the ex-servicemen in Chapter 6, Sheila Hawker and Christine Kerr refer to the process of coding as the process of 'noticing'. They wanted to emphasize the importance of systematically thinking about data and that codes and links between codes are there in the data to be noticed – to be discovered. They also remind us that one of the key evaluative criteria of grounded theory research is 'goodness of fit' between data and the emergent theory. The relative appropriateness of the evaluative criteria outlined in Chapter 2 for each approach will be discussed later in this chapter. What is important here is to note the distance placed between the data and the researcher in the analysis stage of the research.

Adopting a phenomenological (Giorgi and Giorgi, 2003) and hermeneutic philosophy (Palmer, 1969; Ricoeur, 1970), IPA acknowledges that, in trying to explore the meanings and experiences of participants, the researcher engages in an *interpretative* activity. The researcher is trying to make sense of the participants' own struggle to make sense of their world. The researcher's pre-existing knowledge and conceptions are therefore actively implicated in the analytic process as the researcher tries to describe and account for participants' experiences. The role of the researcher is twofold. First they strive to put themselves in the place of the participant and second they ask critical questions of the participants' words, being aware that there is no straightforward and/or direct relationship between what people express and what they experience (see Chapter 3). A superficial reading of this process may lead one to wonder whether here IPA shares with radical constructionist approaches the assumption that speakers construct their realities and experiences to fulfil certain functions in either the micro-conversational context or the macro-ideological context. However, there is a difference between IPA and discursive approaches in that IPA assumes that the researcher can access motives and understandings that the participant is either not aware of or finds difficult to express, whereas discursive approaches do not attribute motives to the participants and do not take their words to reflect experiences that participants may or may not be aware of. Rather they examine the accounts that people offer of their experiences and consider what particular conversational and/or ideological functions are achieved through these accounts.

Narrative analysis is also based on a phenomenological philosophy and sees the task of the researcher as both describing and interpreting the data (see Chapter 9). It assumes that the researcher is able to make sense of the personal and cultural meanings that participants use either in written or oral texts to describe their experiences. Furthermore, the researcher adopts an active and creative role for interpreting the data to create a narrative that is coherent and persuasive.

Discourse analytic approaches see the role of the researcher as constructing or authoring an account of the data (see Chapter 7). Based on the assumption that language is constitutive of reality rather than reflecting it, discourse analytic approaches do not give theories or analytic accounts a special status. The latter are seen as particular constructions of events, as are the data under investigation. The researcher is therefore expected to be reflexive.

The above summary has demonstrated that all approaches acknowledge that the psychological knowledge and experiences of the researcher are inextricably interlinked with the research process. However they differ in their recommendations as to how we should deal with this issue.

Advocates of earlier versions of a grounded theory approach have argued that this 'baggage' is something one needs to try to put aside when starting their research (Glaser and Strauss, 1967). However, one can question to what extent it is possible to be aware of all our beliefs and background knowledge that may be relevant to the way we conduct a piece of research. If we were able to be aware of them, to what extent can we put them out of our minds? If we were to do this, how can we define the parameters of the phenomenon we are investigating and/or what areas/domains we should ask questions about? Other researchers in this area accept that such an approach is utopian and argue that what researchers should do is to make explicit at the start of the project any beliefs and experiences which may influence the way they conduct their research (see Chapter 5 in this volume, and Pidgeon, 1996). For example, Charmaz (1990) suggested that qualitative researchers need to have a perspective from which they actively seek to build their analyses, without merely applying it to new data. Such a perspective includes the substantive interests that guide the questions to be asked, the researcher's philosophical stance, the school of thought that provides a store of sensitizing concepts and the researcher's personal experiences, priorities and values.

IPA invites the researcher simultaneously to put aside their own experiences so that they can enter the world of the participants and also to actively use their background knowledge in order to interpret the experiences participants express. Similarly, narrative analysis assumes that the researcher can access the cultural meanings which surround the participants' narratives and use those to analyse the data and provide the researcher's account. Although this conceptualization of the role the researchers' own understandings and knowledge may play in the research appears, perhaps, more plausible, neither approach satisfactorily theorizes how the researcher's 'baggage' is implicated in the research. They do not tell us how to incorporate our own insights into the final account of the data (Willig, 2001).

On the other hand from a discourse analytic perspective, a researcher can only offer their own *construction* of the research data rather than discover 'facts' or witness participants' 'experiences'. The researcher therefore needs to ask questions about the possible implications of the particular accounts he/she would produce for the discursive and material contexts in which the data and research audiences are located.

Representing 'the Other'

One frequent source of anxiety for qualitative researchers is the issue of how to represent participants. This is a concern which may arise for several reasons. First, this issue may relate to the quest for authenticity: the researcher may wish to ensure that he/she does not 'mis-represent' the accounts and experiences of participants. Second, this is an issue that may have political implications, particularly when participants have experiences different from researchers and belong to groups which are not given opportunities to voice their experiences and claim their rights (Kitzinger and Wilkinson, 1996).

Analysing the transcripts of interviews with the ex-soldiers (see Appendix 2) using grounded theory in Chapter 6, Sheila Hawker and Christine Kerr have pointed out that one of their concerns was that they did not have enough contextual knowledge of how the data were collected and the background of the participants. They were, therefore, anxious to emphasize that they were not fully confident about their interpretation of the data. In this case, they were anxious that the emergent themes and theory may not be grounded in the 'right' interpretation of the participants' words. In other words, they were concerned that their interpretation and conclusions may 'misrepresent' the participants' accounts.

In Chapter 4, when reporting the attempts of the IPA group to analyse the account provided by the ex-soldier David, Lesley Storey commented on the anxiety of the group that the use of particular theoretical constructs to make sense of David's world would distance their interpretation from and 'misrepresent' his experiences. She also discussed the difficulties that may arise from identifying too closely with the participant during the analytic process. This, she felt, might result in researchers forcing 'the data to conform to *their* experiences'. Equally, if the researcher negatively dis-identifies with the interviewee, she argued, it 'can make it difficult to empathize (or at least sympathize) with the interviewee and thus attain the sort of "insider" perspective on the research topic to which IPA aspires'. The researchers were keen to understand the world of the interviewee through his/her own eyes and not to judge him/her or represent him/her in ways that he/she would either not recognize or perhaps not agree with.

In contrast, constructing an account of applying Foucauldian discourse analysis to the interview transcripts, Chris Walton acknowledged that the focus of the analytic group was not on understanding the experiences of David and Brian (see Chapter 8). Instead, their analysis focused on 'the words and phrases that they drew upon when they talked about or constructed their identities, both army and post-army identities'.

In this sense, the discourses the group identified as used by David and Brian to construct their identities were instrumental in representing or reconstructing them in particular ways.

Neil Harbison raises similar concerns in Chapter 10 when he discusses the deliberations of the group that used a narrative analysis approach to analyse the data. Harbison challenges the notion that we can access cultural meanings of the past using oral or written accounts of historical periods and contended that these sources are likely to give voice to the more educated and privileged groups at a particular historical time and place, as these groups are likely to have the power to produce dominant versions of history, thus ignoring the experiences of more disadvantaged groups. Harbison therefore questions the possibility of producing a narrative analysis of the transcripts 'without privileging certain voices or making unacknowledged political commitments'. In addition, Harbison is concerned with the extent to which the social world we inhabit as researchers, which values innovation and creativity, would interfere with the judgments we might be tempted to make about the orderly and disciplined world of the ex-soldiers. In other words, Harbison raises questions about our ability to produce a narrative to account for the participants' reflections of a period of their lives and factors that may influence this production process. He presents us with the dilemmas of how to represent the data in a way which reflects the participants' worlds and takes into account the political implications of our versions of their narratives.

In all four analytic chapters, it becomes apparent that the researchers are constantly preoccupied with the question of how the final report of their analysis will have implications for how their participants are represented. First, irrespective of the approach to data analysis adopted, the authors emphasize the importance of producing an account of the data set which is 'grounded' in the raw data. In this respect, they strive to establish the credibility of their particular versions of David's and/or Brian's accounts by showing that the researchers' accounts are not arbitrary: they are based on empirical evidence. This is not to say, however, that any of the analytic approaches focused on in this volume would see the interpretation of empirical evidence as either a neutral or an objective process. As was noted above, all four approaches acknowledge that researchers engage in an interpretation or a (de/re)construction of the data and that this process is conceptualized within each of the four approaches to a greater or lesser extent as being subjective and political. They all acknowledge that the final analytic account would comprise particular versions of David's and Brian's worlds which would represent/construct David and Brian in particular ways. Furthermore this acknowledgement gives rise to different concerns depending on the epistemological basis of each approach.

Two main factors may influence this process: first, the use of existing theory and psychological jargon and second, the way the researchers construct themselves. Thus, based on a realist epistemology, the version of grounded theory presented in Chapter 5 raises questions about the extent to which the researcher understands the contextual meanings attached to particular events by the participants and therefore the extent to which the emergent theory represents the participants in the same way that participants make sense of themselves.

Based on a phenomenological approach, IPA raises questions about the extent to which the researcher is able to enter the inner world of the participants and interpret the data in a way which elicits the 'real experiences' of the participants. Again the concern here is with ensuring the relevance and perhaps the recognizability of the accounts to the participants. Within the version of narrative analysis presented in Chapter 9, questions arise regarding the validity and privileging of the researcher's narrative over the participant's original narrative. Finally, based on a radical social constructionist epistemology, discourse analysis is concerned with how the researcher's speaking positions may influence how participants are constructed through his/her analysis.

How we represent others becomes particularly important when our participants belong to groups which are often constructed as 'Other' in particular cultures. For example, feminist researchers have argued that women have been traditionally constructed as 'Other' (Kitzinger and Wilkinson, 1996; Ussher, 1991). People with mental illness, lesbians and gay men, economically disadvantaged people, people with HIV/AIDS, non-White people and people with disabilities have also been constructed as 'Other': they are defined in opposition to the norms of 'mentally healthy', heterosexual, privileged middle class, White and able-bodied people (see, for example, Coyle, 1996; Fowler and Hardesty, 1994; Marks, 1996).

The issue here is whether we should speak for these groups in order to empower them and have their voices expressed via our reports, with the hope of shaping a social change, or whether such attempts are presumptuous and are reinforcing the denial of a voice to the 'Other'. This dilemma is aptly summarized in the following two quotations: 'We must take on the whole world; we cannot afford "no go areas" of the imagination; we cannot afford to refuse an opinion on any subject' (Livia, 1996: 36); 'No one should ever "speak for" or assume another's voice . . . it becomes a form of colonisation' (Sinister Wisdom Collective, 1990: 4).

Kitzinger and Wilkinson (1996) have identified four different ways that feminist researchers suggest that we, as researchers, should deal with the issue of 'Othering'. First, some have argued that we can only speak for ourselves – that is, we can only conduct research with groups whose experiences we share. Second, it has been claimed that we should speak of Otherness only to celebrate it.

However, this carries a risk of idealizing the 'Other'. Third, another strand of thought suggests the way we should deal with the issue of Otherness is to try to destabilize the relationship between self and 'Other'. This may mean that we try to reverse the established power relationships by having members of less powerful groups (e.g., a black researcher) researching the more powerful (e.g., white people).

One of the assumptions underlying the debate about the implications of researching the 'Other' is that there is a simple way of grouping people or placing them in particular social categories. For instance, in my work with young people from ethnic minority communities, I often have to write about the experiences of women of South Asian origin. Do they constitute an 'Other'? My participants and I belong to different ethnic and age groups but we can also be categorized as women and as immigrants (as I come from Cyprus). I often find that I interview women who are of a lower socio-economic status to me but we can both recite experiences of discrimination. Which group membership should be the one that defines us in ways that determine whether I and my participants are 'Other' to each other or people from the same group? People belong to multiple groups and it would be both impractical and reductionist if we were to argue that we can only research and speak for people who have the same profile of group memberships as us. Furthermore, as researchers we need to be very careful in assuming that, because our participants belong to a particular group, they necessarily define or construct their identities in terms of these memberships (Camp et al., 2002; Finlay and Lyons, 2000; Lyons et al., 2006).

Box 11.1   WHO IS THE 'OTHER'?

An example of how apparent 'sameness' is not always reflected in the eyes of the researcher and the participants is discussed by Ranti Oguntokun (1998). Oguntokun studied the experiences of black African refugees in the UK and describes how she began her research assuming that, being a black African woman herself, she and her participants would not be 'Other' to each other. As she said:

> 'I assumed that a shared skin colour, shared continental origins and a shared immigrant status would give me the right to represent these women's experiences with legitimacy and authenticity as an 'insider', avoiding the errors that culturally and ethnically dissimilar researchers may make.' (p. 526)

However, she goes on to discuss how she soon realized that she could not continue to claim similarities between her own experiences of feelings of displacement and homesickness and those of her participants, most of whom had fled war-torn areas and endured terrible hardships. Moreover, her participants did not

(Continued)

(Continued)

allow her to make such claims either. One woman, who was a refugee from Somaliland, said to her:

'I do not talk to other people about Somali because it is too much. You cannot understand. You do not have war in your country, no? It is too bad, you yourself will weep for Somali.' (p. 527)

Oguntokun's reflections provide us with a striking example of how apparent 'sameness' can become illusory in the context of diverse experiences between members of the same group and the dilemmas faced by researchers who want to represent people who are different from them. In responding to this, Oguntokun (1998) acknowledged the differences between herself and her participants and endeavoured to produce an account which was knowledgeable about and sympathetic to the experiences of the black African refugee women, positioning her not within the group but knowledgeably alongside the group members.

From a critical, radical social constructionist perspective, it is also important to note that **representing the 'Other'** is not merely a descriptive process. The way we represent the 'Other' does not necessarily reflect the experiences of the 'Other'; it also constitutes us and the 'Other' in particular ways. Alcoff (1994) argues that we need to evaluate instances of speaking for others by asking questions about the reasons why we wish to speak about the Other, the relevance of who we are and the experiences we carry for what we say about the Other and the effects of what we say on the discursive and material context.

Box 11.2   PRACTICES ENABLING CRITICAL ENGAGEMENT WITH THE SELF-OTHER RELATIONSHIP

There are a number of different strategies you can employ to adopt a critical and reflexive approach to speaking for an 'Other'. For example:

- ask your participants to evaluate the validity of your account of them
- listen to how your participants speak of 'your group' so that your own perspective is problematized and its relativity exposed
- listen to how other members of the powerful group (your group) speak about members of the group to which the participants belong (the Other)
- try to provide opportunities to create a dialogue between you and your participants so that no account is privileged.

(Continued)

Some of these are easier to achieve than others. The important point is to employ strategies to interrupt the process of privileging the account of the powerful group to which we as social scientists often belong. For a fuller discussion, see also Fine (1994) and Kitzinger and Wilkinson (1996).

I have chosen to devote significant space to discussing this issue as I think it important to raise questions about the political and social implications of our research. In books such as this, which are concerned with the intellectual and technical debates about how we conduct research, it is easy to think inadvertently of the research process as socially and politically neutral and be overly concerned with the rigour of our methodological skills to the detriment of considering the intended and unintended consequences of our practices. I hope this discussion raises your awareness of the need to question vigilantly the political and social implications of our research endeavours.

Evaluating the four analytic approaches

In this section, I would like to address the different ways we can evaluate research conducted within each of the four methods presented in this book. In Chapter 2, Adrian Coyle pointed out that there are some evaluative criteria which seem to recur in the literature on qualitative research methods. These have to do with ensuring that the contexts in which the participants are located are adequately described, that the analytic process is presented in a transparent and detailed way, that there is a reflexive account of how the researcher's 'speaking position' might have influenced the research at its various stages and that interpretations are grounded in research data. He also focused on the practical implications of the research, which he argued qualitative researchers would do well to engage with. Examining the evaluative criteria that qualitative researchers have put forward (see for example, Elliott et al., 1999; Yardley, 2000), it seems that these relate to either the **rigour and quality of the research activity** or the **usefulness of the research** outcomes. The usefulness of the research is often seen as its potential contribution to theory development and/or its applicability to real life situations.

Coyle suggested that there is no consensus amongst qualitative researchers as to the most appropriate evaluative criteria for qualitative research and such lack of consensus may not be surprising given the variety of qualitative research methods. I want to extend this discussion by focusing on the evaluative criteria appropriate to each of the four methods we considered. What constitutes an appropriate criterion depends on what the method claims to attempt to achieve but one can also evaluate a particular method from an epistemological perspective different to that on which it is based. Therefore, before considering the dimensions along which we can evaluate research carried out within the four methods, it is useful to revisit the goals of psychological enquiry as stated by each method and which stem from the epistemological stance they take.

Within grounded theory, the aim is to develop inductive theory which is closely derived from the data. The emergent theory must be able to explain the data elicited from all the participants, even the cases that provide conflicting data. The aim is to generate a theory which explains the social and psychological processes under study and understand the local network of causal relationships which may result in particular events and how the participants made sense of them. Researchers using grounded theory look for possible and plausible mechanisms by which one event/variable leads to another and examine the complexity of the networks of actions and processes in concrete contexts.

Whilst the aim of grounded theory is to derive an explanatory theory on the basis of data, IPA is mainly concerned with providing a detailed description of the participants' lived experiences. *Why* the participants experience their world in particular ways is only a secondary concern to an IPA researcher. Similarly narrative analysis is more concerned with detailed description than explanation. Moreover the focus is on analysing individual experience and meanings in depth rather than looking for commonalities between different people.

Within discourse analysis, the goal of psychological inquiry is to offer a critical interrogation of the *status quo* by destabilizing taken-for-granted ways of categorizing the world. Discursive psychology examines the social functions performed by particular discursive resources in talk and text. Foucauldian discourse analysis sometimes goes a step further by trying to theorize about the social structures and power relationships which make certain discursive resources available and the implications for the subjectivities of those who use them. In this sense, Foucauldian discourse analysis can provide a theory of how historically some discourses have come to be the way they are or how they are grounded in particular structures and institutions (e.g., see Parker, 1992).

Given the differences in what each of the focal research methods strives to achieve, it is appropriate that we use different criteria to evaluate them (although some criteria are relevant to all, such as the need to evidence interpretations by quoting relevant data). For example, a grounded theory study within a realist epistemology which aims to generate a theory is best evaluated by demonstrating that methods of data collection and the analytic processes captured the 'real' experiences and meanings of the participants. This can be demonstrated by being transparent about the analytic process and sometimes going back to participants to check the validity of the researcher's analysis (although this raises questions about how differences between the researcher's and the participants' interpretations are dealt with). Furthermore, the validity of one's interpretation can be assessed by a method of triangulation (see Moran-Ellis et al., 2006) – that is, the validity of the analysis can be demonstrated by the extent that two or more researchers reach the same conclusions.

On the other hand, methods such as IPA and narrative analysis are often more concerned with detailed description than explanation and are therefore more appropriately evaluated by demonstrating the rigour of the research activity and reflexivity rather than the relative adequacy of the research to access the *real* experiences of the participants. Similarly, it would be inappropriate to criticize research conducted within these approaches for not contributing to the development of explanatory theory.

Within discourse analysis, discursive psychology is concerned with how language constructs particular objects and phenomena and most often aims to challenge the taken-for-granted ways of constructing the world rather than explaining under what conditions certain behaviours would occur. In contrast, Foucauldian discourse analysis is concerned with the influence of social structures, institutions and power relationships on the availability of particular discourses and in turn the possibilities for action that particular discourses afford. In this respect, Foucauldian discourse analysis is more concerned with explaining under what conditions certain discourses would be taken up. However, given that both approaches are based on a radical social constructionist epistemology, it would be inappropriate to evaluate them in terms of the extent to which they accurately represent 'reality'. Rather they should be judged in terms of the rigour and quality of the analysis. For example, Antaki et al. (2003) have discussed six shortcomings with the way that many researchers who engage in discourse analysis treat talk and textual data: (a) under-analysis through summary; (b) under-analysis through taking sides; (c) under-analysis through over-quotation or through isolated quotation; (d) the circular identification of discourses and mental constructs; (e) false survey and (f) analysis that consists in simply spotting features in the text.

However, the question of whether psychology should be concerned with the development of theories or just description of social and psychological phenomena is worthy of our consideration. One answer would be that the state of psychological knowledge is such that we cannot claim that we can strive for explanation since we have not yet described our target phenomena adequately. Another answer could be that psychologists should aim to develop explanatory theories if they are to be involved in finding solutions to real life problems or in bringing about social change.

This last-mentioned argument is linked to a key issue of research evaluation, namely the degree to which we think the research is useful. Consideration of this evaluative criterion raises a number of questions, such as what the research should be useful for and for whom it should be useful. We have already raised the issue of whether research should necessarily always contribute to the development of theory or whether it needs to be readily applicable to real life situations in order to be considered useful. And who should the researcher provide useful information to? Should researchers aim to conduct research that would be useful to the participants, those funding the research or other potential users of the research findings?

Many researchers, especially those who espouse a social constructionist approach, have levelled criticisms at the notion that psychological knowledge can and ought to be readily applicable to real life situations. Willig (1999) identified three different types of critique directed at attempts to apply psychological knowledge to real world situations. First, it has been argued that, by claiming that particular applications are based on 'scientific' and 'objective' knowledge, the stakeholders of a particular application legitimate their activity and therefore prevent others from raising questions about how, why and in whose interests psychological theories are being applied. She calls this the **'ideology of application critique'**. Second, Willig refers to the critique levelled by Cromby and Standen (1996), who argue that those with power, such as governments, use psychological research findings to justify particular policies which they pursue for political or economic reasons. This is often called the **'abuse/power critique'**. Third, she cited Widdicombe's (1995) argument against critical psychologists putting forward recommendations for interventions on the basis that such recommendations tend to disempower rather than empower oppressed groups by reifying particular meanings and discourses attached to them. However, Willig (1999) argues persuasively that discourse analysis can contribute to social and political practice by offering a social critique of the *status quo*, empowering oppressed groups and guiding reform.

Whether we endeavour to produce research which could address real life problems or whether we strive to provide a rich and interesting description of a social or psychological phenomenon and what criteria we think should be applied to evaluate our research are all questions and dilemmas that can only be resolved in the context of a specific project. What is important is that we as researchers take the time to think about the potential usefulness or otherwise of the research we engage in.

Summary

In this book, we aimed to equip the reader with the conceptual and methodological tools to navigate the uncertain waters of qualitative research in psychology. Qualitative research offers exciting opportunities for studying the complexities, contradictions and ambivalences of our emotionally charged, social and psychological worlds in depth. We hope we have managed to enthuse and encourage you to embark on researching into issues that are socially and politically important and especially those that matter to you.

We endeavoured to provide answers to some of the questions that you might have had about conducting qualitative research or that might arise as you embark upon the qualitative research process. We hope that we have raised as many questions as we have answered. Hopefully you will grapple with some of these questions and arrive at your own answers which can contribute to the further development of qualitative research methods. Producing knowledge should after all be a collaborative endeavour!

Further reading

For those interested in studying further the complexities of the relationship between epistemology and method, Michael Smith's (2005) book, *Philosophy and Methodology in the Social Sciences*, provides an excellent discussion of these issues. For those interested in the debates surrounding the relationship between research and real life applications, especially on the applicability of discourse analytic research, Carla Willig's (2001), *Applied Discourse Analysis: Social and Psychological Interventions*, provides useful reading. Finally, for those who are interested in reflecting further on the political implications of how we represent the 'Other', Sue Wilkinson and Celia Kitzinger's (1996) edited volume on *Representing the Other* provides useful insights and examples of how researchers working with different groups of participants dealt with such issues.

Appendix 1
DATA SET

PREFACE

Arnie Reed

The research project from which the data used by the various analytic groups in this book are drawn was a qualitative study of ex-soliders' accounts of renegotiating identity after leaving the army, which I undertook as part of my doctoral training in counselling psychology at the University of Surrey. The study is intimately tied up with my own history. It might therefore be helpful to contextualize the research by outlining some pertinent aspects of my history which provided the impetus for the work.

Having served as a soldier for 26 years, the army is a context with which I have some familiarity. However, at the time of my discharge from the army, I knew nothing about the process or experience of leaving it. I had moved from one army posting to another, gaining experience as a soldier, while at the same time civilian life became more and more distant from me. After leaving the army, my attempt to adapt to civilian life saw me trying to immerse myself in this new and sometimes strange life context and to 'make it work'. In doing so, I tried to distance myself from my military experience – to stop being a soldier and become a civilian. It soon became clear, however, that it is not at all an easy or straightforward process to set aside 26 years of your life as a soldier: the wonder is that I ever thought it might be.

The culmination of this growing realization coincided with my signing up for the doctoral training programme in counselling psychology at the University of Surrey. Here, I was given the opportunity to research a single topic for three years, exploring it from diverse theoretical and methodological vantage points. Although I considered several research options, I suspect it was inevitable that I would be drawn to something that I knew best – namely the army – and, paradoxically, to something I knew little of, apart from my own isolated experiences of it – namely the process of leaving the army. The thought of 're-entering' the army through association with other ex-soldiers in my research was both exciting and challenging. How had other soldiers coped after discharge? How would I feel after being reminded of aspects of army life which I still missed? Would my own sometimes difficult and negative feelings be reawakened? How had other soldiers fared during their own experience of leaving the army and would they be prepared to share these experiences with me?

I conducted first a qualitative research project and then a quantitative one, exploring how ex-soldiers experience and talk about the transition from army to civilian life once they retire. My particular focus was on the implications of this experience for their sense of self, which led me to use Breakwell's (1986, 1996) identity process theory to inform my qualitative work and to structure my quantitative research. However, this theory was used with a lightness of touch in my qualitative work: it did not play an obvious role in the shaping of the interview schedule and never drove the analysis but merely informed it, being invoked only after the data were analysed as far as possible on their own terms.

For the qualitative study, I recruited 10 ex-servicemen, firstly through advertising in a local newspaper in a garrison town in southeast England and then through 'snowballing' from the initial sample that had been recruited in this way (i.e., having participants nominate others who might wish to take part). The men were aged between 40 and 48, with a mean age of 43.5 years. All were white and married. They had spent between 10 and 24 years in the army, with the mean duration of service being 20.5 years. They had left the army between one and 10 years prior to the research interview, with the mean length of time since discharge being 5.6 years. On discharge, one participant had held the rank of major, four had been warrant officers, three had been sergeants and two had been corporals. In terms of their occupational status at the time of the interviews, two were in professional jobs, three were classed as technicians or associate professionals, two were craft workers and three held elementary occupations.

I interviewed each man using a semi-structured interview schedule. I recorded the interviews on audio tape and transcribed them (changing the names of participants and amending any other identifying information in order to preserve confidentiality; three dots in the transcripts indicate where the participants paused) before subjecting them to qualitative analysis. This was a fascinating process, especially the challenge of sometimes trying to bracket my own experiences lest they end up overly shaping my interpretations and at the same time figuring out how best to use my personal experiences to enrich the analysis. It became clear that my own experiences were both similar and dissimilar to those of the participants. Some participants had experienced greater difficulties than others in the transition to civilian life; some apparently had experienced few or none. Despite my concerns that this group might not want to engage in this research, it appeared that – perhaps because I was positioned as 'one of them' or 'one of us' – the majority really wanted to talk about their experiences and feelings during and after their own transition. Although I harboured doubts and concerns about conducting this research, the whole experience was a positive and useful one for me, helping to validate and accommodate my own experiences. Additionally, being allowed to enter the world of this extraordinary group of people and to share their range of rich experiences left me feeling privileged and humbled – and for that I will always be grateful.

I was delighted to be asked to allow part of the qualitative data set to be used by the analytic groups in this book and have been fascinated to see and compare the outcomes of their analyses as they applied interpretative phenomenological analysis, grounded theory, discourse analysis and narrative analysis to the transcripts. Although I have decided not to reveal which specific method of analysis I used in my qualitative research, my reflections in this preface probably make it clear to readers that I did not use discourse analysis.

Time has dimmed my memory of the challenges, frustrations and anxieties involved in trying to make sense of my data (the study was conducted in 2000) so that now, what I most clearly recall are the thrilling moments of break-through and clarity. My hope is that readers who decide to use the transcripts to practise and refine their own qualitative analytic skills will experience some of those high points too.

References

Breakwell, G.M. (1986) *Coping with Threatened Identities.* London: Methuen.
Breakwell, G.M. (1996) 'Identity processes and social changes', in G.M. Breakwell and E. Lyons (eds), *Changing European Identities: Social Psychological Analyses of Social Change.* Oxford: Butterworth Heinemann. pp. 13–27.

Interview transcript: David

1   **Arnie:** In what ways, if any, do you think your sense of yourself has
2   been influenced by being in the army?

3

4   **David:** It gave me more confidence. As a nipper when I first joined
5   the army, I wasn't confident at all. I think I joined the army to see how
6   I could do it for one thing. Number two – I joined to get away because
7   I didn't have a trade. I had no or very little education. The education I
8   did have behind me wasn't up to much, so I needed a job where I could
9   go in and have some money in my pocket. And, as you know, in them
10   days, they were 'Yeah, if you want a job my son, come this way' and
11   that was it. But it definitely gave me confidence – confidence to go
12   out. As we said, once I left the army, I could find a job
13   anywhere . . . within reason.

14

15   **Arnie:** What aspects, if any, of being a soldier were important to you?

16

17   **David:** I was a member of a team and I was an important member of a
18   team and I was recognized as doing something for my country. You
19   know, I was prepared to go. If they say, 'Right, David, Kuwait has
20   been attacked, you know, I was ready to go'. Yeah. It wasn't a case of
21   'Woah, it's their country, it's nothing to do with us'. If the boss wanted
22   to send me, then away I go. That was important to me. It's like, as I
23   say, I had an identity and I belonged to somewhere.

24

25   **Arnie:** You had an identity – could you talk a little bit more about
26   having an identity?

27

28   **David:** Yeah, I was, I was part of a team. I was a driver and, without
29   us drivers, no-one would get their goods, so we were important and I
30   was proud of that. Uh, so that side of the identity was important to me,
31   you know – we were important in doing a job.

32

33   **Arnie:** Do you have that now?

34

35   **David:** [Sigh] People like to tell me I've got that now but I know I
36   haven't got that now. You know, I'm in the school [working as a
37   caretaker] and they say, 'Oh, without the caretaker this wouldn't
38   happen and this wouldn't happen. You know where everything is – we
39   don't'. True. Yeah, you know. If I was to have a week off, it would
40   start falling down because people don't know where everything is. But
41   in the same vein, if I happened to walk out of there and if I was to get
42   run over by a bus, you know, it would be case of, 'Well, that's it.
43   David, you did a good job, we miss him, fine, get someone else in'.

44

45   **Arnie:** It seems to be a little different for you from being a team

46   member within the school and being a team member in the army.

47

48   **David:**   You're not a team member within the school because you're

49   not a teacher. The teachers all sort of get round their . . . I sometimes

50   wonder why the kids of today act like they are and I can understand by

51   the standards of some of the teachers. They can't do simple things.

52   Like, at the end of the day before the class is dismissed, the teacher

53   could say 'Right, we are going to pick bits of litter up'. They don't do

54   that. They just leave it off, you know, as if to say, 'Ah, it's only the

55   caretaker and his staff – they'll do it'. It annoys me because being part

56   of a team as we should be, as we were in the army, you know, we

57   would have all helped right from the top all the way down. Civilians

58   have different ideas of being in teams. They go as far as what's good

59   for themselves and then, 'Right, that's it', and that to me is not being

60   part of a team. That's the difficult part, I find.

61

62   **Arnie:**   I'd like you to think and talk about whether or not your values

63   and personal beliefs have anything to do with your training as a soldier

64   or experiences in the army.

65

66   **David:**   I would say a great percentage of them, yes. As in, as in being

67   honest to your mates – yeah – which, you know . . . if you're not honest

68   to your mates, then God, you were in the dog house, right up to your

69   neck in the dark and murky stuff. Um, discipline. Yeah, I think I

70   learned a great majority of them being in the army. Ah, I wouldn't say

71   I could have learned them at home because my mother died when I

72   was young, when I was little, you know, um, so being brought up by

73   my grandmother, right, I don't think she had a great deal of time so, so

74   yeah, I think I got a lot of them from being in the army.

75

76   **Arnie:**   People tend to experience events like this sort of transition into

77   civilan life in their own unique way. I'd like to hear how you

78   experienced it and what your feelings were.

79

80   **David:**   About leaving? It was an anti-climax. It was a . . . I don't know

81   what I expected but I didn't expect to just . . . You sort of stood in front

82   of this officer who reeled off a load of crap because, you know, the

83   officer I was stood in front of didn't like me anyway. We never saw

84   eye to eye from the day I got there because he knew I was only there

85   for 18 months because of 'Options for Change' [plans for reducing the

86   size of the army in the light of the end of the 'Cold War']. The unit I

87   was at was closing down so they had to send me somewhere. Um and,

88   you know, so he came out of his office and reeled off 'Oh, we've really

89   enjoyed having you' and all this . . . and I thought, 'You lying git'. But

90   then you just walked out of his office and the next thing you know,

91   someone's saying 'ID card – thank you, Mr Jones'. And that hit you,

92   you know. Someone's actually calling you 'Mister'. No-one's calling

93   me 'Sergeant' any more. That was funny. That was a shock. That's

94   when you knew. And then that's it – you walk out and no-one's
95   prepared you for that. I just . . . Once you're out that gate, that's it. I
96   know I can't even get back into the camp where, not ten minutes ago, I
97   was a serving sergeant. I can't get back in. You know, you . . . it's like
98   they're throwing you outside and locked the gate, you know, and that's
99   it – you're on your own. That was painful. And then having to sort of
100 fend your way through the world like . . . If something falls off your
101 house, you can't pick up the phone and get hold of the old housing
102 people any more – you've got to deal with it. In fact, there's no great
103 problem in that but it's a funny feeling. You know, 'Bloody hell, I've
104 got to deal with that now'. Yeah. Um, and going around and, you
105 know, like we were saying, you walk round and you walk down the
106 street and you see ghosts. You know, you walk down streets where you
107 walked down as a serving soldier and you can see all these ghosts,
108 people you've met, you know. Or, come out of this shop and you
109 expect all the lads to come staggering down the road drunk as skunks
110 or something like that and they don't and I still see them today, you
111 know. I can sit down in [named garrison town where he lives] and
112 yeah, the mind goes back to the times and you think, 'Yeah but there's
113 no-one there any more' and, you know . . . you think, 'Jesus, you never
114 expected it to be like that'. You thought that maybe there's someone
115 you could talk to but there isn't. Even, you know, when they say you
116 can go to SSAFA [Soldiers, Sailors and Air Force Association – a
117 charitable organization that offers help to ex-service people] and all
118 that, even they sort of put you on the back burner once you're a
119 civilian because they think 'Yeah, that's it, you've used up, you know
120 you've done your bit – off you go'. And you know they don't realize
121 that you've given the best time of your life to them and you give,
122 which I did, I gave 150 per cent to the stage where I got damaged
123 knees and other things and I'm knackered. And so when I came out, I
124 should be out now enjoying myself because my kids have all grown up
125 and I should be now but I can't and you think to yourself, 'Oh Jesus,
126 what have I done?'. Would I have done that if I had my time all over
127 again? Yes, even for all I've just said. You know, you walk out and
128 there's nothing – there's that void. It's just like an open space, an
129 empty space.
130
131 **Arnie:**   It sounds lonely.
132
133 **David:**   If it wasn't for my wife, I think I'd have done something totally
134 crazy. I don't think I'd be around today to be honest if it wasn't for the
135 missus. She was, she was very supportive and I, um, I tended to be a
136 little wild for about a couple of months after I got out, which one does.
137 Uh, it nearly broke the marriage up at one stage. But she stuck with us
138 and here we are. But yeah, it's . . . it is lonely. I still miss it, I still do. I
139 wish I could get civilianized very quickly.
140
141 **Arnie:**   Can you tell me about what it felt like to be thinking about

142   leaving the army and becoming a civilian?

143

144   **David:** I started leaving the army when I was posted back from [a

145   named German town]. Hence that's why I chose, because I had a

146   choice of my unit, and I thought to myself, well a truck driver, that

147   seems like the obvious route to take, being RCT [Royal Corps of

148   Transport]. So I thought if I go for [name of specific army unit], at

149   least they've got the artics [articulated vehicles] there, so I can get out.

150   Although I had a Class 1 licence, I can get experience on them and get

151   the tacco [taccograph] experience, the rules of the road and the driver's

152   hours. Um, I started building up from then. What I aimed to do was get

153   a job first then find somewhere to live. And so I thought, and you

154   know when you have these briefings [army resettlement briefings] and

155   they tell you how hard it is to get a job, which was right in one respect,

156   um, as I think you need a job to get a job in Civvie Street and so I was

157   gearing up for that all the way through. I was putting favours out and

158   working for firms moonlighting, so I was getting my fingers in quite a

159   few pies. Um, it was the army that wouldn't let me leave. I started

160   gearing up for Civvie Street.

161

162   **Arnie:** It sounds like you were doing a lot of preparation, practical

163   preparation – was there any mental preparation? Did you think about

164   what it would feel like when you were a Civvie?

165

166   **David:** I might have given it one or two thoughts . . . [indecipherable] . . .

167   But one thing I could never sort of visualize was Civvie Street. You

168   know, to me civilians were people that walked around and weren't able

169   to make decisions. That's the feeling you get, you know.

170

171   **Arnie:** Looking back, do you think that you were prepared for civilian

172   life and how being a civilian was going to feel?

173

174   **David:** No.

175

176   **Arnie:** Looking back, do you think there is anything extra that the

177   army might have done to help you adjust to civilian life or did they do

178   enough?

179

180   **David:** Yes, I think the army should allow you to get a feel for civilian

181   life. They should allow you to go and work, um, work experience for

182   instance. In the last six months, they should post you off somewhere

183   and say, 'Right, off you go and we'll see in you in . . . ' – not letting you

184   run wild, having at least to report in once a week or something, um,

185   and let you go and work for somebody. So I think that would have

186   helped a lot. I don't think you can go away on one of these three week

187   [resettlement] courses and, you know, you come back and they think,

188   'Well, he's ready'. You know, I think some of the officers at the top

189   don't realize just how hard it is for someone to get out because I know

190   when they finish, they don't really finish. They go to the officers' clubs
191   and all of those things and they carry on drinking G and Ts for
192   breakfast. They don't think you . . . [indecipherable] . . . has to go out and
193   find his work. He doesn't get the money that they're offered in their
194   package, so he's got to go out and find the work, if you can understand
195   what I mean. And it's . . . you know, it just didn't prepare me at all. Like
196   I said earlier on, you know, one minute I was there and the next minute
197   I was out the gate – I was a civilian, you know. There was no
198   preparation at all.
199
200   **Arnie:**   Some researchers believe that when people leave a distinctive
201   environment like the army, there may be an impact on how they see
202   themselves, feel about themselves or on how they behave. I'd like to
203   explore how your sense of being a soldier might or might not have
204   affected how you felt about yourself in civilian life.
205
206   **David:**   Yes, I think I understand. You're trained to be disciplined and
207   you're trained to look after yourself. When I say 'look after yourself',
208   not like just combat. I mean by 'looking after yourself', I can make my
209   breakfast, I can make my dinner, I can sew, I can iron, I can wash. Um,
210   I know that there's a lot of Civvies out there can't. I was astounded at
211   how many blokes can't iron or sew or can't cook. I just can't believe it,
212   you know. Um, so yeah, that's the thing . . . that was me.
213
214   **Arnie:**   Did you feel differently or the same about yourself in civilian
215   life compared to how you felt about yourself while you were still in the
216   army?
217
218   **David:**   Don't feel as . . . sometimes, not all the times, sometimes I don't
219   feel as though there's a purpose to it. You know, like, going to school
220   [as a school caretaker] and walking along and thinking, 'What the hell
221   am I doing here? Bugger this'. The kids are a bunch of shits, you
222   know. But I've got to do this yet again, today and tomorrow. And you
223   think to yourself, 'This is me for the rest of my life'. I go in there and I
224   just feel, 'Why isn't it like it was in the army?' and hope something
225   will change, yet I get on with it. Um, so I mean the answer to that
226   question is sometimes I feel upset but other times, you know, there's
227   just that void where I just wonder.
228
229   **Arnie:**   Can you say something about how, if at all, being an ex-soldier
230   helped you or caused problems for you, or if you feel it made no
231   difference?
232
233   **David:**   In Civvie Street, being an ex-soldier gives you the confidence.
234   Um, I went for an interview for a job. As I said, I've never been out of
235   work. I've had more jobs than I thought I ever would and I think that
236   the simple fact is that when I go on the interviews, I say, 'Right, this is
237   me. This is what you're getting. Take me and I'll be a great team

238   player', and I tell them that. Where it hinders me is the fact that I like
239   things in lines. I like things in neat packages and so when I go – like
240   when I was driving the truck, when I used to come back at night, I used
241   to park all the wagons up so all the bumpers were level. Funny as it
242   may seem, they had them parked all over the car park. It made it harder
243   to get out. They couldn't see the fact that by lining them all up it was
244   easy to get them out. Um, it was other little things like your paperwork.
245   Keep your paperwork in order – it makes it easy. I think that side of
246   life used to hinder me because all I would do was spend an extra ten
247   minutes. All they wanted to do was in, out and go. Um, so yeah, there
248   is a hindrance somewhere way along the line, in some aspects. I think
249   in most aspects it certainly stood me in good stead.
250

251   **Arnie:** Sometimes spouses, relatives or friends can influence how we
252   feel about ourselves, particularly during important changes, such as
253   changing career or lifestyle. I'd like to focus on whether or not the
254   decisions that you made and how you felt might have been influenced
255   by your spouse, relatives, friends and work-mates. Can you say
256   something about whether or not you felt supported by your spouse?
257

258   **David:** Supported by . . . no, not really. Because the people we knew
259   when we went to live in Civvie Street were up in [named town], north
260   Wales, so we didn't really know anybody there, so as for support, no,
261   no we didn't get any support from anybody. You just had to go out and
262   try and find your own feet and make lots of mistakes – expensive ones
263   at that.
264

265   **Arnie:** Can you say something about whether or not that lack of
266   support affected how you felt about yourself?
267

268   **David:** There was no-one there to give me advice and guide me on
269   things like buying a house. Um, it's all right sitting in a briefing room
270   and someone pointing at a chart and saying, 'Do this and do that'.
271   That's all well and good but, as we know, what you see on paper and
272   what happens on the ground are two different things. Um, we bought a
273   house and it collapsed and we lost everything. I lost all of my money,
274   the lot, in this house in one fell swoop. If I had've been guided, if
275   someone had been there to say, 'Look, this is what you have to look
276   for', if there had been someone up in that area that we could have
277   called on and say, 'Look, I'm buying a house, I've just come out of the
278   army – any chance of coming along and showing me a few pointers?',
279   I think that would've helped. So at least you'd have got the first one
280   over with. I won't be buying another house. I don't want to buy
281   another house ever again. That would have been handy. Um, no, there
282   was no support for me.
283

284   **Arnie:** I wonder if people's feelings or behaviour towards you changed
285   or stayed the same after you became a civilian?

286

287 **David:** Yes I think they did because the people we knew when we

288 were living in [named Welsh town], the people we knew around the

289 area knew me as the soldier from England so they used to come around

290 and we used to have a chat at weekends and all this. But once I got out

291 [left the army], a few of them sort of kept coming round for a while

292 and then all of a sudden they were just gone. They must have thought,

293 'Well that's it, he's got nothing else to offer, the novelty's worn off'. I

294 think people's feelings did change in some respects.

295

296 **Arnie:** Did that have an effect on you or not?

297

298 **David:** No, not really, because I was working permanent nights, so I

299 never used to see them often anyway. Once I got out and I started

300 working properly, no I don't think it did.

301

302 **Arnie:** Working and living in the military environment is different in

303 many ways to civilian life. I was wondering if there are parts of

304 military life which you miss?

305

306 **David:** What, compared to Civvie Street? I miss the social life, I miss

307 the social life . . . I miss the programme of events that we used to get in

308 the army.

309

310 **Arnie:** The social programme or...?

311

312 **David:** Both, the social and regimental programmes . . . in view of my

313 character. Like, we've got days when we're on exercise for a few

314 weeks. Get there and you could plan your life. You knew you were

315 going on exercise and you thought um, you knew that 18 weekends out

316 of the 52 . . . you knew you were going to kill a few beers and you knew

317 you were going to have a good time. I think you've got over that now.

318 You know you can't plan anything from day to day. I miss the danger,

319 the thrill, the adrenalin rush. You don't get that any more. Um, I miss

320 walking out the door and making sure I'm all right. I'm proud to be a

321 soldier. Now I walk out the door in my overalls and I think, 'Well,

322 yeah, that's it'. You try to give an appearance of someone who's been

323 trained and disciplined but it's not the same, it's not the same. You

324 don't have the same effect as anywhere else.

325

326 **Arnie:** Did you feel you needed to replace things about the army that

327 you missed with something else?

328

329 **David:** Well I tried to join the Association but it's full of old people.

330 The RCT [Royal Corps of Transport] Association, I mean. We joined

331 that but I'm the youngest there by 26 years. You know, um, we went to

332 the Christmas function and it was someone with an organ playing 'Roll

333 out the barrel' and other 1940s music, which is no good to me and our

334   lass. Um, we haven't reached that stage yet. We go back up to [named
335   Welsh town] and we have some friends up there and we go back up
336   there and we have a whale of a time up there – totally go wild. So
337   yeah, that replaces it.

338

339   **Arnie:** You talked about moving around in the house in [named Welsh
340   town] and now you're living in [named garrison town]. What made
341   you come back to [named garrison town]?

342

343   **David:** The house we had up there, um, collapsed and we had to sue a
344   solicitor and get another solicitor to sue the other solicitor and it was
345   quite a hard task, you know. They refused to do it or reluctant, I should
346   say, to do it but we did find one but it cost us a lot of money – money
347   which we didn't have so we had to beg, steal and borrow it. In the end,
348   we lost the house altogether. Um, we had to sell it to pay off some of
349   the debts and this job came up which meant I got a house with the job.
350   Hence, I'm back here. And that's it.

351

352   **Arnie:** You had links then with the [named garrison town] area to
353   know about the job here?

354

355   **David:** Oh yes. The father-in-law was a governor of the school and he
356   told me that there was a job coming up. He didn't actually have any
357   say or input into me getting the job because it was totally down to me,
358   you know. Him being a governor, me coming because we were related
359   – he had to take a step to one side and let me get on with it.

360

361   **Arnie:** When I was preparing for this research I came across material
362   which discussed how people from distinctive jobs might try to lessen
363   the impact of leaving. We've talked about the army resettlement
364   package but I'd like to know a little more from a personal perspective.
365   Did you think about what it might be like when you would've left the
366   army lifestyle and how – how you might feel about that?

367

368   **David:** Well one of the reasons why I think I was moonlighting was to
369   get to know my civilian counterparts and try and get into how they
370   thought and how they worked and how they operated, um, but it was
371   very difficult in some respects. That, uh, as soon as they found out that
372   you were a squaddie – a serving squaddie – working in their firm,
373   some of the drivers – not all of them but some of the drivers – just
374   wouldn't speak to you because you were trying to take over their jobs,
375   which I think, you know . . . it's how can I put it, a bit like a Black trying
376   to join the Klu [sic] Klux Klan, you know. You know, we were sort of
377   coming in and we were 'No go', you know. 'You shouldn't be coming
378   in here, you know. You've got a job – what are you doing sort of
379   taking other jobs?', you know. 'There's people out there who are
380   unemployed who want this job', you know. And I'd turn round and
381   say, 'Well, why aren't they here taking the job?' That was hard. It was

382 also giving an insight into how they felt.

383

384 **Arnie:** And that was towards you when you were a soldier?

385

386 **David:** Yeah.

387

388 **Arnie:** But as an ex-soldier it might have been different?

389

390 **David:** Yes, I think it would've been.

391

392 **Arnie:** Um, do you think you've adjusted to civilian life?

393

394 **David:** No. No. I would say that in one easy answer there.

395

396 **Arnie:** Looking back, would you have done anything differently as
397 part of the transition?

398

399 **David:** Yes. I wouldn't have went to [name of army unit]. I would
400 have gone to a TA [Territorial Army] unit, asked for a post as PSI
401 [Permanent Staff Instructor] at a TA unit, knowing that I'd have got
402 extra time off to go and get in there and also um, working with
403 civilians you know, maybe I'd have got a little bit more insight into
404 how they work and how things operate on the other side of the fence.

405

406 **Arnie:** David, that's just about all the questions that I've got. Is there
407 anything on the subject that you want to talk about which we haven't
408 covered?

409

410 **David:** Yeah. I think it's looking at it now in the long term and
411 speaking to other ex-soldiers as well and people who are due to get out,
412 it's that somewhere round the UK there should be a camp or whatever
413 where you could be posted to for six months and then go out and work
414 for the civilians. So you don't have to get paid but you can go out and
415 can get worked in slowly, slowly, slowly and then, at the end of the six
416 months, you'll have a time to be shown possibly how to buy a house.
417 You'd have worked with the civilians, worked in a civilian atmosphere
418 and just totally tried to get yourself civilianized, so when the time does
419 come, you're out and you just slide out instead of fall out.

420

421 **Arnie:** More smooth?

422

423 **David:** Yeah, smoothly. And plus also for the ladies as well, the
424 females as well and the kids because the kids will have gone from
425 pillar to post over that time, so it will obviously give them time to get
426 settled in. And, I don't know about the majority, I don't know what the
427 actual percentage is but it could it be a few anyway, who would be
428 getting out as they are coming to a crucial time in their education and
429 when you just sort of, bang, finished, there's an awful lot of flying

430   around to do. You know, you've got to get yourself a house, you've

431   got to get this, you've got to get that and, you know, the kids are

432   caught in the middle of it. Where that . . . if you have a nice sliding slope,

433   you can get them settled, get them in and they can be cracking on with

434   their education. The wives, again, sliding out slowly but surely, getting

435   settled, you know, and so, at the end of the day, you've got a nice

436   transition to Civvie Street instead of this void and you're sort of

437   wandering around for a few months with your finger up your backside

438   thinking, 'Well, what's this?', you know. 'Where am I?'

439

440   **Arnie:** I'd like you to reflect now just for a moment on the experience

441   of the interview and how's it felt. What have been the positive things

442   and what have been the negative things, perhaps, about taking part.

443

444   **David:** I think one of the positive things is that you're getting it

445   all . . . you're getting the questions, you're letting us speak how we feel

446   and not like when you get a lot of these questionnaires – they get you

447   to answer what they want to hear by the way they've put the question.

448   Um, on the negative side, it's, it's very difficult in some respects

449   on . . . to describe how you feel. I think that if we'd had a chance to slide

450   over from army to civilian in a nice steady flow, I think that might

451   have been easier. I think because we're just sort of door shut, out you

452   go, you know, you still don't know who you are. And, as my brother-

453   in-law said, it's taken him 11 years to become civilianized – and his

454   wife's still in the forces. Um, but that might have been easier if that

455   makes any sense.

456

457   **Arnie:** It makes perfect sense, yeah. Do you think that taking part in

458   the interview has had any effect or perhaps will have an effect on the

459   way you feel about yourself?

460

461   **David:** No, I think we've sort of . . . .I think we're still in the army. If

462   you look around the house . . . I wouldn't call it . . . it's like a married

463   quarter. So, you know, that's drifting away from the question there

464   slightly but . . .

465

466   **Arnie:** Well thanks for participating in the interview.

Interview transcript: Brian

1   **Arnie:**   In what ways, if any, do you think a sense of yourself has been
2   influenced by being in the army and your experiences in the army?
3

4   **Brian:**   I think I've learned in the forces and the thing is you learn these
5   things in the army without realizing it a lot of the time, so that when you
6   come out and start comparing yourself to the people working alongside
7   you, you find that you've got a much greater sense of urgency. You tend
8   to pay more attention to detail, you don't bother about the time so much,
9   you don't clock on or clock off. If the job takes twice as long as it should,
10   you just work on as necessary. We seem to be much more flexible, much
11   more adaptable to situations, and it's all stuff I've learned in the forces and
12   the experience I've had where you need to be adaptable, where the
13   situation might change. You've already learned to adapt to new situations
14   – and that comes through all the time. When I look around I see that all of
15   the time, lack of attention to detail, how they just skimp over things, and
16   no attitude. You know, we do our best all of the time.
17

18   **Arnie:**   What aspects, if any, of being a soldier were important to you?
19   When you were in the army, what was important?
20

21   **Brian:**   I suppose it was actually being part of something really big, doing
22   a worthwhile job and being able to prove yourself by progressing through
23   the ranks. That was very important to me. To have the opportunity to
24   prove what you can do and how well you can do it.
25

26   **Arnie:**   Do you think you've found that in Civvie Street?
27

28   **Brian:**   To some respect but in different ways. The type of job I have now,
29   there is no form of progression through the ranks but that doesn't stop you
30   doing your job well and actually being noticed. But no, there's no real
31   rank structure as such in the job I'm doing at the moment.
32

33   **Arnie:**   So how do you feel about working with those differences?
34

35   **Brian:**   It's something I've accepted and there's not a problem. I enjoy
36   what I'm doing. One of the main reasons I think I enjoy it is because I've
37   been given a job to do in a given area and I get on and do it. I'm not
38   closely supervised. I belong to a team – there are 16 of us in total and we
39   do come together from time to time and we do help out and work together
40   as we need to but a lot of the time I'm left to my own devices and allowed
41   to make my own decisions rather than having people telling you what to
42   do all of the time.
43

44   **Arnie:**   How does that compare with the army?
45

46   **Brian:**   Yes, I suppose to a certain extent, I suppose you were
47   guided all of the time but then, as you progress through the ranks, you
48   have more say in what you do and I've always believed that when I was in
49   the forces if someone gave me a goal, how I achieved that goal was up to
50   me, which is exactly the same as what I'm doing now. I'm given an aim
51   and how I achieve it is up to me at the end of the day. No-one actually sets
52   out the route which I need to take.
53
54   **Arnie:**   People tend to experience events like this sort of transition in their
55   own unique way. I'd like to hear and understand how you experienced it
56   and what your feelings were. So to that end, could you start wherever you
57   want about whatever you want about the whole process of leaving the
58   army and entering Civvie Street.
59
60   **Brian:**   When I first came out, obviously I was totally preoccupied in
61   trying to find a job, finding something to do. That took a while to find a
62   job and I was sending loads and loads of applications off and I was getting
63   loads and loads of interviews and I was going to the interviews and getting
64   down to the last two or three people – no problem at all – but it was
65   obvious from the interviews that when you go to them, the people doing
66   the interviews have preconceived ideas about what the people in the forces
67   are like and their perceptions of military people are totally outdated. And
68   they seem to believe that your style of management means shouting at
69   people and hitting people with big sticks and that's it. They don't believe
70   that we get trained to manage people quietly. And since I've been out, I've
71   noticed that the way ex-military guys manage their staff is much better
72   than the way a civilian-trained person does because the way civilians
73   manage their staff, they see a job – for instance, if their job is to construct
74   a network for telecommunications – that's all they do, just getting the stuff
75   in the ground as cheaply as possible and as quickly as possible. They don't
76   manage the job as a whole – they don't look into the welfare side of life
77   and make sure that their staff are happy. They don't keep that on track –
78   they see it as very narrow. When I was in the forces, you were given a
79   resource which included your guys to do the job and you had to look after
80   that resource, so it was all geared around that you see. But em, once I
81   found a job, I ended up taking probably the first job that was offered to me
82   which wasn't probably a good idea but I didn't want to be out of work and
83   then I found when I was doing the job, I was going about it differently to
84   how everyone else did. Everyone else did what was expected and I was
85   going that extra sort of mile every time and I found that was causing a lot
86   of problems because I was doing it and no-one else was. The thing is the
87   job I was doing at the time was an enforcement job and a lot of the time
88   you had to go round and tell people they had to do something in a certain
89   way or they couldn't do something what they was doing and because
90   going round and doing the job which I thought I was doing it as I was
91   supposed to be doing, a lot of complaints were coming back to me at the
92   office of my superiors about the way I was doing the work and um there

93   was a couple of times I was asked 'Well why are you generating all these
94   complaints?' and I said 'Well I'm only doing what I'm supposed to be
95   doing. You've asked me to do this work and I'm actually doing it'. And
96   when they looked into it, they saw, well, that's what I was doing but the
97   other people, if they felt it was going to be confrontational, they just shied
98   away from it and they didn't actually do that part of the job – they just
99   used to let it ride, you see, and find something else to do.

100

101   **Arnie:** It sounds like this was all part of the military overlap which you
102   talked about before – doing your job properly and the military discipline
103   as well.

104

105   **Brian:** And not shying away from confrontation really. If it was going to
106   be confrontational, then try and manage it in a certain way but if it needs
107   to be done, it needs to be done.

108

109   **Arnie:** Can you tell me what it felt like for you when you were
110   considering leaving the army? You've told me that you came out on the
111   redundancy phase. When you started thinking about what it was going to
112   be like being a civilian, can you remember how that felt?

113

114   **Brian:** Well, to be perfectly honest I didn't really want to leave. Although
115   it was my choice, I felt my hand was being forced really. I was making the
116   best of a bad job really. As I said before, part of the reason I came out was
117   partly medical reasons and I felt that, had I stayed in, I wouldn't be able to
118   fulfil my full potential so I decided to come out early and that was making
119   the best of it. But if I had the choice, I would have stayed in. I wouldn't
120   have come out early at all. So yeah, I was a bit . . . but other than that, I
121   wasn't particularly bothered. The area we decided to settle, we already had
122   a house here. My children were at school, my wife had a job so really all I
123   had to do was find myself a job and I was quite prepared to do anything if
124   necessary, so I didn't envisage being out of work. When I was applying
125   for jobs, I wasn't just applying for one job, I was reading through the job
126   adverts and thinking, 'Oh I can do that', and so I applied for it. And in
127   total I probably applied for about 20 to 30 different types of jobs because I
128   thought, 'Yeah, I can do that'. And I didn't really have anything set in my
129   mind about what I wanted to do at the time. I just wanted to . . . I was
130   coming out, I was going to get a job and take it on from there. I didn't
131   expect to be in the first job all the time and, in the end, it was probably
132   about 18 months to two years I had my first job before I changed. The job
133   I'm doing now I've had for four years now and I'm quite happy to do that
134   and, if I change my work now, I'll probably go for a similar job in a
135   different company.

136

137   **Arnie:** Can you say something about how it felt when you were actually
138   discharged? You've talked a little bit about what you were thinking about
139   when you were thinking about leaving. What did it feel like when you

140   were actually discharged, do you recall?

141

142   **Brian:**   No, not really. No. No I don't think . . . personally I don't think it had

143   much of an effect or if I worried too much about it but I probably did and

144   my wife seems to think that, when I was in the forces, I was much happier

145   than what I have been since I've been out. But, no, I don't really recall any

146   particular feelings at the time.

147

148   **Arnie:**   I'd like to talk about the army resettlement package now – pre-

149   release stuff. I'm aware that the army has got a resettlement package for

150   people leaving the army and I'd like to get an idea of how useful it was for

151   you.

152

153   **Brian:**   Well yes, um, the army took me to one side and they gave me

154   training and that's the training I now . . . is the basis I've used . . . the basis to

155   get the work I'm doing now. So yes, it was fine, it was adequate. It puts

156   you in the right direction. The only thing is um because I decided to come

157   out a year before I actually left, it wasn't really long enough to put

158   everything into . . . all the plans I would have like to have gone into, into

159   motion. Really I should have started two or three years in advance rather

160   than try and fit it in one year. You just can't do it – it's too much to do.

161   And the problem is everything you do in the forces, all the experience you

162   gain, it doesn't transfer very well to civilian life so you need to sort of

163   adapt all your skills and qualifications into such a way as civilian

164   employers can actually pick up on it and understand. And that's what I

165   didn't have time to do, you just don't have time to do it in the year. But

166   other than that, yeah, it was great you know.

167

168   **Arnie:**   Looking back, do you think that you were prepared for civilian life

169   and how being a civilian was going to feel? You've said that perhaps a

170   year wasn't long enough and you might have liked two or three years to

171   prepare but on the whole do you think you were prepared – and

172   particularly about how being a civilian was going to feel?

173

174   **Brian:**   Well, when I first came out, the thing I found most strange was the

175   job I had, I was finishing work about four o'clock in the afternoon. With

176   starting fairly early and finishing about four, I was getting home for about

177   half past four and thinking 'What I do now?' Because before, I'd never get

178   home that early, even when I was based just up the road I used to um . . . the

179   type of job I was doing – used to be doing that job all day and then you

180   had to do all the admin side and sometimes I didn't get home until about

181   six or seven anyway and I found I had a little more time on my hands and

182   I wasn't quite sure what to do with it. One thing I felt strange was, in the

183   civilian environment, everyone sort of dress and everyone looks the same

184   and in the military you can tell just by looking at someone where they are

185   in the pecking order and where they are and so you can temper what you

186   say to them and how you say it to them. In civilian life in the company,

187   everyone dressed the same, everyone looked the same – you didn't know

188   who you were talking to, whether someone at the same level as you or
189   some of the more senior directors. And I found that very disconcerting
190   until you get to know who the faces are but that was strange. But other
191   than that, I treated my first move into civilian life, especially the job, as
192   another posting really and it worked quite well because the first job I went
193   to . . . I was working in a small department of about ten people and six of
194   those were ex-forces and they were all from my old regiment and some I
195   knew from before anyway so really it was very similar to another posting,
196   just another job.

197

198   **Arnie:** Did that help, having ex-servicemen around?

199

200   **Brian:** Oh it certainly did help, yeah. Yeah and these guys had been out
201   ranging between um, like a couple of years to probably ten or twelve
202   years. So we had a whole range of experiences and they'd all sort of
203   learned different things and it was quite helpful to speak to them and find
204   out what was going on. Just coming out and being a bit of the new boy
205   there and it is a slightly different environment but that . . . I felt, I think
206   things would have been different if I hadn't gone for that job first off and
207   been surrounded by ex-forces people, especially some of the guys I'd
208   known from before as well, or if . . . and even ones I didn't know, we had
209   mutual friends with other people we knew between us, so that worked out
210   really well.

211

212   **Arnie:** You've touched on this next thing I was going to ask – and still
213   will. Looking back, do you think that you were mentally prepared for
214   civilian life?

215

216   **Brian:** Yeah. Yeah, I think so and mainly because I believe that the forces
217   learned me how to adapt to new situations and this was just another
218   situation to adapt to and, other than that, it's not been a particular problem.
219   Initially I found it very hard in that way to fit in with civilian workmates
220   because I came across as aggressive, abrupt, arrogant . . . which is the way
221   other people would describe me, the type . . . but I was just sort of being
222   what I was doing really and in the military environment that was . . . it
223   wouldn't even have been picked up on. In fact, when I was serving in the
224   military, I was often being pulled up for not being as aggressive as some
225   of my peers. And when I came out, then they were saying, 'Well, you're
226   overly aggressive', which of course I found very strange. But um, I
227   have . . . it's several years I've been out now and I've mellowed but even so,
228   people still describe me as being aggressive, overbearing and but um, I've
229   mellowed to such an extent and I suppose you have to . . . in such a way
230   to . . . you have to sort of change your style. A lot of my work, I train people
231   up . . . my work is training and I've had to adapt my training style to be more
232   civilian friendly than in the military because it was . . . people used to say,
233   'Well, we come to you and you don't teach us – you shout at us', which
234   was – all I was doing was projecting my voice so that people would hear
235   me at the back but I've had to adapt it in such a way that people are more

236   happy with it and it's slightly less structured than what it was when I was
237   in the forces – a bit more casual.
238
239   **Arnie:** More civilianized.
240
241   **Brian:** Yeah. Civilians have a preconceived idea of ex-forces anyway and
242   it's based on fact but obviously as it's gone through different people, it's
243   been sort of changed and exaggerated and made bigger and so if you
244   spoke to the average civilian about what a service guy is, they'd probably
245   say, 'Oh he's um, he's very fit and he's aggressive and he's loud', and
246   they're not all like that, but again, so you're losing before you start really.
247   Whenever they wanted someone to head up a sports team or something
248   they'd say, 'Oh, Brian, you're ex-forces you can do that, you know how to
249   do that'. Or when they want someone to take control of a situation, 'Oh,
250   you've done that. You can do that role on these sort of leadership training
251   courses', or anything like that, anything that has a military connotation,
252   'Oh you know what you're doing; you can do that'. So they have
253   preconceived ideas.
254
255   **Arnie:** Mmm. It sounds like they were happy with some of the military
256   qualities that you were bringing to them but unhappy with others.
257
258   **Brian:** Well the thing is, when I first obviously, when I joined my first
259   company I was . . . six out of ten of us were ex-military, so they obviously
260   liked military people because they got good value for money from them.
261   They knew the military guys would work hard and they didn't shy away
262   from the work and they did a good job. So, yeah, once they . . . and I found
263   even in my other job as well, when I first, the job I'm doing now, I was the
264   first military guy they took on in my department and at one stage we had
265   five people in that department who were ex-military – obviously some
266   have left now – and I find that when you get one guy and if he does a good
267   job, then the company is quite open to bring more people into the same
268   department. And the way it normally works anyway is that you end up
269   then working with people you've know from before because when you
270   know they're going to take military people, then you recommend the
271   people that you know and um, out of the five military guys we had
272   working in my department, three of them I knew from before anyway so . . .
273
274   **Arnie:** Again we've touched on some of these issues but I'd like to talk
275   now about the influence of your personal values and beliefs on the
276   transition to becoming a civilian. Some researchers believe that, when
277   people leave a distinctive environment like the army, there may be an
278   impact on how they see themselves, feel about themselves or in how they
279   behave. I'd like to explore how your sense of being a soldier might or
280   might not have affected how you felt about yourself in civilian life and, as
281   I say, you've touched on some of these issues and you can expand on
282   those or you can move onto other areas if you like. Did you feel
283   differently or the same about yourself in civilian life compared to how you

284   felt about yourself while you were in the army?

285

286   **Brian:** No, not really. Because when I was in the forces, you feel good

287   about yourself anyway. You've got an identity there and you feel good

288   about yourself. And since I've been out, it's almost the same I think – not

289   much has changed there really. Obviously what I do now is different but I

290   don't think I've changed a great deal. I still try to maintain my ideals and

291   the principles that I had from before, which is perhaps why, every now

292   and again, I've caused a few ructions because I've still tried to maintain

293   and perhaps enforce my ideals on other people perhaps.

294

295   **Arnie:** Other people's influence, sometimes spouses, relatives or friends,

296   can influence how we feel about ourselves and particularly during

297   important changes like this, such as changing career or lifestyle. I'd like to

298   focus on whether or not the decisions you made and how you felt might

299   have been influenced by a spouse, friends, colleagues. Does that make

300   sense?

301

302   **Brian:** Yeah. No, I don't think . . . I suppose I must have been influenced in

303   such a way because the first job I took was fairly local – it was based at

304   [named town] when I lived here. So, and I suppose that must have been

305   influenced by the house we ha- and schooling – my daughter was going to

306   . . . so I didn't have to go too far afield. But um, and when I changed my

307   second job, I chose a job even closer to home, so yeah, there must have

308   been some kind of influence there but at the time I wouldn't have probably

309   admitted that I was being influenced or even realized it I suppose.

310

311   **Arnie:** Can you say something about whether or not you felt supported by

312   your wife?

313

314   **Brian:** Oh yeah, yeah. When I decided to come out, my wife was all for it

315   and she said, 'Well if that's what you want to do, then go for it' and she

316   didn't attempt to sway me or influence me in any way really but if I was

317   happy, she was happy.

318

319   **Arnie:** Do you think that people valued you more or less when you were a

320   soldier or as a civilian? Or the same?

321

322   **Brian:** Don't know really. Um, I know . . . I suppose I valued myself higher

323   when I was in the forces than now I'm outside because you had a much

324   more definite identity which other people could relate to, even if they had

325   a warped view of what you were doing. So, personally I feel I had greater

326   status when I was serving than now I'm out but, as opposed to people in

327   the company I'm with, I don't suppose there's any difference at all. In

328   fact, I'm probably valued greater by the company I'm working for than I

329   ever was when I was in the forces because of the size of the organization.

330   I'm in a smaller organization here and the job I'm doing is quite key to the

331   company and they need someone . . . when I was just one sergeant in the

332   Royal Engineers, there's lots of other sergeants in the Royal Engineers.
333   Now, I am a bigger fish in a smaller pond and so I'm probably valued
334   more by the company than I ever was in the forces, yeah.

335

336   **Arnie:**   By the sound of it, your own self esteem was higher while you
337   were in the army?

338

339   **Brian:**   I think that's because I had a definite label I could pin to myself
340   really.

341

342   **Arnie:**   A label? Sergeant?

343

344   **Brian:**   And obviously it took a lot of time and effort actually to get to that
345   level as well. You know, what I'm doing now, I joined the company as
346   that from day one and, although my job has changed a great deal, I have a
347   lot greater area of responsibility. I have more people to cover and look
348   after now than what I had when I first started but I'm still basically the
349   same – I'm still a health and safety adviser and I was that from day one so
350   it hasn't taken a great deal of effort to actually do that and um, as I
351   progress through the company, I'll be given like more and more
352   responsibilities but I'll only be a health and safety adviser. And so you
353   have to work hard and you have to earn your titles in military life.

354

355   **Arnie:**   Has any of what we've talked about so far affected how you felt
356   about yourself?

357

358   **Brian:**   No but um, it's probably made me look a lot closer at what I was
359   doing and what I'm doing now and what I was thinking then and now than
360   I ever done before. It's just something you get on and do it really without
361   actually thinking about it a great deal. This has prompted me to think back
362   and think through a few things.

363

364   **Arnie:**   I'd like to focus on any parts of military life which you've missed.
365   I was wondering if there were any parts of military life which you miss?

366

367   **Brian:**   The main bit really was the social life but I've managed to sort of
368   keep links with that. I still . . . I'm an honorary member of the Mess [a place
369   where members of the armed forces have their meals or spend their free
370   time] up at the barracks which I go to every now and again and that's
371   handy because, especially with it being a training establishment, you've
372   got people coming through all the time and it's a good way of meeting up
373   with people that you've not seen for many many years because everyone
374   comes through there eventually. So that's ideal, so I've managed to retain
375   links up there and other than that, that was probably the only thing that I
376   really ever said I missed. But thinking about some of the answers I've
377   already said, then there's perhaps a few other things in there I've missed
378   as well, such as the status and the esteem and everything else but, um, as I
379   would have said, the most important one was the social side of life which I

380   missed. Work is work really and, although I'm working in different
381   environments with different people now, I've managed to replace one type
382   of work with another type of work and I'm quite happy with that but the
383   social side is a lot different and um, I will keep the links. It's not quite the
384   same, but yeah, it's a good compromise.
385
386   **Arnie:** So it's mostly the social side you miss and you've managed to
387   retain links with that and you enjoy that by the sounds of it. And you
388   touched on other things that you miss and you touched on self esteem and
389   status and I guess that was linked to the hierarchical situation in the
390   military, that you were a sergeant within that system.
391
392   **Brian:** That's right, yeah.
393
394   **Arnie:** Could you say a little bit more about that? About how you felt and
395   what it feels like now not to be in that situation?
396
397   **Brian:** Well, I think before it was just um, belonging and being part of a
398   system and able to work your way through that system and be able to
399   achieve and now you just . . . it's not the same. There's no real rank structure
400   the same. No, really the only thing I felt I might miss when I first came out
401   was the . . . obviously the social side. I knew that I'd miss that, but then I got
402   round that by . . . as soon as I came out I joined the Mess straight away. That
403   only lasted for eighteen months because pressures of work wouldn't allow
404   me to go, to attend the Mess as regularly as I would have liked, so that fell
405   flat after a couple of years. But um, I've since been able to juggle things a
406   bit better and I can fit it in now. And um, initially when I first came out as
407   well, I went straight into the TA. Again that didn't last for long because I
408   was a bit disillusioned with the way the TA was run. Obviously I had one
409   idea of it which it didn't sort of meet up with the reality really. So yeah, I
410   thought I'd sort of miss out on sort of the military life. I thought, 'Well if I
411   can join the TA, it's . . . ' – again it's not quite the army but it's run on
412   similar lines. And I thought that would help ease me into civilian life but
413   again that didn't last particularly long. One was, being working, it was
414   difficult to get there a lot of the time and two um, I was a bit disappointed
415   with the way it was run. It wasn't being run on the same lines as the
416   regular forces and when they started moaning about me not being fully fit
417   because of my eye, I said, 'Well fine, I didn't join the TA for any hassle'. I
418   more joined for the . . . having a bit of fun and the social side again but there
419   wasn't a great deal of social side in the TA so I decided, when they made a
420   few waves, I just decided to pack it in and just leave because I had other
421   things to focus on anyway. I had to focus on working on my job and that
422   stuff so I just left.
423
424   **Arnie:** It sounds like it was a little bit of a stepping stone.
425
426   **Brian:** It would have been but that was the aim of doing it in the first
427   place. I thought that would help coming out but, as it happened, I wasn't

428   in there long enough really to get any real benefit from it.

429

430   **Arnie:** Can I ask you to think about whether or not you feel now that

431   you're fully adjusted to civilian life?

432

433   **Brian:** Yes but um people know I'm ex-forces whether or not I tell them

434   or not. Quite often I train people from all round the company and, at the

435   end of the presentation, another ex-serviceman will come and ask me

436   about my military life and I didn't refer to it. It's just that they pick up on

437   the way I act, the way I behave and the way I speak as well – they pick on

438   it straight away and they know, so other ex-servicemen would stop me

439   straight away or other people who've had some involvement – perhaps

440   that their parents had been in the forces or their husband had been in the

441   forces – they recognize it as well and pick up straight away. So, although I

442   feel I have quite adjusted to civilian life, um, really I'm still an ex-

443   serviceman. I'm not a civilian as such.

444

445   **Arnie:** How do you feel when people can readily identify you and

446   approach you in the knowledge that you're an ex-soldier?

447

448   **Brian:** Oh, I suppose it pleases me really I suppose because I've still

449   retained links with this certain part of my life I had, so yeah. It doesn't

450   displease me in any way. It's probably a benefit rather than anything else.

451

452   **Arnie:** Looking back, would you have done anything differently? Or not?

453

454   **Brian:** No, I don't think so. No, everything's worked out as I would have

455   hoped. Yeah.

456

457   **Arnie:** That's all the questions that I've got that I wanted to ask. Is there

458   anything on this subject that you wanted to talk about?

459

460   **Brian:** I don't know, no. I think everything's come out really. Before you

461   came here, I was thinking about what of my experiences would be most

462   useful for other people to hear . . .

463

464   **Arnie:** And again you touched on this yourself briefly and I'd like to ask

465   you to reflect for a moment on the experience of this interview. How has it

466   felt? What have been the positive things about taking part and what have

467   been the negative things about taking part?

468

469   **Brian:** Well, I don't think there's any negative things really. On the

470   positive side, it's made me look a little bit closer perhaps how I did feel

471   or . . . when I did come out and um, perhaps it's made me realize that uh,

472   perhaps there was more of an impact in coming out than what I realized at

473   the time. And perhaps there's more to military life that I missed than

474   perhaps I would have previously admitted to. But other than that . . . but one

475   of the positive parts of it was actually now um, after this you've got all the

476   reports together. I will be able to see how everyone feels rather than just
477   myself and see how closely I match other people and whether I'm actually
478   out there alone or whether I'm just the same as everyone else and had
479   similar experiences.
480
481   **Arnie:**   So there's part of you which wants to compare yourself to other
482   ex-servicemen and your experiences to other ex-servicemen's experiences.
483
484   **Brian:**   Because in the department I work for now, there's another two
485   guys at the moment, ex-forces, both of whom I knew from before when I
486   was serving. One of the guys he also attends the Mess as well and we go
487   up there quite regularly together and the other guy has cut himself off
488   completely from the military and doesn't attend any of these functions and
489   doesn't . . . not interested in going back. So obviously there's two different
490   people. There's one who wants to retain the links and another person who
491   wants to forget about it.
492
493   **Arnie:**   Do you think that taking part in this interview has had any effect,
494   or will have any effect on the way you feel about yourself? And again
495   you've touched on some of those issues. You said that you think it's given
496   you a little bit more insight into what you really did feel when you were
497   coming out.
498
499   **Brian:** No, I don't think so. Obviously, yes, it's made me a bit closer and I
500   probably have gained something from it but whether I'm actually going to
501   go away and build on that or having a lasting effect, I wouldn't have
502   thought so, no. It's just like . . . it's provided some information and that's it
503   really.

Appendix 2

REPORTING QUALITATIVE RESEARCH

PREFACE

Adrian Coyle and Evanthia Lyons

Whether a researcher conducts qualitative or quantitative research, the research process does not end until the study has been written up and presented to a wider audience. This audience may initially be quite a local one in the case of student research, where supervisors and examiners will review the work. However, ultimately the researcher's aim should be to convey their findings to an even wider audience so that, if the study is of sufficient quality, it can add to our knowledge of the research topic, inform debate and, in the case of applied research, shape policy and practice. This entails writing up the research for presentation at conferences and ultimately for publication in academic journals and other relevant outlets. Yet, the process of writing up research can be rather daunting, whether the research is qualitative or quantitative. The researcher may harbour fears about whether their work will withstand public scrutiny. They may be unsure about how best to represent in writing what they have done because relatively little practical guidance is offered in qualitative methodological texts on how to write up qualitative research (for an example of a notable exception, see Holliday, 2002).

We felt that, having taken readers through the principles and practicalities of four qualitative research methods, something of vital importance would be missing from this book if we did not address the process of writing up qualitative research. We have done this by inviting the authors of the chapters which present the principles of interpretative phenomenological analysis, grounded theory, discourse analysis and narrative analysis to write reports of studies they have conducted (by themselves or with other researchers) in the form of journal articles. Readers can thus gain some insight into how the outcomes of analyses using each method may be presented and can have access to templates for writing up research that may prove useful to those who have not previously written for publication (and to students who are uncertain of how best to write up their qualitative research). Each report deals with a fascinating topic (a woman's reported experience of anger, the experiences of relatives of organ donors, counselling psychologists' talk about 'psychopathology' and diagnostic categories of mental disturbance and one man's account of adapting to life with oral cancer) and so has value above its usefulness here as a template for writing up qualitative research.

Of course, readers should also consult other published journal articles which employ each of these methods in order to obtain a sense of the variety of ways in which research using these approaches can be presented. This is important to bear in mind. Just as, in the chapters on the four methods, authors have emphasized that there is no definitive way of using their method, so there is no definitive way of organizing the presentation of qualitative research when writing it up. Most academic journals in psychology that carry research reports will expect articles to conform to a general accepted structure, even if that simply takes the form of an introduction, a method section, the presentation of findings and some sort of discussion or conclusion, followed by references. Yet, within that broad framework, there is scope for creativity, especially in the presentation and interpretation of findings. Some non-academic publications (such as publications that are not primarily concerned with research and are aimed at professionals working in applied areas of psychology and related disciplines) may allow even greater scope for the creative reporting of qualitative research.

We felt, however, that straightforward templates would be of limited value because they would only present the finished product without giving a sense of the issues that the authors had to consider in producing their research report. We therefore asked authors to provide reports that featured 'reflective boxes' in which they identified and explained some of the decisions they had made in presenting their research or identified questions that other researchers might usefully consider when writing up their work. Some of the issues raised were general ones that confront the qualitative researcher; others were particular to specific methods. They concerned matters that need to be considered when engaging with relevant literature in the introduction to a research report (addressed by Virginia Eatough and Jonathan A. Smith in their report on IPA (Interpretative Phenomenological Analysis) work, Magi Sque and Sheila Payne in their report on grounded theory research and Mark Craven and Adrian Coyle in their report on discourse analytic work); the sampling process (Sque and Payne); how to describe a sample in the method section (Eatough and Smith; Craven and Coyle); strategies for data collection (Sque and Payne; Craven and Coyle); decision-making about what to present in an analysis – something that is necessary because of the amount of material generated by many qualitative analyses and the word limits faced by researchers who are writing journal articles (Eatough and Smith); related to this, how much data and what sort of data should be presented in research reports (Eatough and Smith; Sque and Payne; Craven and Coyle); interpretative style (Eatough and Smith); the role of theory in the analysis (Michele Crossley in her report on narrative analytic work); and the most appropriate location for discussing interpretations (Sque and Payne; Eatough and Smith).

We hope that the reports presented in this Appendix will assist readers in navigating through the process of writing up qualitative research in order to create engaging stories from their analyses and to bring their work to the attention of audiences that can benefit from it.

Reference

Holliday, A. (2002) *Doing and Writing Qualitative Research*. London: Sage.

Report 1

MAKING SENSE OF ANGER: A CASE STUDY USING INTERPRETATIVE PHENOMENOLOGICAL ANALYSIS[1]

Virginia Eatough and Jonathan A. Smith

In this report, we present an abridged version of a paper from our study on anger and aggression in women. The paper presents a case study of one woman, different from the one considered in Chapter 3. We have edited the paper by leaving out some material which covers very similar ground to that in Chapter 3 – for example, the argument for interpretative phenomenological analysis (IPA) and the description of how analysis was conducted. We have also only been able to present the first half of the results from the paper because of space restrictions. However we hope that what we have presented here gives you a strong indication of what is involved in writing up an IPA paper. For the complete paper, see Eatough and Smith (2006a).

Introduction

This report considers what it feels like when explanations for one's anger and its behavioural expression begin to break down. The report aims to illustrate the experience of meaning-making and how such meaning-making can be ambiguous, ambivalent and confused. In addition, we will argue that sense-making is always both an individual and social product (Riessman, 1992). Although, inevitably, cultural discourses inform individual meaning-making, this process also involves individual re-experiencing and reinterpreting of the events in one's life. This report demonstrates this dual enterprise by presenting an interpretative analysis of interviews with one female participant.

Box R1.1   ENGAGING WITH THE LITERATURE

In an IPA study, the 'literature review' is often less extensive than for other approaches. Reference is made to work which helps orient the study but the aim

(Continued)

(Continued)

is not to test a hypothesis derived from extant work. It is recognized that issues may arise during the analysis which were unanticipated and which will therefore be picked up by engaging with the appropriate literature in the discussion. What happened in this study was that attributional concerns emerged during analysis and were debated in the discussion. However we felt we also wanted to help the reader through our analysis by giving a reasonable amount of coverage of the attributional literature in the introduction as well.

Few emotion theorists would doubt that a relationship exists between cognition and emotion and many 'non-cognitive' theories incorporate some sort of cognitive component (Strongman, 2003). Much of the important social psychological research on cognition and emotion has been concerned with appraisal and attribution. Schachter's (1964: 51) two-factor theory of emotion is a cognitive–arousal theory which proposes that 'an emotional state may be considered a function of a state of physiological arousal and of a cognition appropriate to this state of arousal'. Importantly, according to the theory, individuals interpret physiological arousal in light of the circumstances that they believe brought it about. For example, in a romantic context, a pounding heart and trembling hands are interpreted as passionate love (Dutton and Aron, 1974).

Weiner's (1985) attributional theory of emotion proposed that emotions are the outcome of a temporal sequence of different cognitive processes. In the first instance, individuals evaluate the success or failure of an outcome. Second, if the outcome is evaluated negatively, then a cause is looked for. The final step involves classifying the cause according to three attributional dimensions: causal locus (is the cause dispositional or situational?), stability (is the cause transitory or constant?) and, finally, controllability (is the cause under volitional control?). There is evidence that specific emotions are associated with these categorical and dimensional attributions. For example, internal locus and controllability have been related to guilt, whereas controllability and external locus have been related to anger (Neumann, 2000). However, causal attribution models are normative in that they state ideal positions of what people ought to do rather than what people actually do when they think and explain their emotions (Fiske, 2004). Such models have a restricted notion of 'explanation' (Harré, 1981) and what people actually do is typically constructed as deviations and biases.

More recently, the claim that attributions exert a causal effect on emotions has been challenged by appraisal theorists (Smith et al., 1993). They argue that attribution is a particular form of knowledge, which assists the appraisal process by making inferences about the perceived causes of an event. Causal attributions are not sufficient to bring an emotion into being. On the contrary, the 'facts' of an event must be appraised and evaluated for emotion to arise. From this perspective, emotions are a consequence of evaluations of the personal significance of events and objects and their impact on well-being (Lazarus, 1991). 'Appraisal' is the psychological term for these evaluations and is typically understood as a distinct stage in an information-processing sequence which culminates in the emotional reaction (Parkinson, 1997). However, empirical evidence for a simple causal relationship between appraisal and emotion is weak (see Parkinson, 1997, for detailed discussion of the appraisal–emotion connection).

From the perspective of this report, our concern is that the interpreting, meaning-making person is reduced to the internal cognitive activity of hypothesized causal relationships. This concern is also expressed by some emotion theorists and discursive psychologists. For example, Parkinson and Manstead (1992) suggest that emotional experience is a consequence of our social interactions with other people, our own and other bodies and our physical environment, as well as cognitive evaluation processes. Moreover, emotional events have a temporal dimension and unfold over time. These features are not well captured in vignette studies, which are often used to investigate appraisals (Levine, 1996) and rely on simulation or directed imagery tasks (e.g., Smith and Lazarus, 1993). The study reported here emphasizes how individuals talk and make sense of their emotions and of being emotional in the very particular context of their unfolding lives.

Method

Participant

The participant is referred to throughout as Marilyn. At the time of the study, Marilyn was 30 years old and living with her partner, John, and their son, Andrew, in a council house in an inner city area in the Midlands area of England. The area is categorized as extreme in terms of social need and has correspondingly high levels of crime. Marilyn left school at 16 years of age and has worked in a variety of unskilled jobs. Since having Andrew, she has not worked outside the home. All names have been changed to safeguard confidentiality.

Box R1.2 'PEN PORTRAIT'

Providing some biographical information about the participants makes them 'come alive' for the reader. The aim is to provide the reader with some holistic sense of the person which contextualizes the analytic material.

Data collection

Marilyn responded to a mail drop in her area asking for volunteers to participate in a study on how women experience and resolve conflict in their lives.

After an initial telephone conversation, the first author met Marilyn at her home to discuss participation in the study. This first meeting was an attempt to make Marilyn feel as relaxed and informed as possible by detailing what the study would involve and to address any concerns she might have. This can be referred to as attempting to achieve symmetry between the researcher and participant (Hollway and Jefferson, 2000). Subsequently, an interview schedule was developed and two semi-structured interviews were carried out over a period of three weeks which resulted in four hours of data. The interviews were conducted by the first author in Marilyn's home and were recorded onto a mini disk recorder. There were specific issues we were hoping to address but the primary aim was for Marilyn to tell her story and not simply to be a respondent. The aim was to capture the richness and complexity of Marilyn's meaning-making by being an active listener and by allowing the interview to progress down avenues she opened up rather than those dictated by the interview schedule.

Box R1.3   ADOPTING A CONVERSATIONAL STYLE

IPA interviews are participant led and researchers treat participants as experiential experts on the topic under investigation. The aim is to facilitate the giving and making of an account in a sensitive and empathic manner, recognizing that the interview constitutes a human-to-human relationship. Thus, interviews are narrative in style and do not follow a simple question and answer format.

Analysis

Analysis of the data established three higher order themes that encapsulated Marilyn's lived experiences of anger and conflict. This report presents part of one of these, which is described as a meaning-making theme. It examines how personal and cultural frameworks of meaning mesh with each other and are lived and experienced by the individual person.

Results

One interrelated aspect of this sense-making theme is presented. The analysis shows how Marilyn invokes cultural frameworks of meaning to explain her anger and aggressive behaviour. The first of these frameworks draws heavily on biological discourses, namely the influence of hormones and alcohol. The analysis demonstrates how Marilyn's attempts to produce a strong and convincing account of these influences are undermined by alternative explanations.

Box R1.4   SELECTING ANALYTIC THEMES TO REPORT

When writing for publication and, indeed, often when writing up a student dissertation, it is not usually possible to report detailed analyses in full so the researcher
must make a decision about what to include. In part, this might be determined by
the focus of the journal or audience you want to reach. Alternatively, the choice
might be influenced more by issues of breadth or depth. One question you may
wish to ask is whether your aim is to provide a close reading of one particular
theme or a less detailed, more expansive account.

'That's all hormones'

Drawing on medicalized discourses that explain behaviour as a consequence
of hormones is a culturally powerful way of making sense of one's experiences.
Attributing aggressive and violent behaviour to an imbalance in hormones
implies a faulty biology and ignores how the individual's material, social and
cultural environment also shapes who we are, how we deal with emotional pain
and how we manage difficulties in life. A narrative of hormonal influence
weaves a potent thread throughout Marilyn's story. In this first extract, Marilyn
makes an explicit connection between her hormones and her aggressive behaviour. At the time, she was almost 17 years of age, she very much wanted a baby
and her aggression was directed at both her partner at that time and herself:

> I started off with just you know pushing him or hitting him type thing but then it was, it
> was sort of got worse where I'd start hurting myself as well, like throwing my arms at a
> mirror and cutting, cutting you know just self-mutilation but not to harm myself. Looking
> back now it was a cry for help but I mean nobody answered (laughs) basically. And
> erm I suffered really badly from depression where I had to go on medication. As well
> as that I had a fertility problem where I had polycystic ovaries . . . It's awful but I mean
> that's all hormones as well which explains away a lot of my moods and aggression and
> that. But I mean I don't know whether it I mean I have got a lot of hang ups about my
> family but I think a lot of it is hormonal my aggression and things like that.

This data extract reveals that in addition to being aggressive towards her partner, Marilyn engaged in deliberate self-harming behaviour. For Marilyn, the
phenomenological experience of this narrative episode is one of escalation. She
moves from relatively harmless acts of physical aggression to those with potentially dangerous and damaging consequences with herself becoming the target.
What is interesting here is how Marilyn's hormonal narrative develops throughout our conversation and gains ground as an explanation. In the first instance,
Marilyn describes her aggression as a cry for help which went unanswered. This
is possibly a relatively new interpretation and is a consequence of the counselling sessions that she has received. Next, Marilyn introduces her depression

and fertility condition, the latter of which sets the scene for Marilyn to make the link between her aggression and hormones. The statement 'that's all hormones' illustrates how Marilyn employs the condition of polycystic ovary syndrome to highlight the pervasive control of hormones over her physical body and possibly her mental state. In the extract, she moves towards stating a blanket, categorical relationship between her hormones and her behaviour. The power of this statement lies in its ability to negate alternative understandings of the anger and aggression events in Marilyn's life and seems to serve as a linguistic climax of this extract. However, there is evidence that she doubts the robustness of her hormonal explanation when she says 'but I mean I don't know whether it I mean I have got a lot of hang ups about my family but I think a lot of it is hormonal my aggression and things like that'. The mention of family difficulties is introduced, then quickly dismissed. The phrase 'explains away' might be ironic, reflecting an awareness on Marilyn's part that she is invoking a 'catch-all' explanation which belies the complexity of what is actually going on.

Box R1.5   INTERPRETATIVE STYLE

This section illustrates the style of IPA analysis. We begin with a close attentiveness to and reading of Marilyn's words. However, as we proceed, we are moving from being with Marilyn to thinking about Marilyn in considering her different own reflections on her invocations of the 'hormones' explanation.

'It was the alcohol'

In addition to inferring that the causes of her anger and aggression are hormonal, Marilyn utilizes an equally powerful physiological discourse: alcohol. Describing an incident involving a fight with a partner named Simon, Marilyn says:

It was the alcohol, I do remember I did feel angry, really angry, I mean raged angry but (pause) it was more because I think being humiliated, being shown up, he made me feel stupid in front of my friends do you know what I mean? It's not, I didn't actually think well you're going to have to pay for that but it was that sort of thing. I just don't think I actually thought about the emotional side of it. I just thought right you've shown me up, you're not leaving me alone. I just walked him away, tried to push him away that way but I mean that was really weird that night because I mean like a lot of it was alcohol but I cannot remember a lot of it. It was like a blind rage, it was really and there's been quite a few times that I've been like that without the alcohol, that I really can't recall a lot of what I've done until I've actually looked at the damage. And sat down afterwards and looked at what I've done.

There are several points of interest in this extract. At the outset, Marilyn makes a clear causal statement, which, by the end, is seriously weakened. First, she describes her rage as 'blind' and the end state is of emerging from the fury with little or no memory and of time being lost. Elsewhere we have reported that such intense emotion can be felt without alcohol, something which Marilyn herself comments upon (Eatough and Smith, 2006b). Second, the rage Marilyn feels appears to be fuelled less by alcohol and more by what she experiences as public humiliation, which requires some sort of revenge. Thus it is not simply to do with the effects of intoxication but also to do with issues of integrity and self worth. Third, 'you're not leaving me alone' can be viewed as a telling statement and it is interesting to speculate on why Marilyn said this to herself. It might simply be that being left alone would increase her mortified feelings or that she no longer had a target for her anger and aggression. However, since leaving home, Marilyn has always been in an intimate relationship. Arguably, these relationships provide evidence that she is a person who is capable of being loved and the unconscious motivation might be to avoid (reliving) the experience of her relationship with her mother. Finally, as with the hormonal accounts, there are cracks beginning to appear in the extract, which undermine its strength as an account. At the end of the extract, she acknowledges a certain culpability for her behaviour when she says 'and looked at what I've done'. There is also a recognition made in passing that the focus on alcohol allows her to bypass other contributory factors such as feeling hurt and humiliated and how this made her feel about her sense of self.

Box R1.6 BUILDING A NARRATIVE ACCOUNT

The final narrative account should be persuasive, illuminating the participants' experience through a mix of interpretative commentary and the participants' own words. It is not possible to say how many excerpts from the data should be presented. However, enough should be provided so that the reader can assess the interpretative claims made.

'I think I got depressed'

In contrast to the rather simple causal accounts of hormones and alcohol, the next extract gives a moving account of the distress Marilyn was experiencing and her specific set of circumstances:

> Paul was the first relationship that when I was sort of violent. Erm, I remember I was happy at first at the beginning of the relationship and then we started living together, we were in a grotty bedsit for a long time. He was working nights, I mean it was, I think I got depressed. And erm I think we'd been together about a year, year and a half and we both wanted a baby erm I remember I was having treatment at the hospital but I was also getting more and more aggressive where I was hitting him. I mean not in the face but in the arms and things like that. Erm I was more verbally abusive and trying to hurt myself more than anything in that relationship where I wanted to cut myself . . . I think

I was in you know like an emotional pain you know, like when your heart aches, I felt heartbroken over something you know, it was probably my mum again and I thought, I think I thought if I hurt myself it wouldn't hurt as much, do you understand what I mean?

Once again, a narrative of escalation is present and Marilyn's emotional pain is felt bodily. At first, Marilyn seems to invoke social or sociological reasons for her aggression (e.g., living and working conditions, depression) but these are superseded by more personal reasons. The metaphor of a broken and aching heart is a culturally powerful one and signifies a loss of something precious, be that a person, goal or relationship. This is a much more multifaceted narrative and differs from the previous ones in that Marilyn's almost casual observation, 'I think it was a cry for help' (see the first extract), is openly acknowledged to have been a time of pain and anguish. Marilyn's loneliness suffuses the account: Paul is physically absent a lot of the time, she is having difficulty becoming pregnant (so is not with child) and her pain is such that she wants to hurt herself.

Thus, in the narrative episodes presented above, there are a number of competing explanations. Marilyn draws on the effects of hormones and alcohol as narrative resources to make sense of her anger. These frameworks of meaning are powerful because they satisfy the desire for a simple causal explanation and, at the same time, remove responsibility from her. However, as we have demonstrated, the emphatic statements 'that's all hormones' and 'it was the alcohol' are threatened and begin to break down as Marilyn begins to realize other ways of sense-making.

It is essential that the material and social conditions that make up Marilyn's life world are noted. At the time of her relationship with Paul, she was 16 years of age and, before moving in with him, had slept for several weeks in a van outside his house. Marilyn was not in touch with her mother (and possibly with none of her family), Paul worked nights and her material circumstances were far from ideal. In addition, she found she was unable to conceive and describes her state of mind at the time as depressed. Finally, there is a move from a general explanation of a cry for help and 'hang ups about my family' in the first extract towards a more specific, if somewhat hesitant, account involving her mother.

Discussion

Box R1.7   PLACING THE ANALYSIS IN A CONCEPTUAL CONTEXT

The discussion is a dialogue between the analytic findings and the extant psychological literature. This dialogue can be critical, drawing attention to how qualitative analyses bring a fresh perspective to our understanding of human beings.

In this section, we build on some of the analytic observations already made by examining them through a theoretical lens. We look at the two long-standing frameworks of meaning Marilyn makes use of: hormones and alcohol.

We contend that this sort of interpretative analysis illuminates how traditional social cognition perspectives of 'explanation' neglect the experiencing, meaning-making person and what she/he brings to the telling of a life. Paradoxically, the prescriptive and reductive aspects of both approaches are brought to the fore through Marilyn's attempts to understand. The normative and unidirectional causal sequences found in attribution and appraisal research are undermined when faced with the messy and turbulent reality of individual meaning-making.

Marilyn's meaning-making is crumbling and this experience bears little relation to causal attribution models that aim to establish relations of cause and effect. Within the context of the individual life–world, these relations are often difficult to discern and speculative. We would suggest that attribution approaches, with their reliance on matching cause with effect, are simply unable to explain the complexity of a person's meaning-making. Similarly, cognitive emotion theories, which give the concept of appraisal centre place, neglect meaning-making and the interpersonal communicative function of emotional experience (Parkinson, 1997). Undoubtedly, emotional reactions have an evaluative component but to reduce this simply to a function of cognitive processing is to ignore the experiencing intersubjective person. For example, elsewhere we have reported how the body plays a crucial role (Eatough and Smith, 2006b) in women's meaning-making around anger. The meaning-making activity of the individual sometimes involves rational appraisal but it also entails being imaginative, intuitive and intentional.

Likewise, although we recognize that personal meaning-making is constrained by available cultural discourses and social conventions, individuals struggle and realize them differently in the context of their unique personal and social history. As Rosenwald (1992: 269) rightly states:

> If a life is no more than a story and a story is governed only by the situation in which it is told, then one cannot declare a situation unlivable or a life damaged.

Marilyn's accounts of her lived experiences are illustrative of how her sense of self, her stories and her situations both challenge and embrace understanding through contemporary cultural discourses. The remainder of this section discusses the restrictive nature of these frameworks of meaning. Our view is that causal attribution and rational appraisal theories need to be elaborated upon before they can adequately contribute to an understanding of the sorts of conceptually complex and multilayered attributions and appraisals that are involved in human meaning-making. Similarly, we argue that individuals' meaning-making is constituted, at least in part, by cultural discourses and conventions but is not determined by them.

The analysis demonstrated that Marilyn made associative links between her infertility, her depression and her anger and aggression. This is not surprising given that the influence of hormones on women's behaviour is a culturally powerful discourse which denies women moral agency. In terms of explaining women's anger and aggression, hormonal explanations form one half of a 'mad or bad' dichotomy. Cultural discourses of women's anger construct their experience of this emotion as negative and deviant in terms of their gender. Research suggests that, when women get angry, they feel themselves to be in a no-win situation (Campbell and Muncer, 1987). Lashing out either physically or verbally is experienced as a loss of control and as not conforming to dominant norms of femininity (bad). However, if women exercise control and express their anger through crying, they are often perceived as 'hysterical' (mad). This is not to say that fluctuating hormonal levels do not have some role in Marilyn's potent feelings of anger and in her aggressive behaviour. There is the fertility problem when she was younger, she had been treated for depression with a tricyclic antidepressant and it is possible that, at the time of the interviews, Marilyn was suffering from post-natal depression. Moreover, it is highly probable that the fertility problem would have influenced Marilyn's menstrual cycle.

However, whether or not hormones are actually an important contributory factor in Marilyn's anger and aggression cannot be ascertained from the interview data. What is important is that she believes they do. The analysis illustrates clearly how hormones are a crucial component of Marilyn's meaning-making and the question as to why this is the case can be addressed. Causal explanations that invoke hormones are part of a medicalized discourse, which suggests that there is a solution in the form of treatment to rectify an ostensible imbalance. They work by denying individual moral agency.

Marilyn's adherence to a hormonal account constructs the experience of her anger and aggression as one that renders her passive in the face of forces beyond her control. Equally, it is unsurprising that alcohol plays some sort of role in Marilyn's stories of her anger and aggression. As with hormonal explanations, there is a wealth of empirical evidence that concludes that alcohol consumption often increases levels of aggressive behaviour (Bushman and Cooper, 1990). Alcohol disrupts how individuals process information; researchers call this 'alcohol myopia' (Steele and Josephs, 1990). Nevertheless, despite this evidence, the relationship between the two is oversimplified and overstated in dominant lay and psychological frameworks of meaning. When Marilyn says 'it was the alcohol', she is invoking a simple causal attribution that ignores the wider interpersonal context in which her behaviour takes place. This sort of oversimplification encourages the individual to view her/himself as passive and as having no control because making alcohol responsible is an easier option. Although it does not make the behaviour socially acceptable, it is a socially acknowledged and understood statement, which can often go unchallenged. This is in spite of the fact that such causal attributions are never wholly convincing at either the intrapsychic or the interpersonal levels.

The analysis above highlights the contradictions within Marilyn's accounts as she wrestles with the internal and external challenges to her hormonal and alcohol explanations. For example, in the extract in which she offers an explanation of her fight with Simon, the role of alcohol is weakened when it becomes clear that Marilyn's rage is more to do with the experience of public shame that requires redress. In this incident, Marilyn's aggression was not simply a consequence of intoxication levels but also to do with personal worth and integrity. Researchers have demonstrated that aggression is one consequence of threats to the self (Baumeister et al., 1999). Explanations centring on public humiliation or a fear of rejection require a conscious and inwardly reflective scrutiny and point to a sense of self that is experienced as fragile and ruptured. By invoking alcohol, any real attempt to understand what is happening beyond immediate antecedent events is effectively closed down.

Summary

This report has provided an illustration of how an IPA analysis might be presented, while offering continued reflections upon the analytic process. Although it has put forward a case study analysis, the same basic presentational principles apply when formatting an analysis of data from larger samples. We hope that this report, in conjunction with the chapters on the principles and procedures of IPA, will help readers who are interested in IPA to undertake and write up their own analyses using this method.

References

Baumeister, R.F., Smart, L. and Boden, J.M. (1999) 'Relation of threatened egotism to violence and aggression: The dark side of high self-esteem', in R.F. Baumeister (ed.), *The Self in Social Psychology*. Hove: Psychology Press. pp. 240–279.

Bushman, B.J. and Cooper, H.M. (1990) 'Effects of alcohol on human aggression: An integrative research review', *Psychological Bulletin*, 107: 341–354.

Campbell, A. and Muncer, S. (1987) 'Models of anger and aggression in the social talk of women and men', *Journal for the Theory of Social Behaviour*, 17: 490–511.

Dutton, D.G. and Aron, A. (1974) 'Some evidence for heightened sexual attraction under conditions of high anxiety', *Journal of Personality and Social Psychology*, 30: 510–517.

Eatough, V. and Smith, J.A. (2006a) 'I feel like a scrambled egg in my head: An idiographic case study of meaning making and anger using interpretative phenomenological analysis', *Psychology and Psychotherapy: Theory, Research and Practice*, 79: 115–135.

Eatough, V. and Smith, J.A. (2006b) 'I was like a wild wild person: Understanding feelings of anger using interpretative phenomenological analysis', *British Journal of Psychology*, 97: 483–498.

Fiske, S. (2004) *Social Beings. A Core Motives Approach to Social Psychology*. Hoboken, NJ: John Wiley and Sons.

Harré, R. (1981) 'Expressive aspects of descriptions of others', in C. Antaki (ed.), *The Psychology of Ordinary Explanations of Social Behaviour*. London: Academic Press. pp. 139–156.

Hollway, W. and Jefferson, T. (2000) *Doing Qualitative Research Differently: Free Association, Narrative and the Interview Method*. London: Sage.

Lazarus, R.S. (1991) 'Progress on a cognitive-motivational-relational theory of emotion', *American Psychologist*, 46: 819–834.

Levine, L.J. (1996) 'The anatomy of disappointment: A naturalistic test of appraisal models of sadness, anger and hope', *Cognition and Emotion*, 10: 337–359.

Neumann, R. (2000) 'The causal influences of attributions on emotions. A procedural priming approach', *Psychological Science*, 11: 179–182.

Parkinson, B. (1997) 'Untangling the appraisal-emotion connection', *Personality and Social Psychology Review*, 1: 62–79.

Parkinson, B. and Manstead, A.S.R. (1992) 'Appraisal as a cause of emotion', in M.S. Clark (ed.), *Review of Personality and Social Psychology, Vol. 13: Emotion*. Newbury Park, CA: Sage. pp. 122–149.

Riessman, C.K. (1992) 'Making sense of marital violence: One woman's narrative', in G.C. Rosenwald and R.C. Ochberg (eds), *Storied Lives: The Cultural Politics of Self-Understanding*. London: Yale University Press. pp. 231–249.

Rosenwald, G.C. (1992) 'Conclusion: Reflections on narrative self-understanding', in G.C. Rosenwald and R.C. Ochberg (eds), *Storied Lives: The Cultural Politics of Self-Understanding*. London: Yale University Press. pp. 265–289.

Schachter, S. (1964) 'The interaction of cognitive and physiological determinants of emotional state', in L. Berkowitz (ed.), *Mental Social Psychology*, Vol. 1. New York: Academic Press. pp. 49–80.

Smith, C.A. and Lazarus, R.S. (1993) 'Appraisal components, core relational themes, and the emotions', *Cognition and Emotion*, 7: 233–269.

Smith, C.A., Haynes, K.N., Lazarus, R.S. and Pope, L.K. (1993) 'In search of the "hot" cognitions: Attributions, appraisals and their relation to emotion', *Journal of Personality and Social Psychology*, 65: 916–929.

Steele, C.M. and Josephs, R.A. (1990) 'Alcohol myopia: Its prized and dangerous effects', *American Psychologist*, 45: 921–933.

Strongman, K.T. (2003) *The Psychology of Emotion. From Everyday Life to Theory* (5th edition). New York: John Wiley and Sons.

Weiner, B. (1985) 'An attributional theory of achievement motivation and emotion', *Psychological Review*, 92: 548–573.

Note

1   This chapter is closely based on a paper which appeared in the journal, *Psychology and Psychotherapy: Theory, Research and Practice* (published by the British Psychological Society) in 2006 (Vol. 79, No. 1, pp. 115–135). We are grateful to the British Psychological Society for granting permission to produce a revised version of the paper in this book.

Report 2

CRITICAL CARE EXPERIENCES AND BEREAVEMENT AMONG FAMILIES OF ORGAN DONORS: A REFLECTIVE ACCOUNT OF GROUNDED THEORY ANALYSIS[1]

Magi Sque and Sheila Payne

The purpose of this report is to provide readers with a clear sense of what the outcome of a grounded theory study looks like and how it might be presented when writing a journal article or a student dissertation. The study that this report focuses on explores the experiences of relatives of organ donors. Throughout the report, text boxes are used at pertinent junctures to highlight important issues in the writing of the journal article upon which the report is based and also some issues specific to the grounded theory process. For the complete journal article, see Sque and Payne (1996).

Introduction

Box R2.1   INTRODUCTION OR BACKGROUND TO THE STUDY

There is much debate about how much a grounded theorist needs to know about the field they wish to explore. Grounded theory was considered the methodology of choice in this study as little was known about the bereavement experience of families who donated organs of a deceased relative. We could have chosen not to write such a detailed literature review and could have included it in the discussion of the findings but we felt that this introduction was essential to make a good case for the study and to show where there were outstanding gaps in the literature and in the knowledge base about the topic. We also had to take into consideration the particular style of the journal for which we were writing, where an elaborated introduction or background was expected.

Every year approximately 700,000 individuals die in the UK, yet very few become 'beating heart donors' (i.e., donors of major organs). While relatives of potential donors are an important group in the donation process (as their lack of objection is needed before organ retrieval can take place), little is understood about their experiences (Pelletier, 1992).

Empirical investigation into the experiences of donating relatives has been limited both in its scope and design. First, the small numbers of donating families, the anonymity that surrounds them and the often wide geographical spread makes access to relatives difficult, except by survey methods (e.g., Bartucci, 1987; Perez-San-Gregorio et al., 1992) which are limited in their ability to describe the meaning of the experience. Second, the emotive nature of the research and theoretical debates (de Raeve, 1994) which surround the ethics of interviewing any bereaved group make investigation problematic.

La Spina et al. (1993) investigated the psychological mechanisms related to families' decisions to donate by interviewing 20 families 6 to 12 months after donation. Results indicated that the primary reason for donation was the desire to keep the deceased relative alive through identification with the recipients. This was considered to be a defensive mechanism against the anguish of death. The collapse of this projection, for whatever reason, left the relatives with feelings of guilt that they had somehow lost track of the deceased. These events manifested themselves in depression, anxiety and elaboration of bereavement.

Coupe (1991) addressed the issues of support and perceptions of information given to 17 families at the time the issue of organ donation was raised. Six themes emerged from the study: informing the family, dealing with brain death, organ donation, grief, family needs and facilities and nursing and medical staff. Organ donation was seen as a difficult subject to raise. However, the request for donation rarely offended the relatives and was often accepted as something the staff 'had to do'. Some families felt that they were given insufficient information about retrieval, particularly about how the body would look post retrieval. The research indicated that individual assessment of families is required to establish when the issue of donation should be raised and who should do it.

Pelletier (1992) used semi-structured interviews with nine relatives of organ donors to appraise what family members identified as the most stressful aspects of the donation process. She identified the most stressful situations as the threat of losing a loved one, the diagnosis of brainstem death, the failure of health professionals to identify the potential organ donor and adjusting to the many changes associated with the loss. Pelletier (1993) further used this donor family sample to extrapolate the emotions experienced and coping strategies used during their stressful situations. During 'the threat to life', a range of emotions such as helplessness, sadness, numbness and panic were reported. Coping strategies involved seeking information, seeking emotional support, keeping the connection (remaining near the relative), escape and avoidance, planned problem solving and exercising control of emotions. Emotions experienced with the confirmation of brain death were disbelief, shock, numbness, anger and sadness. Organ donation was the coping strategy used on this occasion as it provided a mechanism for changing the death into something positive.

Prior to the present study, investigation into donor relatives' experience by qualitative methods had been limited, patchy and incomplete. No investigation had attempted to describe the totality of relatives' organ donation experience or to suggest inductive theory which could explain it. This was the aim of the present study. It was anticipated that such a theory could provide a framework for future investigation through the identification of variables and the generation of hypotheses. It could also suggest pertinent factors necessary in the education of health professionals to ensure appropriate care for donor relatives.

Method

Box R2.2   REFLECTING ON SAMPLING AND DATA COLLECTION

While always bearing in mind the constraints imposed by the word limit for articles in a particular journal, one of the most important items that need to be explained is the sample. In a grounded theory, as indicated in the first paragraph below, we wished to capture the widest set of participants' experiences that we could. Hence it was important to show the reader that we had made great efforts by using more than one geographical location, which might have had different support services, different age groups of donors, time since donation and cause of death. Some of these factors are usefully pulled together in Table R2.1. In Chapter 5, Sheila Payne has written about over-sensitizing the researcher to the field and we could have chosen not to carry out a pilot study but felt that, because of the sensitive nature of the research and the participant group, plus the questions that the interviewer (Magi Sque) could be asked, as well as her role as a novice researcher, it was appropriate to carry out a pilot study. This strategy did prove invaluable as many difficult issues were often raised during the interviews and Magi was able to give reassurance or was able to suggest referral routes for participants to find answers to their questions or resolve issues. We have therefore stated that a grounded theory *approach* was used rather than classic grounded theory where the researcher would enter the field with little knowledge of the issues that would be likely to arise. It was also important in sensitive research of this nature to be kept informed of the effect interviews had on participants – hence our interview evaluations. Data validation and analysis are briefly reported. This is often a choice one has to make and the debates about data analysis and about checking analyses with participants in grounded theory could run on, so we simply mention the validation process here and that data were analysed in accordance with general principles of grounded theory, which become apparent in the reporting of the findings.

Relatives from 42 donor families were invited by letter to participate in an interview study. Since geographical spread might have been important (due to differences in local practices), families were recruited via three regional transplant co-ordinating centres within England. Relatives were chosen to cover a range of experiences, such as the time since donation and their relationship to the donor. 16 families (24 relatives) agreed to participate. A detailed sample profile is provided in Table R2.1.

All the participating families had agreed to multi-organ retrieval. Four donations were spontaneously offered, while 12 were requested. Interviews were carried out in the homes of the participants: these lasted between one and a half to two hours.

In dealing with this sensitive topic, it was important for the researchers to be fully informed about the subject of their exploration. Also, specific preparation for the interviewer role was developed through pilot interviews carried out with two donor families who had made donations several years previously. These families had both spoken publicly about their experiences. The objective was to explore salient issues and to gain confidence in conducting such an interview.

All the interviews were carried out by the first author (Magi Sque). Following an introduction to the procedure for the interview, participants were asked to

Table R2.1   Participant sample to show family relationships, age of donor, critical injury and months since donation

Relatives interviewed	Age of donor (years)	Critical injury	Time since donation (months)
Parents	27	Cerebral haemorrhage	5
Parents	25	Cerebral anoxia following cardio-pulmonary resuscitation	7
Parents	20	Head injury from a riding accident	36
Parents	22	Head injury following a road traffic accident	8
Parents	26	Marphan's Syndrome	18
Parents	10	Viral meningitis	16
Mother	22	Cerebral anoxia following an asthma attack	11
Mother	0*	Cerebral anoxia following asphyxiation	11
Father	26	Head injury following a road traffic accident	4
Husband	44	Cerebral haemorrhage	7
Husband	56	Cerebral haemorrhage	8
Husband	48	Cerebral haemorrhage	17
Wife	47	Cerebral haemorrhage	4
Wife	47	Cerebral haemorrhage	18
Wife & mother	22	Head injury following a road traffic accident	7
Wife & daughter-in-law	50	Cerebral haemorrhage	4

* baby 10 weeks old.

tell the story of their experiences. Only after the story was complete did the researcher use the interview guide, developed from the pilot interviews and relevant literature, in further questioning. This guide was modified throughout the data collection process to incorporate new concepts. Participants were later invited to provide evaluative feedback on their experience of being interviewed.

Analysis of the data was carried out using a grounded theory approach (Strauss and Corbin, 1990). Transcripts were coded for themes which were clustered to form named categories. These categories closely fit the data, as they were derived from the inquiry. Nine participants were asked to review a summary of their interviews to validate the researchers' interpretations.

Results

Box R2.3   REPORTING THE FINDINGS

There are many ways of reporting a grounded theory study and if we were writing this section again, we would entitle it 'Findings' rather than 'Results' (which is how we described it in the original journal article). The term 'Findings' better describes the outcomes of a qualitative investigation, which are not the sort of measurable 'Results' obtained from a quantitative study. We chose to report the findings in three parts starting with the number of categories and the core variable, their titles and Figure R2.1, which shows their configuration. The second section gives a description of the categories into which explanatory literature is interwoven in accordance with reporting grounded theory. The third part focuses on the theory developed and the literature that lends support to its development.

In describing the categories, we have included illustrative quotations from the interview transcripts as evidence. Choosing quotations can often be problematic for researchers because it can be difficult to decide which quotations are most representative of a specific theme or category. Often there is a conflict about using the most 'startling' quotations that may be particularly memorable or ones that really embrace the substance of the category. Then there is the decision of how many quotations to use. Often there are many good descriptive quotations and the process of elimination can be mentally 'painful' as there is so much you would like to share with the reader. It is also important in reporting grounded theory to give a selection of opposing views if these differ from the main pattern of themes, as is illustrated in this section. However it must be borne in mind that a journal article relies mainly on the authors' interpretation of events, which should be the substantive part of the findings, with the quotations acting as confirmation of this interpretation. This is how we have tried to report the nature of the categories here.

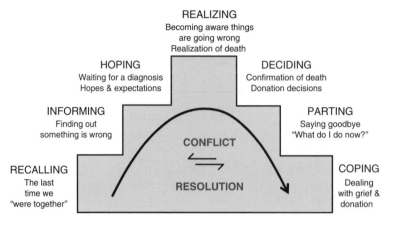

Figure R2.1 A model of donor relatives' experience

The analysis of the data produced 11 categories which conceptualized participants' experience. These categories were arranged around the central theme of the research, 'donor relatives' experiences', to form an analytical version of the story, shown in Figure R2.1.

The model in Figure R2.1 indicates a sequential relationship of categories that described participants' commonly constructed realities of the donation experience. These were 'the last time we were together'; 'finding out something is wrong'; 'waiting for a diagnosis', 'hopes and expectations'; 'becoming aware things are going wrong', 'realization of death'; 'confirmation of (brain-stem) death', 'donation decisions'; 'saying goodbye', 'what do I do now?'; and 'dealing with grief and donation'.

There appeared to be particular behaviours through which each phase was acted out by participants. These were: 'recalling', where participants talked about the attributes of their relative and the last occasion they shared together; 'informing', when they were first told something had gone wrong; 'hoping' during the hospital experience; 'realizing' that their relative would not recover; 'deciding' about donation; 'parting', leaving the relative; and 'coping' with grief and donation. These behaviours were explained through a process of conflict and resolution which pervaded the categories and formed the core variable of participants' experience. A theory of 'dissonant loss' was developed to explain participants' psychosocial concerns during the donation experience, using this core variable. This process of conflict and resolution will now be examined with reference to the categories concerning donation and its outcome.

Deciding – donation decisions

Deciding about donation was often the first time during the period when their relative had been hospitalized that participants were given some control. Up to this point, events had developed around them as they sought to understand

and come to terms with their situation. Decisions about donation created further conflicts for participants, such as whether to donate and what to donate.

Participants were approached about donation at various stages during the relative's illness. Nevertheless, they were all consulted following the confirmation of brainstem death. Requests were usually made in an interview with the doctor and the next of kin who had a supporting relative with them. Participants were sympathetic toward requesters, as they had empathy with this sensitive task. Decisions about donation were discussed between significant family members and were mainly consensus decisions. Arbitrators and principle contributors to the decision-making process were the parents or spouses of the deceased relative and final decisions rested with them. The agreement to donate was in these cases made easier when there was tangible evidence of the relative's wishes, such as a donor card. On occasion there was disagreement within families about donation. In these cases the principle contributor made the decision to support the relative's wishes or their own preference. This did cause resentment within families. Deciding to donate sometimes caused conflict for principle contributors, as they may not have wished for donation themselves but felt they had to fulfil the wish of their relative. Participants from whom requests were made felt that they probably would not have thought of organ donation and were glad they were approached. They felt it would have been distressing not to have fulfilled the pre-mortem wish of their relative.

Motivation to donate   There appeared to be four major contributing factors about making the decision to donate organs: the wishes of the relative; the attributes of the relative; the realization of the death of the relative; and the confirmation of brainstem death. However, the relative's wishes were of primary importance as the donation was seen to be their gift. A participant, for instance, remembered how she had taken a donor card from her 10-year-old son saying, 'Don't be so silly, you don't want that'. The episode helped her believe that her son, now 22, had intended to help other people after he died and she supported his wife's decision to facilitate the retrieval of his organs.

In some cases, making a decision without the explicit knowledge of the wishes of the deceased was very difficult for participants. The category of 'recalling' – 'the last time we were together' gained importance as the attributes of the relative helped to make the decision:

> We said, well yeah, I think G would like that because she did talk about having a card, only she never got around to having one and being a caring and sharing person that she was, we said yeah we'll do that . . . she would be more than pleased and proud that we did really.

For more on motivations for donation, see Sque and Payne (1996: 1363–1364).

Concerns about donation   Participants had two main concerns about donation: mutilation of the body and the possible suffering the relative might sustain as a result of the operation. It was important to participants that the retrieval of organs was carried out with dignity and propriety. Participants found the knowledge that retrieval was carried out as a regular surgical procedure comforting:

I thought G was going to be carved up and everything else but it was not so, it was done clinically and I don't think this is ever explained openly . . . It is done like a surgical operation and there is no fear of the patient being hurt in any shape or form.

There was another type of suffering which was of concern to participants. They felt that the relative had already suffered so much so was it fair to subject them to further indignities by allowing their organs to be removed? A father was concerned about the vulnerability of his child at retrieval:

I wanted to protect her more because I mean, she was very vulnerable, wasn't she? For all intents and purposes she was dead but I did not want her to be cut about. I didn't want her to be injured. You see she was not injured in my eyes because there was no marks. So anything done after that would be an operation and I couldn't comprehend that too much at that particular time. So really that was my reservation – I didn't want her to be hurt.

Conflicts for participants concerning donation were about fulfilling the pre-mortem wishes of their relative and assumptions about contributing to their perceived posthumous suffering. These concerns were conceivably exacerbated by a poor understanding of brainstem death or affected by the notion of harming the dead. Callahan (1987) highlighted the sentiment that it is possible to 'feel sorry' for the dead person because we do think of the dead as they were ante-mortem. Therefore, it is possible to experience compassion for the dead and to feel genuine moral outrage at broken pre-mortem promises which respect the wishes of the dead. Although the subject of posthumous harm has been debated, Callahan (1987) feels that our empathetic responses to the dead are in part due to our inability to identify with the dead: we are only capable of identifying with pre-mortem states. Feinberg (1985) details these sentiments in that a dead body is a natural symbol of a living person and when a corpse is mutilated it looks very much like one is harming a real person: horror is felt at the mere proposition of such action. This is the way we imagine the dead person and sorrow and outrage can justifiably be felt on their behalf.

However, Callahan (1987) points out that the express wishes of the dead generally merit respect in their own right. This may explain the gratitude that was felt by families who were asked about donation and were able to facilitate this wish for their relative. The question that naturally seems to follow is whether we feel so morally bound when what is willed is wasteful. This could be a painful dilemma for relatives involved in donation requests when the wishes of their loved ones were explicitly opposed to it. Likewise, relatives in this study agonized over the decision to donate if the wishes of the dead were unknown.

Information about donation   While some participants seemed well informed about retrieval procedures, others felt that adequate information was not available to support their decisions about donation. For more on this, see Sque and Payne (1996: 1365).

Parting – saying goodbye

Once donation was agreed, participants needed to make decisions about leaving the relative and 'saying goodbye'. This created further conflict and difficulty for participants in equating death with the appearance of the relative when making the decision to leave them:

Interviewer: How did you actually make that decision to go and say goodbye?

Participant: Well, it is very difficult to. All I kept thinking was that I kept saying to my brother-in-law, 'How can you say goodbye to somebody who is still breathing?' I mean, oh God, I kept on saying, 'He's warm, he's still perspiring, he's warm' because to me he wasn't dead really . . . because he was still breathing. And I know it was the machine and that but he was too warm.

Except in one case, all the participants in this study chose to leave the hospital soon after the results of the second brainstem test were known and confirmed brainstem death. In no case did hospitals offer participants a full range of options for seeing the relative post-organ retrieval, such as back on the ward, which might have been appropriate for some. This did cause regrets among participants, as they felt that viewing the newly dead would have been more preferable than, in some cases, days later at a funeral home.

In some instances, the nurses offered to inform participants when the retrieval operation had been completed. Some participants found the time waiting for this telephone call and the declaration of cessation of the heartbeat difficult. It did mark a kind of finality but it was an end to any hope of existence for the relative:

We got the phone call 4.30 Christmas Eve to say they had switched off the ventilator. That was terrible waiting for the phone call. We dreaded the phone to ring. I mean, we knew that he had gone then.

Retrospectively, participants wished that they had had more guidance from hospital staff about options and about the possible effects of choosing how and when they said goodbye.

Parting – what do I do now?

'What do I do now?' was asked of intensive care staff by a father when he was about to leave the hospital. It was the bewildering stage of leaving hospital and dealing with immediate concerns of the hospitalization and its outcome. Families most often felt that once they had left the intensive care unit, 'A door had closed behind us'. They had very little support from anyone to do with the donation, with one participant saying:

We sort of felt as if they had the organs and at the moment we had been left.

Hospitals generally did not provide any advice about grief, give any bereavement support contacts or carry out any follow-up. Only in two cases did consultants and transplant coordinators suggest participants should get in touch if they had any unanswered questions. Here the needs of some relatives are explained:

We came away from that hospital with no support, nothing – just a plastic bag with his belongings in, nowhere where you could get in touch with anyone if you needed any counselling . . . It's like you just walk away empty, you know . . . If only they could find a nicer way of doing it rather than just writing out a death certificate and sending you away with a plastic bag.

Coping – dealing with grief and donation

The most important thing about grief and donation is that donation does not appear to reduce grief but it changes the emphasis of death to focus on the achievement of the donor and that their kindness and caring are living on. Here a father describes the feelings he had following the death of his son and his donation:

It's not a reward that you get – it's something that happens as a result of a loved one wishing to give their organs to somebody else. They give their organs to somebody else so that they can have the gift of life and what they give to us is almost not an easy road in grief but a different road through grief – a less harsh road and a less final death because it is a death filled with different emotions. It's filled with the joy of knowing good has come out of his death, as opposed to us having to know that, just, ah, nothing has come out of his death, only pain and sorrow and sadness, and also knowing that it is not only the recipient that receives, it's their family, their friends . . . It is a tremendous thing, it ripples out to hundreds of people . . . Almost unending the relief and saving of pain that just giving something that is not needed can produce.

Participants reported that the most important thing in providing respite from grief was the ability to talk to others about their bereavement when they needed to. Participants tended to seek out their own social supports but grief was largely managed within the family. A few participants who did not have this internal support sought the help of bereavement organizations, which seemed ill-prepared to be of assistance in this particular circumstance. Families who used bereavement services did not feel that the experiences had been particularly helpful; in one case, the counsellor expressed her objection to organ donation.

Participants received a letter from the transplant co-ordinating units which gave information about organ distribution. Participants found this initial information helpful but desired more information about recipients, as they faced the conflict of part of their relative still living on. This desire for information did not necessarily abate as time went by. In some cases, participants realized that they may not wish to know if the transplant had failed. Others thought this was unimportant as help had at least been offered. Participants put great value on the concept of their relative living on:

> She is not dead and gone sort of thing, you know. She is still out there walking around, which is very pleasing to know . . . that her life is still going on, in that context really, life still goes on. She's out there in the big wide world, in four different places at once (laughing) which is unbelievable, unbelievable.

At the time of the interview, although some participants had experienced difficulties with aspects of their bereavement, all remained supportive of their donation decision:

> At the end of the day, it was right, it was the right decision to do, I'm quite happy, I'm quite content, I've got no remorse, no regrets or doubts because I know somebody out there got life.

Donation decisions may have consequences which will affect the rest of donor relatives' lives. Unfortunately, this can only be speculation, as there are no longitudinal studies about donor relatives. However, this study has suggested that, even as time goes by, the effects of the donation are perpetuated in the desire for continuing information about recipients.

Bowlby (1980) proposed that bereaved people generally experience a strong need for continuation of a relationship with the dead person. It is possible that the way the relationship continued to play a central role in participants' lives is manifested in the often intense and sustained yearning for information about recipients because of the attachment participants felt for the part of the donor that 'lived on'. In some instances, this need for information seemed to be influenced by the intensity of the relationship that had existed with the relative.

Theory of dissonant loss: Conflict and resolution in the donation experience

---

> ### Box R2.4   REPORTING THE THEORY
>
> We started the section on the theory by defining the theory and the core variable. We then integrated the literature into the discussion that supported the way families' decisions were made. In this section, we have presented Figure R2.2 which shows the events that impinged on the process of conflict and resolution (core variable) for participants.

This study has suggested that the experience of organ donation can be explained by a theory of 'dissonant loss'. Dissonant loss is defined as 'A bereavement or loss which is characterized by a sense of uncertainty and psychological inconsistency. The loss is assured but the effects of the loss on those involved are unknown'. Dissonance occurs as the loss is encompassed by a series of complex decisions. These decisions are made necessary by the ubiquitous and pervasive elements of conflict and resolution (see Figure R2.2).

The notion that people who hold conflicting or incompatible beliefs are likely to experience dissonance and distress has a long history in psychology (Higgins, 1987). Therefore, the conflict/resolution concept provides an appropriate explanation of the psychosocial influences that families encounter during their donation experience. Conflict is defined in this sense as 'The simultaneously opposing tendencies within the individual or environment which cause discrepancy, discord or dissonance and the distress resulting from these instances'. Within this study, participants described the factors that created resolutions to their conflicts and helped them to move through the phases of the donation process (see Figure R2.2).

Conflict originated in the contracted and intense emotional period of hospitalization (which has not been reported here but is described by Sque and Payne, 1996: 1361–1363). During this time, participants seemed to lose control to the experts, as they were functioning outside of their assumptive world, which includes all we know, our interpretations of the past and expectations of the future (Parkes, 1993). Higgins (1987) described how construct availability or our stored experience of a given situation will influence the possessor's response. Higgins maintains that individuality of response to the situation is due to construct accessibility, which refers to the readiness with which each stored construct is used to process new information.

Since the donors were relatively young, their next of kin were young parents or spouses, who were inexperienced with critical injury, death and hospital protocol and without the life experience or information to support their choices. The degree of conflict and uncertainty experienced by participants was exacerbated by a lack of experience and knowledge about the events of organ donation. It was in this environment that participants were asked to make complex decisions about donation, which had implications for their own emotional well-being and ability to manage their bereavement process.

Conflict in the donation experience existed for participants in two major forms. On the one hand, conflict unfolded as a series of extraneous events over which they had no control, such as the perceived realization of their relative's death. Other conflicts arose as a result of decisions which needed to be made about donation. These decisions did not take place in a vacuous and impartial environment but in one that was emotionally provocative. Therefore, conflict may have been experienced more poignantly at this time as participants were persuaded, even against their own convictions, to honour the wishes of the deceased. Participants' decisional conflict was increased when they were asked

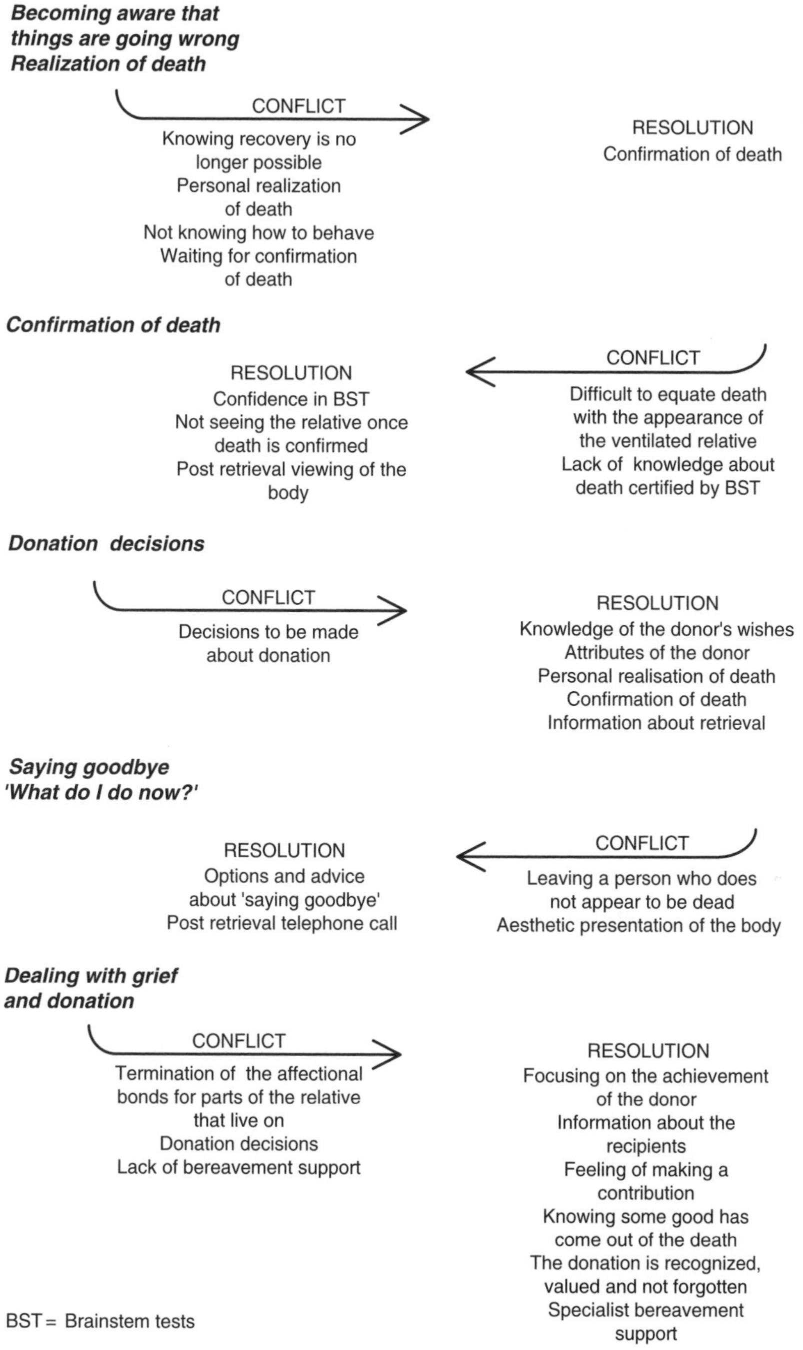

Becoming aware that things are going wrong
Realization of death

CONFLICT

Knowing recovery is no
longer possible
Personal realization
of death
Not knowing how to behave
Waiting for confirmation
of death

RESOLUTION
Confirmation of death

Confirmation of death

RESOLUTION

Confidence in BST
Not seeing the relative once
death is confirmed
Post retrieval viewing of the
body

CONFLICT

Difficult to equate death
with the appearance of
the ventilated relative
Lack of knowledge about
death certified by BST

Donation decisions

CONFLICT

Decisions to be made
about donation

RESOLUTION
Knowledge of the donor's wishes
Attributes of the donor
Personal realisation of death
Confirmation of death
Information about retrieval

Saying goodbye
'What do I do now?'

RESOLUTION

Options and advice
about 'saying goodbye'
Post retrieval telephone call

CONFLICT

Leaving a person who does
not appear to be dead
Aesthetic presentation of the body

Dealing with grief
and donation

CONFLICT

Termination of the affectional
bonds for parts of the relative
that live on
Donation decisions
Lack of bereavement support

RESOLUTION
Focusing on the achievement
of the donor
Information about the
recipients
Feeling of making a
contribution
Knowing some good has
come out of the death
The donation is recognized,
valued and not forgotten
Specialist bereavement
support

BST = Brainstem tests

Figure R2.2   A theory of dissonant loss

to accept a non-traditional definition of death, brainstem death, as death (see Sque and Payne, 1996: 1362–1363). The implications of brainstem death transcend the usual experience of the lay individual, so there are few role models for participants to emulate in their decision-making.

Decision-making to reduce conflict in the context of organ donation fits the criteria of complex decision-making. Among other features, Orasanu and Connolly (1993) suggest that an important characteristic of a complex decision problem is the uncertainty experienced by those involved in the resolution. Some participants were unsure of the wishes of the deceased and even those who possessed explicit knowledge of their wishes were faced with a number of concerns. Some of these were the mutilation of the body and the perceived continued suffering of the relative during organ retrieval. Participants needed to resolve these issues before they gave consent for organ donation. The participants' value system, information sets, relative power, commitment and affective component influenced the outcome.

What were some of the underlying influences that might help us to understand the processes of decision-making by participants? Janis and Mann (1977) point out that, when embarking upon important decisions, individuals become aware of the risk of suffering serious losses from whatever course of action is selected. They will use a number of strategies to cope with this. One of these strategies, 'buck-passing', involves shifting the responsibility for the decision to someone else. Might this be the strategy that donor relatives largely used, by sharing the decision with family members? This seemed likely, as the support they sought would give their decisions legitimacy when they 're-entered' their assumptive world. This may be the reason that these decisions were shared only with close family members. Where participants were aware there might be disapproval from some family members and friends, they kept the donation secret.

The pre-decision situation is generally regarded as one in which the person experiences conflict. The conflict exists because of the simultaneous presence of at least two mutually incompatible tendencies. Janis and Mann's (1977) theory suggests that, to prepare for donation decisions, participants would first gather information about the wishes of the relative and ensure that the preconditions for donation, such as confirmation of brainstem death, had been met. Coupled with this information, they would evaluate the information that they had about retrieval and the possible outcomes. Participants relied on medical and nursing staff for this information.

So how did participants make their decisions? Etzioni (1992) argues that choices are made on the basis of emotional involvements and value commitments. Information-processing is often excluded or is a secondary concern. The main context for making decisions lies in moral commitments, affects and social factors such as norms and habits. The importance of emotions and values and the way they fashion choice shows that information and reasoning have limited roles. Also emotions and values affect the information we are able to absorb, the way it is absorbed and our interpretations. Decision-making is not an individualistic event that takes place in isolation within the individual mind but is motivated by values that are culturally embedded. This stands in direct opposition to humans as rational actors. Indeed, as suggested by Whittaker (1990), it would raise the question whether more participants may have consented to organ retrieval than would do so, were they not in a state of emotional distress. It appears that participants used decision strategies from Janis and Mann's (1977) rationalist perspective but were also influenced by factors suggested by Etzioni (1992).

Discussion of the method

Box R2.5   REFLECTING ON THE METHOD

Having integrated the literature with the findings, we *only* discuss the method in the following section. We believe that grounded theory worked very well for this study and, even with a small sample, we were able to provide a potentially useful framework, which has added to knowledge in this area and provided a guide for clinicians who wish to examine their practice.

This study has offered an explanation of donor relatives' experience through the development of the inductive theory of 'dissonant loss'. A grounded theory approach to analysis allowed us, even with a small sample, to derive a theoretical perspective, which we believe helps to explain donor relatives' experiences. While caution must be exerted in generalizing the results from a small sample, we believe that the emergent theory suggests a number of potentially useful interpretations.

Making the donation experience explicit may contribute to an understanding of the psychosocial issues involved in donation and transplantation. Increased understanding of this process could provide indicators for the appropriate care of other populations of donor relatives and a theoretical foundation for the education of care professionals. The theory provides a plausible basis for continued research with populations we clearly know little about, such as those relatives who refuse donation. The study has provided supportive evidence for other studies concerning donor relatives (e.g., Coupe, 1991; MORI Health Research Unit, 1995; Pelletier, 1992).

One of the main criticisms levelled at qualitative research is that of reproducibility. If this cannot be done, is the work credible? Strauss and Corbin (1990) have made clear that a social phenomenon is not reproducible insofar as being able to match conditions exactly to those of an original study. However, the themes identified in this study are open to support or refutation by other investigators.

Narrative knowledge does place the narrators, researchers and readers in a hermeneutic circle of interpretation, as their own values and interests will affect the meaning of the activity in which they are engaged. Therefore, information about settings, the reflective processes of the researcher and the reciprocal impact of the researcher on the researched does gain a focal importance. The researchers are nurses who are committed to the donation process. This does raise the question about the nature of the information collected and its interpretation. The professional background of the first author (Magi Sque) may have had an impact on the interaction with participants and the development and pursuit of the research agenda. Magi felt that identifying herself as a nurse and researcher was an important element in developing rapport with relatives in this delicate situation. She felt her professional background had prepared her to conduct such interviews with sensitivity and empathy and she was able, as far as it is possible, to gain the co-operation of the participants, who were grateful for the opportunity to express their sorrow and to talk about their deceased relative (for more on this approach, see Coyle and Wright, 1996). As one commented:

I found the interview very helpful to me. Just to talk to somebody who understands was most welcome. In a roundabout way, it was a sort of therapy.

For some participants, the interviewer's opinion about donation was important as they would not have felt comfortable talking with someone who was opposed to donation. Where this information was not requested, Magi maintained an impartial stance as far as possible. While her professional background could have created some inhibition for participants to confide certain experiences to nurses, we do not believe this to be so, as participants were aware that the researchers were not affiliated with any transplant co-ordinating centre or hospital. This does highlight the issue of interview data validation by participants. While the value of this activity remains questionable (Henwood and Pidgeon, 1995), we feel this exercise allowed us to establish that we had a good grasp of the issues, while the interview evaluations kept us informed about the impact of the interview experience on relatives.

Summary

While there are many theories of loss and separation, there has been no theory which explains the experiences of donor families. Our theory suggests areas where help may be focused. The theory of dissonant loss may usefully be applied to other situations of loss that involve conflicts and complex decision-making. Clearly, there is still a lot we do not yet understand or know about the donation process and its psychosocial effects. Dissonant loss theory may provide a framework for further investigation. We also hope that this presentation of our work and our reflections upon the analytic process will give those who are interested in pursuing grounded theory a clear sense of what the end-product of grounded theory research may look like and how such research may be written up.

Note

1   This report is an edited version of an article by the authors, entitled 'Dissonant loss: The experiences of donor relatives', which was published in *Social Science & Medicine*, 43: 1359–1370 (reproduced with permission from Elsevier). The authors wish to thank the participants in the study and Dr Jan Walker for her thoughtful comments on earlier drafts of the article. The research upon which the article was based was supported by a British Department of Health Nursing Studentship.

References

Bartucci, M.R. (1987) 'Organ donation: A study of the donor family perspective', *Journal of Neuroscience Nursing*, 19: 305–309.

Bowlby, J. (1980) *Attachment and Loss 3: Loss, Sadness and Depression*. London: Hogarth Press.

Callahan, J.C. (1987) 'On harming the dead', *Ethics*, 97: 341–352.

Coupe, D. (1991) 'A study of relatives', nurses' and doctors' perceptions of the support and information given to the families of potential organ donors'. Unpublished MPhil thesis, University of Wales College of Medicine, Cardiff.

Coyle, A. and Wright, C. (1996) 'Using the counselling interview to collect research data on sensitive topics', *Journal of Health Psychology*, 1: 431–440.

de Raeve, L. (1994) 'Ethical issues in palliative care research', *Palliative Medicine*, 8: 298–305.

Etzioni, A. (1992) 'Normative-affective factors: Toward a new decision-making model', in M. Zey (ed.), *Decision Making: Alternatives to Rational Choice Models*. Newbury Park, CA: Sage. pp. 89–111.

Feinberg, J. (1985) *The Moral Limits of the Criminal Law: Volume II – Offence to Others*. New York: Oxford University Press.

Henwood, K. and Pidgeon, N. (1995) 'Grounded theory and psychological research', *The Psychologist*, 8: 115–118.

Higgins, E.T. (1987) 'Self-discrepancy: A theory relating self and affect', *Psychological Review*, 94: 319–340.

Janis, I.L. and Mann, L. (1977) *Decision-making: A Psychological Analysis of Conflict, Choice and Commitment*. New York: The Free Press.

La Spina, F., Sedda, L., Pizzi, C., Verlato, R., Boselli, L., Candiani, A., Chiaranda, M., Frova, G., Gorgerino, F., Gravame, V., Mapelli, A., Martini, C., Pappalettera, M., Seveso, M. and Sironi, P.G. (1993) 'Donor families' attitudes toward organ donation', *Transplantation Proceedings*, 25: 1699–1701.

MORI Health Research Unit (1995) *Report of a Two Year Study into Reasons for Relatives' Refusal of Organ Donation*. London: Department of Health.

Orasanu, J. and Connolly, T. (1993) 'The reinvention of decision making', in G.A. Klein, J. Orasanu, R. Calderwood and C.E. Zsambok (eds), *Decision-making in Action: Models and Methods*. Norwood, NJ: Ablex. pp. 3–20.

Parkes, C.M. (1993) 'Bereavement as a psychosocial transition: Processes of adaptation to change', in M.S. Stroebe, W. Stroebe and R.O. Hansson (eds), *Handbook of Bereavement: Theory, Research and Intervention*. Cambridge: Cambridge University Press. pp. 91–101.

Pelletier, M. (1992) 'The organ donor family members' perception of stressful situations during the organ donation experience', *Journal of Advanced Nursing*, 17: 90–97.

Pelletier, M. (1993) 'Emotions experienced and coping strategies used by family members of organ donors', *Canadian Journal of Nursing Research*, 25: 63–73.

Perez-San-Gregorio, M.A., Blanco-Picabia, A., Murillo-Cabezas, F., Dominguez-Roldan, J.M. and Nunez-Roldan, A. (1992) 'Psychological profile of families of severely traumatized patients: Relationship to organ donation for transplantation', *Transplantation Proceedings*, 24: 27–28.

Sque, M. and Payne, S.A. (1996) 'Dissonant loss: The experiences of donor relatives', *Social Science and Medicine*, 43: 1359–1370.

Strauss, A. and Corbin, J. (1990) *Basics of Qualitative Research*. Newbury Park, CA: Sage.

Whittaker, M. (1990) 'Bequeath, bury or burn?', *Nursing Times*, 86: 34–37.

Report 3

COUNSELLING PSYCHOLOGISTS' TALK ABOUT 'PSYCHOPATHOLOGY' AND DIAGNOSTIC CATEGORIES: A REFLECTIVE ACCOUNT OF A DISCOURSE ANALYTIC STUDY

Mark Craven and Adrian Coyle

The purpose of this report is to provide readers with a sense of what the outcome of a discourse analytic study may look like and how it might be presented when writing a journal article or a student dissertation. In the study presented in this report, counselling psychologists were interviewed about their views and understandings of 'psychopathology' and the use of diagnostic categories in counselling psychology practice, as discussion of these concerns has been part of the domain's construction of its professional identity. The analysis presents participants as drawing upon two contrasting repertoires in constructing their positions on these issues, with the same participants drawing upon both repertoires. Throughout the report, text boxes are used at pertinent junctures to highlight important issues in writing up discourse analytic research and analysing data through discourse analysis.

Introduction

Counselling psychology is a relatively new psychological domain in Britain, with the Counselling Psychology Section of the British Psychological Society (BPS) having been established in 1982. While BPS Sections are concerned with specific branches or aspects of psychology, BPS Divisions are concerned with particular professional and practical domains of psychology and focus upon standards of professional education, knowledge and conduct among their members. After a sustained campaign, the Counselling Psychology Section attained Divisional status in 1994.

Throughout this process and subsequently, counselling psychology in Britain has been engaged in a (sometimes explicit) process of constructing its identity as a profession. It has done this in various ways. Over time in its texts, counselling psychology moved towards increasingly fine-grained constructions of difference from and similarity to related professions (particularly clinical psychology) in terms of value systems and standard models of psychological science (Pugh and Coyle, 2000). The professional positioning of counselling psychology has also been attempted through debate on issues relevant to other therapeutic professions such as evidence-based practice (the contention that the delivery of therapeutic interventions should be informed by 'evidence' of their 'effectiveness') (Milton, 2003), the use of psychometric instruments to assess and measure psychological 'problems' (Kanellakis, 2004) and the use of diagnostic categories of 'psychopathology' to 'describe' clients' difficulties (Strawbridge and James, 2001). In many of these debates, attempts have been made to construct a position on these issues, which is distinctive to counselling psychology, at least in the basis of the position, if not in its nature.

In the debate on 'psychopathology' and the use of diagnostic categories, the basic tension or dilemma is said to relate to whether counselling psychology ought to embody a stance that reflects a humanistic value base – emphasizing clients' understandings and processes rather than trying to use therapeutic 'expertise' to classify clients' 'disorders' – or should embrace the symptom- and diagnosis-focused approach epitomized by the American Psychiatric Association's (2000) *Diagnostic and Statistical Manual of Mental Disorders* (DSM). This latter approach has been constructed as a 'medical model' of mental distress and as embodying the fundamental assumptions of positivist-empiricist science (see Chapter 2 in this volume), such as the idea that distress can be legitimately and accurately categorized (Boyle, 1999). This stance has dominated scientific and psychotherapeutic world views with regard to 'psychopathology', although it has been subjected to sustained critique (e.g., see Fee, 2000; Parker et al., 1995).

In order to obtain insight into how counselling psychologists may make sense of this issue, the study presented in this report examined how counselling psychologists talked about 'psychopathology' and the value/use of diagnostic categories within their clinical practice, with the aim of identifying how these 'objects' are constructed and the discursive resources that are employed in their construction.

Box R3.1   PITFALLS IN WRITING LITERATURE REVIEWS FOR SOCIAL CONSTRUCTIONIST STUDIES

The introduction to this report may seem very brief, which is not only due to the word limit imposed on the report. We did not want to discuss counselling psychology, 'psychopathology' and diagnostic categories in more detailed terms because we would then be deemed to have overly engaged in the process of construction that we wanted to explore in the study. Of course, it is impossible to avoid this entirely. Can you see how, even in this brief introduction, we have constructed 'counselling psychology', 'psychopathology' and 'diagnostic categories' in particular ways?

(Continued)

Our short introduction has also largely helped us avoid some of the pitfalls associated with writing a literature review for a social constructionist study. In composing such a review, you need to adopt a social constructionist stance, even though you may be reviewing writing and research that comes from a very different epistemological position. This can be difficult but it can be helpful to present viewpoints in the literature as constructions of your research foci and to consider research not as revealing 'truth' about your research topic but as positing and legitimating a particular version of events.

Method

Eight chartered counselling psychologists (six women and two men) were recruited through personal contacts and by 'snowballing' from an initial sample (that is, having participants nominate others who might wish to take part). Four had qualified within the previous five years and four had attained 'chartered counselling psychologist' status on the basis of their professional experience (this latter possibility was available for a limited time when 'chartered psychologist' status first became available). Participants had a range of clinical experience in private, primary, secondary and tertiary health care contexts and in private settings.

Box R3.2   SITUATING THE SAMPLE IN DISCOURSE ANALYTIC REPORTS

It has been recommended that qualitative researchers should situate their samples – that is, they should 'describe the research participants and their life circumstances to aid the reader in judging the range of people and situations to which the findings may be relevant' (Elliott et al., 1999: 228). Some qualitative research reports do this in great detail. Discourse analytic work also needs to situate samples but researchers (and readers) should remember that, no matter how much detail is provided, these 'descriptions' can never capture all the potential positions from which participants may speak in the data. For example, it would be a mistake to assume that, just because all the participants in our study were counselling psychologists, they spoke consistently from that position throughout their interviews. As was noted in Chapter 7, any individual may assume some positions fairly consistently within their talk while other positions are more temporary. Hence, participants could have spoken from a wide range of possible positions across their interviews – for example, positions as counselling psychologists, psychologists, therapists, men, women, radicals or good employees. Nevertheless, samples in discourse analytic reports

(Continued)

(Continued)
should be situated with sufficient specificity to allow readers to assess the contexts to which the analyses most readily apply and to identify which people and contexts might usefully be studied in future research.

Data were collected through individual interviews. A relatively open interview schedule was developed which asked participants about their personal and professional views or understandings of 'psychopathology' and the use of diagnostic categories for mental distress within counselling psychology practice. Interviews were carried out by Mark Craven in participants' places of work, their homes or in a university setting. Interviews were audiotaped and transcribed using a basic version of the notation scheme developed by Atkinson and Heritage (1984).[1]

Box R3.3 DATA COLLECTION STRATEGIES IN DISCOURSE ANALYTIC STUDIES

During its short history within psychology, discourse analytic research has moved away from gathering data through interviews and towards naturally occurring data, such as media materials and recordings of 'unstaged' social interactions. Where interviews are used, these tend to be focus group interviews rather than individual interviews, which carry a greater risk of the participants orienting consistently to the artificial interview context. It can be argued that data from individual interviews are so specific to the research context that they may be of limited value. Focus group interviews carry the same risk but perhaps to a lesser extent as it may be possible – with care and skill on the part of the interviewers – to foster a relatively free-flowing discussion. Given that we sought to gather data from very busy professionals in the present study, it would have been difficult to have organized them into one or more focus groups. For practical reasons, we therefore opted for individual interviews. While we were aware of the limitations this would impose on our analytic outcomes, we felt that it was preferable to have limited data on this important topic for counselling psychology rather than no data at all.

Transcripts were subjected to a relatively micro-level form of discourse analysis, looking at the rhetorical functions and action orientation of the data, but with attention also being paid to the discursive resources through which these discursive practices were produced (Potter and Wetherell, 1987; Wetherell, 1998; Willig, 2001). In a preliminary coding process, interviews were read line by line at least twice to identify portions of text that were relevant to the research question and appeared analytically interesting. The analytic process then involved further reading and rereading of data extracts, attending to the questions, 'Why is this particular utterance here?', 'What might this particular utterance be doing?' and 'What discourses are being invoked in this utterance?'

The analysis that we have produced reflects not only the data but also our theoretical commitments and interests as a critical counselling psychologist (Mark Craven) and social psychologist (Adrian Coyle) (and doubtlessly other factors which we cannot name). We do not claim to have uncovered 'truth' about counselling psychologists' views, merely to have illuminated some local and contingent 'truths' on the research issues. However, our analyses are accompanied by quotations which demonstrate the basis of the interpretations in data, so readers can assess their persuasiveness and offer alternative readings. Note that, in the analyses, quotations from participants are either in a distinctive font or within double quotation marks; single quotation marks are used to signify constructed ideas that are important to the research questions.

Analysis

Two opposing accounts/constructions predominated in participants' talk about 'psychopathology' and diagnostic categories. We have identified these as the 'empiricist' and 'contingent' repertoires. We shall now present what we found to be the salient features of these repertoires before examining the interplay of these repertoires in one data excerpt.

'Empiricist' repertoire

What we refer to as the 'empiricist' repertoire concerned modernist notions and assumptions regarding such basic issues as 'reality', 'knowledge', 'science', psychological 'disorders' and their 'cure', together with the principles of modern science implicit in contemporary psychology. This perspective is often referred to synonymously as 'positivism', 'naïve realism' or the 'received view' (depending upon the speaker's position) and provides the ground in which the empiricist repertoire is rooted. Throughout the interviews, participants explicitly and implicitly made use of an empiricist discourse as they described, explained and made attributions about the 'objects' towards which they were orienting. This appeared to serve many functions, the most salient of which was to construct a version of events wherein 'psychopathology' was granted ontological status as a 'thing' that 'exists' independently in the world. This particular construction appeared intimately bound up with legitimating the use of diagnostic categories. The operation of the empiricist repertoire can be seen in the following brief extracts:

> I suppose you're looking for things that would (4) yeah (.) I haven't thought about this like this before but er (.) but that would (.) differentiate them from how anybody might react in a particular situation for instance or if they have (1) if they're thinking in ways that wouldn't be within what you'd think to be the normal range.
>
> (Diana)

She's a paranoid–schizophrenic (1.5) with CLEAR <u>EVIDENCE</u> of that (.) auditory and
visual hallucinations (.) many-many symptoms (1)

(Nathan)

The 'out-there-ness' of 'psychopathology' is achieved here by using the
metaphor of scientific discovery and visual, observational and legal terms, such
as "looking for things" and "CLEAR <u>EVIDENCE</u>". Crucially, the use of this
metaphor constructs the discoverer (the psychologist) as merely revealing something that had been there all along: 'psychopathology' exists in an objective sense
so it can be discovered. In these extracts, the 'facts' of psychopathology come in
the form of "evidence" which is constituted by the identification of "symptoms".

The sense of 'objectivity' is made intelligible through recourse to an empiricist discourse which operates in dualistic terms by creating a clear separation
between the subject and object or between the knower and the known. This
duality is evident in the extract from Nathan's interview, where he says of a
client, "She's a paranoid–schizophrenic", invoking a diagnostic category and
then further legitimating this ascription through professional vocabulary in his
reference to "auditory and visual hallucinations". Likewise, in her interview,
Diana referred to, "if they're thinking in ways that wouldn't be within what
you'd think to be the normal range". Such talk positions the speaker (the psychologist) (and also the listener/interviewer) as the 'knower' – an 'expert' who
holds a privileged position in relation to the experiences of the client so,
through their professional logic, they can legitimately define a client's thinking as abnormal and categorize them as pathological.

The features of the empiricist repertoire identified in these brief extracts were
common across the interviews, such as when Annabel said of the psychologist,
"you're the one with (.) the experience and knowledge (.) the <u>expertise</u> (.) you
know (.) to make offers of treatment", when Janine referred to "someone
presenting with a clear panic disorder" and when Kate said of 'anorexia', "you
can <u>see</u> it (.) no doubt about it".

'Contingent' repertoire

Though the empiricist repertoire appeared to be central to participants' accounts,
they also drew upon what we have termed a 'contingent' repertoire. Whereas the
empiricist repertoire provided a means of talking about 'psychopathology' and
diagnostic categories at a more impersonal, theoretical and 'objective' level, the
contingent repertoire constructed the use of diagnostic categories as a less than
straightforward endeavour, which was influenced by a number of factors – for
example, "client understanding and desired outcome" (Diana), "personality factors" (Nick), "individual experiences" (Charlotte), "training" (Sue), "therapeutic
orientation" (Janine) and "philosophical viewpoint" (Nathan). For example,
speaking about diagnostic criteria and categories, Nick said:

I think it depends (.) you know some criteria or some labels are quite useful some really
aren't [ ] so I guess I take it with a pinch of salt really (.) so at the end of the day it's

what it means to the client (.) it's what concerns the clients (.) erm (.) what they're
expressing or able to express which I find most important rather (.) that I go on (.) rather
than whatever diagnosis they've received.

Here Nick positions himself as somewhat ambivalent about the possibility of achieving any fixed or 'objective' truths regarding 'psychopathology' and the utility of diagnostic categories. This redirects the focus of his account towards his actual concerned involvement and interaction with clients ("it's what it means to the client (.) it's what concerns the clients") and helps to work up and legitimate a contrasting account where the diagnostic venture and the utility of diagnostic categories only make sense in relation to their context of usage. As such, 'understanding' can be interpreted as being discursively linked to action and conduct.

Dilemmatic dances

Box R3.4 HOW MUCH DATA TO PRESENT IN DISCOURSE ANALYTIC REPORTS?

Discourse analysts vary in the amount of data they present in their research reports. Some offer many brief extracts of data; some present a few relatively lengthy data extracts; and some present a combination. Thus far, we have presented analyses that are based on relatively short data excerpts in order to establish the positions that will be examined in their interplay in this section. We are aware that this could be seen as problematic. The data have been presented in a decontextualized form, so the reader cannot see what questions elicited the data and cannot ascertain the role played by the interviewer in shaping the data. While we would have liked to have provided more data, including the interviewer's interventions, the word limit that we faced in writing this report made this impractical. Discourse analytic researchers routinely face this problem when writing up their work for publication and need to balance the requirement to ground interpretations in textual evidence with the desire to cover adequate interpretative ground. We felt that we could tolerate presenting limited data in the previous sections as we present a more extended data extract in this section. However, again compromises have had to be made because ideally we would have wanted to present more than one detailed extract to avoid creating the impression that our analyses lack a wide or empirical basis. Note how we try to manage this by presenting snippets of data at the start which we hope serve to deflect that impression reading when our analyses.

Rather than participants having access to or only using an empiricist or contingent repertoire, both repertoires often occurred within accounts from the same participants, with the contingent repertoire acting in contrast to the empiricist one. The opposing nature of these repertoires was often explicitly constructed as problematic for participants or as locating them within a dilemmatic position. For example, participants said of these opposing repertoires, "there are radically opposing philosophical views" (Sue), "that's where the problems start" (Charlotte), "so you're automatically in a funny position" (Diana) and "it was a huge dilemma" (Janine). Here we focus specifically on the dilemmatic nature of participants' accounts as they orient to the issues of 'psychopathology', diagnostic categories and their therapeutic practice. There were several pervasive themes across the texts relating to the dilemmatic aspects of ideology associated with these repertoires (Billig et al., 1988). Here we focus upon the tension between authority and equality.

In the following extract, as Charlotte orients to the use of diagnostic categories, we find ambivalences between authoritarian expertise on the one hand and democratic egalitarianism on the other as she manages her identity as a counselling psychologist:

368	**Charlotte:** I mean not in the sense that I think that diagnostic categories are absolutely
369	necessary and that's what we should use and that's how (.) we should think (.) you know
370	(.) how we should formulate client problems or whatever but (.) in terms of the necessity
371	of (1.5) erm not necessarily the necessity but (.) yeah in terms of the necessity me to
372	have an understanding of the DSM (.) and be able to use it (.) and be able to you know
373	speak this language (2) but this doesn't necessarily (.) affect me (.) my practice when I
374	am with a client on a one-to-one basis
375	**Int.** Right
376	**Charlotte:** I wouldn't you know call anybody borderline [personality disordered] or
377	something or I wouldn't you know do you see what I mean?
378	**Int.** Yeah I'm trying to sort of (.) it seems as though there are different levels to
379	it in a way you're saying that it's different in your clinical work [ ] so I was just
380	wondering can you maybe expand on what those differences are of possibly how come
381	that it's like that?
382	**Charlotte:** Well erm say for example I have this client who has been diagnosed as
383	borderline personality and she has a severe personality problem erm the way I would
384	speak with other professionals is going to be different than when I'm with her you know
385	(.) I'm not going to perhaps say to her (.) "You have borderline" or "Given your
386	borderline personality disorder this is what is best for you" I would probably say
387	something to her like
388	**Int.** [Mmm]
389	**Charlotte:** '(.) "You know we're here together to think together what your needs are (.)
390	and you know how can we best (.) erm help you" '
391	**Int.** Right (1) so okay so the right okay yeah
392	**Charlotte:** and er perhaps I might have in mind what might be helpful or best for her but
393	I won't necessarily (.) I will not say to her "Well I think because you are borderline I
394	think you should be referred to [named hospital]" or something
395	**Int.** Yeah yeah okay
396	**Charlotte:** but I will try to work with her (.) to see what she wants and to see what's best

The extract begins with Charlotte distancing herself from the view of diagnostic categories that is embedded within the empiricist repertoire, in which the psychologist is positioned as an 'expert' who has the power scientifically and objectively to identify, categorize and treat 'psychopathology'. Her narrative functions at an implicit level to challenge the correctness of the standard view that diagnostic categories provide the appropriate or only means of understanding 'psychopathology' and of formulating treatment. Initially this challenge is personalized as Charlotte uses first person pronouns which position her in opposition to this standard view, albeit in a qualified way, as in lines 368–369 ("I mean not in the sense that I think that diagnostic categories are absolutely necessary"): it is the *absolute* necessity of diagnostic categories that is questioned. What immediately follows in lines 369–370 makes the inference available that what is advocated by the view she is opposing is that diagnostic categories should be used as the basis for understanding client problems ("and that's what we should use and that's how (.) we should think (.) you know (.) how we should formulate client problems or whatever"). Note that she does not present her opposition to the standard viewpoint in explicit terms, perhaps to manage her institutional accountability as a counselling psychologist. The use of "we" in lines 368–370 possibly functions to further manage the accountability of the speaker's views by providing a line of insulation against rebuttals or the criticism that solely personal interests motivate her account. Of course, it is always possible that her lack of explicit opposition could demonstrate a sensitivity to her audience – in this case a counselling psychologist interviewer whose views on diagnostic categories were not known to her at the time of the interview.

As the account develops, Charlotte shows some hesitation and ambivalence before positioning herself as being held to account institutionally. In the midst of pauses, linguistic stumbles and what conversation analysts call 'repair' (Nofsinger, 1991) in lines 370–373, she constructs herself as having no real choice in using diagnostic categories ("in terms of the necessity of (1.5) erm not necessarily the necessity but (.) yeah in terms of the necessity me to have an understanding of the DSM (.) and be able to use it (.) and be able to you know speak this language (2)"). She positions herself at the professional and institutional level as being required or obligated to work within a particular professional framework of understanding and associated vocabulary. Though this is presented as a concrete reality, she nonetheless partially resists this forced positioning by constructing her own therapeutic practice with clients as not necessarily being affected (lines 373–374). This could be seen as a response to the dilemmatic position of the counselling psychologist as someone whose professional discourse in counselling psychology foregrounds the therapeutic relationship but who works within a mental health context where the empiricist discourse and the apparatus of diagnosis are generally accepted. However, in spite of this, the speaker constructs herself as having some choice and agency within this dominant empiricist discourse. In lines 383–384, reflecting on how she might talk about and to a client diagnosed with borderline personality disorder, she constructs a contrast between her talk with other experts (professionals) and with non-experts (clients). This allows her to position herself as an agent who selectively uses the technical vocabulary and diagnostic language grounded in the expertise of professional authority (the empiricist repertoire) depending on its context of usage (the contingent repertoire). Talking about therapeutic practice provides Charlotte with a context for rejecting an authoritative expert position in favour of a more egalitarian one. She employs two resources in particular to construct a position of equality. First, in

---

Box R3.5   MAKING USE OF POSITIONS THAT ARE NOT EXPLICITLY INVOKED IN THE DATA

In the analysis above, we suggest that Charlotte may find herself in a dilemmatic position because of her position as a counselling psychologist operating within a context where the empiricist discourse dominates. However, Charlotte does not explicitly position herself as a counselling psychologist in the data extract. This raises the question of whether it is permissible, when formulating interpretations, to invoke positions and other material that are not (explicitly) mentioned in the data. Discourse analysts differ on the extent to which they consider this to be permissible, with some contending that interpretations of positioning must be explicitly reflected in the data presented while others favour greater leeway for interpretation. Of course, if a speaker has positioned him/herself in a particular way elsewhere in the data set and that positioning is alluded to in the extract under analysis, it is perfectly acceptable to invoke that positioning (provided the analyst can convince the reader of the allusion). What can be more problematic is when analysts assume that a speaker is speaking from a position that is assumed to be salient but where, even with some interpretation, the analyst does not present a convincing case for the relevance of that positioning. For example, as we noted in Box R3.2, it would be a mistake to assume that, just because all the participants in our study were counselling psychologists, they spoke consistently from that position throughout their interviews. We feel justified in invoking Charlotte's position as a counselling psychologist here because (a) she positions herself explicitly in this way elsewhere in the interview and (b) the way in which she distances herself from the empiricist repertoire and constructs her approach to a hypothetical client in the data extract in many respects echoes literature on the defining characteristics of counselling psychology (e.g., see Strawbridge and Woolfe, 2003).

---

lines 385–386 ("I'm not going to perhaps say to her (.) 'You have borderline' or 'Given your borderline personality disorder this is what is best for you' "), she presents hypothetical reported speech that is implied as how an expert authority would respond to a client with borderline personality disorder. This enables her to work up the difference between this approach and her own. Second, there is a notable use of democratic semantics in the form of "we" statements in lines 389–390 ("we're here together to think together what your needs are (.) and you know how can we best (.) erm help you"). The discursive form is one of polite invitation rather than imperious command. The ethos is one that expresses democratic aspirations and utilizes the language of free and equal exchange. This works to construct the therapeutic encounter where Charlotte is the therapist as a joint venture wherein 'we' (Charlotte and the client) discover and create meaning together rather than 'I' (the expert) telling 'you' (the client) the 'facts' of your case. This construction allows Charlotte to resist the authority of her expert position and to reposition herself in a softer, more egalitarian way. However, this position seems to be charged with ambivalence because the right to speak authoritatively has not been abandoned. Albeit in a tentative way, Charlotte still holds the therapeutic 'maps' (as in line 392 – "perhaps I might have in mind what might be helpful or best for her"). The ambivalence may be seen most clearly in line 396 ("I will try to work with her (.) to see what she wants and to see what's best") where the line begins with a statement of co-operative intent before switching to prioritize the desires of the client ("to see what she wants") and ending with a phrase that leaves it unclear who has the ultimate right to determine "what's best" in this interaction. This pattern of discourse has been described as 'unequal egalitarianism' or 'non-authoritarian authoritarianism' (Wetherell et al., 1987).

Conclusion

Given the relatively small sample in the present study, we cannot claim with confidence to have discerned all the major discursive resources that counselling psychologists employ to make sense of 'psychopathology' and the use of diagnostic categories in counselling psychology practice. Yet, although the sample was diverse, it is notable that the empiricist and contingent repertoires (and their intricate and dilemmatic interaction) were readily identifiable across the interview data. It may be the case that these are standard sense-making repertoires for counselling psychologists in relation to their contextualized professional practice. Indeed, these repertoires appear to be standard resources for other mental health professions too, as was found by Harper (1994) in his study of how psychiatrists and lecturers in clinical psychology talked about 'paranoia'. Other researchers may wish to explore the relevance of these repertoires with different samples of counselling psychologists on these and other professional issues.

In relation to counselling psychology, the present study indicates that there may be a gap between the 'ideal' and the 'real' in terms of 'psychopathology' and the use of diagnostic categories – that is, between theory and reports of situated practice. The principles and values expressed in counselling psychology theory – such as a humanistic value base, a reaction against a medical model of professional-client relationships and an emphasis on well-being rather than pathology (Strawbridge and Woolfe, 2003) – stand in opposition to the prevalent reported discourses that shape the applied contexts in which counselling psychologists often work. Given that current practices are culturally sanctioned and increasingly reinforced by an ideological framework of professionalization, this creates ongoing dilemmas for individual practitioners at a local level (as was discerned in the data) and more general dilemmas for the status, identity and development of counselling psychology as a discipline. If counselling psychology is to be a cultural enterprise that reflexively questions its relevance to society and its role in maintaining and/or challenging existing social structures and practices, then it may be worthwhile for counselling psychologists to take a critical and deconstructive posture towards their theories and practices – especially in relation to fundamental issues such as 'psychopathology' that can hold serious implications for those to whom relevant discourses are applied.

Summary

This report has provided an illustration of how a discourse analytic study might be presented. However, it should be remembered that there are different forms of discourse analysis with different emphases, which may require alternative presentational formats. We hope that our study, together with the other chapters on discourse analysis, will persuade readers of this value of this research approach and inspire them to venture into discourse analytic research themselves.

References

American Psychiatric Association (2000) *Diagnostic and Statistical Manual of Mental Disorders* (4th edition – text revision). Washington, DC: American Psychiatric Association.

Atkinson, J. and Heritage, J. (eds) (1984) *Structures of Social Action: Studies in Conversation Analysis*. Cambridge: Cambridge University Press.

Billig, M., Condor, S., Edwards, D., Gane, M., Middleton, D. and Radley, A.R. (1988) *Ideological Dilemmas: A Social Psychology of Everyday Thinking*. London: Sage.

Boyle, M. (1999) 'Diagnosis', in C. Newnes, G. Holmes and C. Dunn (eds), *This is Madness*. Ross-on-Wye: PCCS Books. pp. 75–90.

Elliott, R., Fischer, C.T. and Rennie, D.L. (1999) 'Evolving guidelines for publication of qualitative research studies in psychology and related fields', *British Journal of Clinical Psychology*, 38: 215–229.

Fee, D. (2000) *Pathology and the Postmodern: Mental Illness as Discourse and Experience*. London: Sage.

Harper, D.J. (1994) 'The professional construction of "paranoia" and the discursive use of diagnostic criteria', *British Journal of Medical Psychology*, 67: 131–143.

Kanellakis, P. (ed.) (2004) 'Counselling psychology and psychological testing', *Counselling Psychology Review*, 19(4): 4–44.

Milton, M. (ed.) (2003) 'Evidence-based practice', *Counselling Psychology Review*, 18(3): 3–35.

Nofsinger, R.E. (1991) *Everyday Conversation*. Thousand Oaks, CA: Sage.

Parker, I., Georgaca, E., Harper, D., McLaughlin, T. and Stowell-Smith, M. (1995) *Deconstructing Psychopathology*. London: Sage.

Potter, J. and Wetherell, M. (1987) *Discourse and Social Psychology: Beyond Attitudes and Behaviour*. London: Sage.

Pugh, D. and Coyle, A. (2000) 'The construction of counselling psychology in Britain: A discourse analysis of counselling psychology texts', *Counselling Psychology Quarterly*, 13: 85–98.

Strawbridge, S. and James, P. (2001) 'Issues relating to the use of psychiatric diagnostic categories in counselling psychology, counselling and psychotherapy: What do you think?', *Counselling Psychology Review*, 16(1): 4–6.

Strawbridge, S. and Woolfe, R. (2003) 'Counselling psychology in context', in R. Woolfe, W. Dryden and S. Strawbridge (eds), *Handbook of Counselling Psychology* (2nd edition). London: Sage. pp. 3–21.

Wetherell, M. (1998) 'Positioning and interpretative repertoires: Conversation analysis and post-structuralism in dialogue', *Discourse & Society*, 9: 387–412.

Wetherell, M., Striven, H. and Potter, J. (1987) 'Unequal egalitarianism: A preliminary study of discourses concerning gender and employment opportunities', *British Journal of Social Psychology*, 26: 59–71.

Willig, C. (2001) *Introducing Qualitative Research in Psychology: Adventures in Theory and Method*. Buckingham: Open University Press.

Note

1   Although this transcription notation is not used in Chapters 7 and 8, it is a standard notation in discourse analytic work. Readers may find it helpful to know what is denoted by some of the features that appear in the data extracts. Numbers in brackets indicate pauses timed in seconds. A full stop in brackets indicates a pause which is noticeable but too short to measure. Underlining indicates that words are uttered with added emphasis. Words in upper case letters are uttered loudly than the surrounding talk. Round brackets indicate that material in the brackets is either inaudible or there is a doubt about its accuracy. Square brackets indicate that some transcript has been deliberately omitted. Material in square brackets is clarificatory information.

Report 4

ADAPTING TO LIFE WITH ORAL CANCER: A REFLECTIVE ACCOUNT OF A NARRATIVE ANALYTIC STUDY

Michele Crossley

This report illustrates narrative analysis by presenting a summary of a detailed case study of the experience of a patient living with oral cancer and the way in which this experience is linked to the tacit cultural process of 'therapeutic emplotment'. This refers to the process by which people facing illness make sense of the story of their illness and determine what is really going on and what is likely to happen as the story progresses. On the basis of the analysis, questions are raised concerning the interpretative process which are relevant not only to narrative analysis but also to other forms of qualitative analysis that have some sort of phenomenological commitment.

Introduction

'Somebody said the other day that it must be like being on death row, being me. The comparison is closer than they can know. The sentence has been delivered, and every so often a call comes through from the state governor's office postponing the date of execution, but never in such terms that I'm allowed to believe that one day the sentence itself might be commuted to something less irreversible.'(Diamond 2001: 244)

This report is based on a more detailed empirical study which used narrative analysis to explore the experiences of one man living, coping and eventually dying from oral cancer (Crossley, 2003). It originally emerged from my work with Canadian colleagues on a feasibility project assessing the possibility of providing psychological interventions to improve the quality of life (and potential survival rates) of patients diagnosed with oral cancer. In the course of this work, it became clear that there was a paucity of research investigating oral cancer from the patient's point of view. A comprehensive literature review failed to find any studies which provided in-depth information about the emotional and psychological issues faced by patients living with oral cancer.

Previous research has shown that although living with serious illnesses can have potentially devastating psychological effects, one of the primary challenges facing people is to reascribe a sense of meaning to their lives. Numerous studies investigating the way in which people cope with chronic and terminal illnesses such as cancer and HIV infection, have emphasized the central importance of stories and processes of 'narrative reconfiguration' in adapting to the massive shock and insecurity that such illnesses impose on people's lives (see Crossley, 2000a). Research has shown that suffering is produced and alleviated primarily by the meaning people attach to their experiences. As one of the primary mechanisms for attaching meaning to experiences is through narrative and story telling, such activities assume a central role in adapting to serious illnesses.

In *Reading for the Plot*, Brooks (1984: xi) conceptualizes narrative as 'one of the large categories or systems of understanding that we use in our negotiations with reality, specifically . . . with the problem of temporality . . . with time-boundedness and with the consciousness of existence within the limits of mortality'. Brooks wrote of an active process of 'emplotment' by which people imaginatively engage in the process of making sense of a story and determine what is really going on and likely to happen as the action of the story progresses. Applying this concept to people making sense of illness, Del Vecchio Good et al. (1994: 885) proposed that such a process of emplotment constitutes a 'crucial imaginative response of those who face the sudden threat of an illness'. Using a concept of 'therapeutic emplotment', they argue that the emplotment of illness constitutes a major task between clinicians and patients in the treatment of cancer (for more on these narrative concepts, see Chapter 9).

It was in the process of looking around for in-depth studies of oral cancer patients' experiences that the published work of the journalist, columnist and broadcaster, John Diamond, came to my attention. Diamond first published his autobiographical account depicting his experience of oral cancer in 1998 in *C: Because Cowards Get Cancer Too*. Alongside this book, he also wrote a serialized diary column in *The Times* which began with his suspected diagnosis in September 1996 and continued until the week before his death in March 2001. This 'diary' constitutes a serialized exploration of the impact of the cancer on his life. The complete serialization was later posthumously published in the form of a book entitled *Snake Oil and Other Preoccupations* (Diamond, 2001). The material on which this report focuses is based on the serialized diary entries presented in this autobiographical document.

Reading Diamond's diary entries over the course of a four year period, I was struck by the way in which they provided an illustrative case study of the 'therapeutic emplotment' Del Vecchio Good et al. (1994) characterized as so central to the treatment of cancer. However, in their work, Del Vecchio Good et al. explored such 'therapeutic emplotment' from the perspective of oncologists, looking at how they attempted to formulate experiences for patients by structuring time and horizons in a way which instilled hope, encouraged investment in arduous and toxic treatments and avoided a sense of despair.

By contrast, Diamond's diaries are unique insofar as they provide essential insight into what it is like to have to live as a cancer patient. One of the main aims of a narrative psychology approach is to explore the social construction of experience and the way in which implicit cultural narratives are used to make sense of (traumatizing) events. Simultaneously, this approach attempts to keep hold of the experiential reality that the patient is undergoing. Accordingly, this report presents a summary of a detailed case study of the experience of a patient living with oral cancer and the way in which this experience is centrally linked to the tacit cultural process of 'therapeutic emplotment'.

Method

This case study uses the theoretical concept of 'therapeutic emplotment' to make further sense of John Diamond's experience. This concept refers to the way in which illness is oriented to in a manner which incorporates a particular temporal structure, with specific implications for the treatment of cancer patients. Diamond's diaries are used to elucidate this theoretical concept by depicting them as illustrative of some of the dominant themes characteristic of 'therapeutic emplotment'. This is achieved by a creative and imaginative engagement with the theoretical literature, which results in an application to the written material (see Box R4.1).

In an empirical paper reporting on a study that used narrative analysis, the Method section would address standard methodological issues, including a detailed account of how the analysis was conducted. As the details of narrative analysis have been presented in Chapters 9 and 10, here I have chosen to devote space to reporting findings rather than repeating material from those chapters.

Box R4.1   REFLECTIONS ON THE RELATIONSHIP BETWEEN THEORY AND EMPIRICAL DATA

Within narrative psychology, it is an entirely open question as to whether the researcher first engages with the theoretical literature before applying this to empirical data or, instead, first analyses the empirical data and only then proceeds to the theoretical literature in order to make further sense of the analysis. In most cases, the process of engaging with theoretical and empirical data will be reciprocal and interactive.

Analysis: The patient's 'timetable'

The detailed case study on which this chapter is based divides Diamond's diary into six main stages. In doing so, it depicts the dominant themes and underlying temporal structure characterizing Diamond's attempts to adapt to the reality of oral cancer. These six stages include the following:

1 Pre-cancer: 'touch wood'
2 Learning to live in 'therapeutic emplotment'
3 In limbo: 'holding one's breath'
4 Recurrence: 'therapeutic emplotment' continued
5 Through the mirror: the 'unspoken narrative'
6 Endings or the end?

The details of each of these will be briefly outlined.

(1) Pre-cancer: 'Touch wood'

On 14 September 1996, John Diamond ambushed his own whimsical and humorous weekly column in *The Times* with a contribution entitled 'I thought I had cancer'. The very title of the column, however, serves to create a distance between Diamond and the reality of cancer. Using the past tense, 'I *thought* I had' (my emphasis) immediately signals to the reader that Diamond believed something that turned out to be incorrect. Although dealing with a serious subject matter, Diamond's distance is maintained as, in characteristically parodic style, he intellectually 'plays' with what it is like to *imagine* oneself as someone who has just been diagnosed with cancer. 'It's easy for me to say', he tells us, 'but there is a certain sort of liberation in learning that *one might* have cancer' (p. 159, my emphasis). Playing the same kinds of superstitious tricks we all play, it is almost as if saying the words out loud, writing the words down, will make them *not* be true. Six months later, however, Diamond's consultant informs him that he has had cancer all along.

(2) Learning to live in 'therapeutic emplotment'

Over the next six months, between April and September 1997, Diamond's column takes on a very different tone – one which is dominated by the repetitive and seemingly endless description of various treatments and their side effects. At times, Diamond's fears about his future slip through but, for the most part, he does not allow himself to look beyond the horizon of the specific treatment and focuses his sights on the hoped for outcome – recovery. To a large part, intellectual rumination and distancing disappears as Diamond enters the new world of 'therapeutic emplotment', placing his faith in the radiotherapy which is going to 'do its stuff' and return him to normality.

(3) In limbo: 'Holding one's breath'

Six months on, on 22 November 1997, Diamond reports that his surgery and radiotherapy have now finished but he now has a new barrier to overcome – or at least to learn to live with. Just before his treatment, in April 1997, Diamond was caught up in 'therapeutic emplotment' which encouraged him to live in the 'immediacy of treatment' and to believe that after 'six weeks of daily radiotherapy, the loss of half my salivary system . . . and a temporary hiatus in my broadcasting career' (p. 178), some kind of certainty might be reached – hopefully, the cancer would be treated. But now, he realizes, 'the truth is . . . I still don't know whether I'm cured. Nor will I know for weeks, or months, or possibly years' (p. 206). Here we see Diamond struggling with the reality of cancer, which, as other autobiographical accounts report, is its assault on the very 'fabric of hope' (see Crossley, 2000b, Chapter 5). Over the next 10 months, there are very few references in Diamond's diary column to cancer. It is almost as if he is holding his breath, waiting, in limbo, too scared even to mention it.

(4) Recurrence: 'Therapeutic emplotment' continued

12 September 1998 – ten months on from the 'end' of treatment. 'It turns out the cancer is back. Or, more likely, has been here all the time' (p. 227). This time, Diamond gets straight down to 'business'. What more is there to say? 'So, here's what happens', he reports:

'Last time they cut away about a third of my tongue and pulled the two cut ends together. This time most of the other two thirds goes. They replace it with a lump of skin-covered muscle taken from my back which will form some sort of mass in my mouth against which I can bounce words' (p. 228).

(5) Through the mirror: The 'unspoken narrative'

On 3 October 1998, after his transplant surgery, Diamond's hope and, as he parodies himself, his 'almost childish belief in the power of modern medicine' (p. 229) is gradually eroding. 'Last time I was here', he tells us, 'I know I said there was a chance that the operation would actually improve my voice, but that turned out to be as probable as Shergar coming back to win the next Grand National' (p. 229). 'There is some part of me', he continues, 'which feels I've fallen foul of some medical con trick' (p. 230). It is not his tongue or other 'glottal accoutrements' which the surgeons have spent time and skill 'whipping away' but rather 'the creeping and unseen inevitability of it all, the swiftness with which black turned to white and I was through the mirror into a new world' (p. 230).

(6) Endings or the end?

'There are times', Diamond wrote on 10 February 2001, 'when I feel I'm covering a long and particularly futile war' (p. 280). The first time he mentioned his cancer, almost four years previously, it was, as far as he was concerned, 'big news'. But now:

'the novelty has worn off and the story has become: cancer comes, surgery, cancer goes, nothing happens, cancer comes back, radiotherapy . . . and so on through, so far, diagnosis, seven operations, three lots of radiotherapy, some chemotherapy and various smaller medical interventions. And so when I say, 'Guess what? The cancer is back', that's almost all I have to say. It's been back before. If it goes, then it will come back again. It's what cancer does . . . It's become so mundane that I thought of not mentioning it, save as a footnote to a tale of ordinary life' (p. 280).

One week later, while writing his book against alternative therapy, ending with the words 'Let me explain', Diamond was rushed to hospital where he died the next day. His earlier hope that 'one day there will be a proper denouement' to his plot – by which he obviously meant recovery – remained unfulfilled. Death provided the alternative ending.

Discussion

As noted earlier, Del Vecchio Good et al. (1994: 855) developed the concept of 'therapeutic emplotment' to characterize the way in which oncologists helped patients to adjust to cancer by creating and negotiating 'a plot structure within clinical time', one which places particular therapeutic actions within a larger 'therapeutic story'. Of particular relevance to this story is the way in which oncologists attempt to formulate experiences for their patients by 'instilling hope' and structuring time horizons in a way which avoids creating a false sense of hope or despair. They do this by utilizing a number of narrative strategies. One such strategy is to express time 'without horizons' or of highly foreshortened horizons as they attempt to create an experience of 'immediacy' rather than of 'trivial chronology'. Through therapeutic discourse and interaction, the patient's experience is consciously composed 'for the moment' which means that information about treatment and prognosis is provided in carefully calibrated step-by-step stages. Oncologists focus on relatively mundane, practical aspects of treatment such as which therapy will be undertaken first, what side effects will be experienced and what the sequence of treatment is likely to be. As 'immediacy' is emphasized, the horizon of the future is 'deliberately blurred, even as patients may struggle to live into the future'. Endings, although palpably present for participants in clinical encounters, remain unspecified within the therapeutic narrative.

In their clinical observations, Del Vecchio Good et al. found that, although the creation of hope via emphasis on 'for the moment' is fraught with anxiety for patients, they do nevertheless participate and collude in this process. Patients join with clinicians in constructing stories which provide a commitment to treatment and a hope for positive endings. It is in the process of learning to live in the immediacy of treatment decisions and therapeutic activities set within the social context of the clinic that they enter into a narrative form in which endings are rarely made explicit and 'progression' is measured in calibrated bits.

The analysis of Diamond's diary entries presents an interesting illustration of the way in which Diamond's narrative very quickly appropriates this characteristic form of 'therapeutic emplotment'. For instance, from his early diagnosis to first recurrence, Diamond focuses on the 'immediacy' of specific treatments, expressing (in retrospect) a naïve faith in their efficacy. As Del Vecchio Good et al. (1994: 857) predict, this process is fraught with anxiety, especially given that the emplotment of life-threatening illness implicitly speaks to much more profound questions such as 'What is likely to happen?', 'Will the treatment be successful?' and 'What *really* will happen next?' Accordingly, it is not at all surprising that therapeutic narratives of immediacy often coexist with other 'unspoken narratives'. These refer to the uncertainty and fear, the 'frontal assault' against the 'very fabric of hope'.

Such 'unspoken narratives' come to the forefront in Diamond's narrative in later stages of his diary. Here, he begins to doubt his previous, 'almost childish belief in the power of modern medicine'. He had been told his chances were 'excellent', then 'good', then 'mediocre', that he would probably only need one more operation, that he would be back to his old self in 'one month, two, or six'. After all this, he still does not know if he is 'cured'. 'Good news' no longer means 'cure' but remission. He can no longer believe 'the surgical word' and is engulfed in the dreadful uncertainty of the illness.

'Endings', Del Vecchio Good et al. (1994) argued, are frequently part of oncologists' stories. Yet the fear that 'endings' will not only be 'undesirable but precipitous' leads to resistance – on the part of both physicians and patients – to their explicit formulation during the course of therapeutic treatment. Hence, it is often the case that decisions about whether to undertake treatments which offer remission continue to be made to the very end. To do otherwise, to abstain from further treatment decisions, would mean that the 'therapeutic narrative' of immediacy and hope, of struggle and progress, would break down. In the case of Diamond, as has already been suggested, the final sections of his diaries indicate a breakdown of the therapeutic narrative as his faith in specific treatments gradually erodes. Stage 6 ('Endings or the end?'), in which his oncologist admits his hunch that the cancer has returned, also potentially indicates that the therapeutic narrative of immediacy and hope is collapsing from the professional point of view. Nevertheless, the diary ends, with Diamond in the terminal stages of disease, steeling himself for three lots of chemotherapy at three-weekly intervals. One is reminded of Bauman (1992), who characterizes modern life as one in which we 'deconstruct mortality', exorcising our fear of death by breaking it down into smaller and smaller units. Contemporary medical practice, with its division into specialities and sub-specialities, is designed to effect this deconstruction.

In his final diary entry, Diamond (2001: 280) expressed concern with the endless, mundane nature of the cancer plot repeating itself: 'cancer comes, surgery, cancer goes, nothing happens, cancer comes back, radiotherapy . . . and so on . . . '. 'If it goes', he said, 'then it will come back again'. But this time it never went and the cancer created its own ending – one that broke the plot Diamond was in the process of creating. On the day after his death, as his brother-in-law commented, his computer screen still flickered, an 'extinguished intelligence', no longer there to explain his point.

Reflections on methodological and theoretical issues

Methodologically, it is important to consider whether it is valid to use selected published texts such as Diamond's in order to provide an in-depth exploration of certain experiences. I would argue that this is valid, as long as one does not merely accept such texts as a 'naïve' representation of reality. The preface to *Snake Oil and Other Preoccupations*, written by Dominic Lawson, Diamond's brother-in-law, in itself reminds us of the fact that the personal accounts provided by people living with illness (whether orally in interviews or written in autobiographies and diaries) cannot just be taken as a simple representation of what is going on in that person's life. Instead, such accounts constitute a form of life in their own right, a constitution of reality in which the individual ongoingly makes sense of and struggles to adapt to their condition.

Diamond (2001: 275) became famous, in his own words, as an example of 'chirpy positivism and its imminent injunction to live on the bright side', 'the name which has become synonymous with cheery death'. Indeed, the front cover of *Snake Oil* depicts him standing shrugging his shoulders with a whimsical smile on his face, stoically amused at the unkind fate life has to offer him. In psychological parlance, he would constitute a typical example of a patient with an 'optimistic' coping style. Yet, as Lawson poignantly articulates:

> 'It is important not to fall for the idea that John's "Diary of Courage" . . . was a complete opening of his soul to his readers . . . in fact, his public never knew just how black his moods could become, how great his physical pain, how deep his mental torment. The John Diamond in those columns was in part an idealised version of himself, designed to help him cope with his illness' (Diamond, 2001: Introduction).

As these comments make clear, it is important to understand that people writing or talking about their thoughts and experiences are *doing* something with their words – in this case projecting and constructing a certain image in order to cope with the everyday reality of life with a serious illness (see Box R4.2).

Box R4.2   AN ANALYTIC DILEMMA

When analysing a patient's narrative, is it possible to retain a commitment to the personal, experiential nature of their experience *and* to provide a deconstruction of that experience in order to reveal its socio-cultural nature? Does this process of deconstruction undermine the person's psychological reality?

Theoretically, it is important to point out that dividing the diary in the way I have done imposes a greater sense of coherence and linearity than actually existed in the original diary documentation. Not least, this increased coherence derives from the way in which the temporal unfolding of events itself brings meaning to narrative. As Brooks (1984: 22–23) proposed, narrative contains a 'necessary retrospectivity' in the sense that 'only the end can finally determine the meaning'. When reading Diamond's serialized diary format in full, we are doing so with the retrospective vantage point of his death. Hence, as readers of Diamond's serialized diary entries, we immediately have a 'fuller' and more coherent picture than the central protagonist himself had. We know the 'ending' of the story, something that, presumably, Diamond did not know as he wrote the words that were found on his computer screen before he was rushed to hospital for what turned out to be the last time – 'Let me explain'.

Perhaps more important is the question of whether or not the analysis presented here constitutes an exploration of the 'patient's timetable', as is postulated in the analytic section. This study purports to provide a case study of the experience of a patient living with oral cancer and the way in which this experience is centrally linked with the process of 'therapeutic emplotment'. But is this just a theoretical concept imposed on Diamond's experiences? Would it not be more accurately described as 'the patient's timetable as perceived through a specific analytic framework', namely that informed by the concept of 'therapeutic emplotment'? Yes, I think this probably would be a more accurate characterization but I do not think this in any way undermines the analysis. Diamond himself may not have thought of his experiences in terms of the concept of 'therapeutic emplotment' but this does not make it any less relevant for helping us to develop a more in-depth understanding of his experiences – one which links into existing literature in the field and thus facilitates comparisons between this particular person's experiences and others undergoing similar processes. Indeed I would argue that it is this ability to relate existing theoretical ideas to experiential accounts in a manner which creates wider depth and discussion, which constitutes an essential component, perhaps *the* essential component, of a comprehensive and competent narrative style of analysis (see Box R4.3).

Box R4.3   WHOSE UNDERSTANDINGS ARE FOREGROUNDED IN NARRATIVE ANALYSIS?

- In conducting an analysis of a patient's narratives, does the patient have to be consciously aware of the narratives they are using for the analysis to be valid?
- If not, is narrative psychology still maintaining its commitment to respect the emotional integrity of the patient's point of view?
- Is the attempt to unpick the cultural components of a person's story incompatible with the attempt to preserve the individual's 'psychological reality'?

Summary

This report has briefly explored the concept of 'therapeutic emplotment' and how it implicitly works to structure the narrative produced by one man attempting to adjust to life with oral cancer. It has shown that, although in the early stages of the diagnosis the influence of 'therapeutic emplotment' was clearly in evidence, as Diamond's illness progressed he started to question his own faith in the 'surgical story' and the contrasting, largely 'unspoken narrative' of fear and uncertainty began to supercede the therapeutic plot. In a manner typical of modern oncology, Diamond eventually died while still enmeshed in the details of three-weekly intervals of chemotherapy treatment. This raises interesting questions about the ability of both patients and oncologists to deal with 'endings' and whether various treatments are being used as a substitute for the more difficult task of engaging with the reality of death. The main aim of this report, however, has been to provide a summary example of a narrative psychological analysis of one man's experience of illness.

References

Bauman, Z. (1992) *Mortality, Immortality and Other Life Strategies*. Cambridge: Polity Press.

Brooks, P. (1984) *Reading For the Plot: Design and Intention in Narrative*. New York: Vintage.

Crossley, M. (2000a) *Introducing Narrative Psychology: Self, Trauma and the Construction of Meaning*. Milton Keynes: Open University Press.

Crossley, M. (2000b) *Rethinking Health Psychology*. Milton Keynes: Open University Press.

Crossley, M. (2003) 'Let me explain: Narrative emplotment and one patient's experience of oral cancer', *Social Science and Medicine*, 56: 439–448.

Del Vecchio Good, M., Munakata, T., Kobayashi, Y., Mattingly, C. and Good, B. (1994) 'Oncology and narrative time', *Social Science and Medicine*, 38: 855–862.

Diamond, J. (1998) *C: Because Cowards Get Cancer Too*. London: Random House.

Diamond, J. (2001) *Snake Oil and Other Preoccupations*. London: Vintage.

REFERENCES

Abraham, C. and Hampson, S.E. (1996) 'A social cognition approach to health psychology: Philosophical and methodological issues', *Psychology and Health*, 11: 233–241.

Alcoff, L. (1994) 'The problem of speaking for others', in S.O. Weisser and J. Fleischner (eds), *Feminist Nightmares – Women at Odds: Feminism and the Problem of Sisterhood*. New York: New York University Press. pp. 285–309.

Allport, G.W. (1942) *The Use of Personal Documents in Psychological Science*. New York: Social Science Research Council.

Allport, G.W. (1962) 'The general and the unique in psychological science', *Journal of Personality*, 30: 405–422.

Anfara, V.A. and Mertz, N.T. (eds) (2006) *Theoretical Frameworks in Qualitative Research*. Thousand Oaks, CA: Sage.

Antaki, C., Billig, M., Edwards, D. and Potter, J. (2003) 'Discourse analysis means doing analysis: A critique of six analytic shortcomings', *Discourse Analysis Online*. Retrieved 13 October 2006, from www.shu.ac.uk/daol/articles/v1/n1/a1/antaki2002002-t.html

Ashburn, A., Murphy, C., Payne, S. and Wiles, R. (2004) 'Discharge from physiotherapy following stroke: The management of disappointment', *Social Science & Medicine*, 59: 1263–1273.

Ashworth, P. (2003) 'The origins of qualitative psychology', in J.A. Smith (ed.), *Qualitative Psychology: A Practical Guide to Research Methods*. London: Sage. pp. 4–24.

Atkinson, J.M. and Heritage, J. (eds) (1984) *Structures of Social Action: Studies in Conversation Analysis*. Cambridge: Cambridge University Press.

Augoustinos, M. and Walker, I. (1995) *Social Cognition: An Integrated Introduction*. London: Sage.

Barker, M., Hagger-Johnson, G., Hegarty, P., Hutchinson, C. and Riggs, D.W. (in press) 'Responses from the Lesbian & Gay Psychology Section to Crossley's "Making sense of barebacking"', *British Journal of Social Psychology*.

Barnes, R., Auburn, T. and Lea, S. (2004) 'Citizenship as practice', *British Journal of Social Psychology*, 43: 187–206.

Bartlett, D. and Payne, S. (1997) 'Grounded theory – its basis, rationale and procedures', in G. McKenzie, J. Powell and R. Usher (eds), *Understanding Social Research: Perspectives on Methodology and Practice*. London: Falmer Press. pp. 173–195.

Benton, T. and Craib, I. (2001) *Philosophy of Social Science*. New York: Palgrave.

Billig, M. (1988) 'Methodology and scholarship in understanding ideological explanation', in C. Antaki (ed.), *Analysing Everyday Explanation: A Casebook of Methods*. London: Sage. pp. 199–215.

Billig, M. (1991) *Ideology and Opinions*. London: Sage.

Blumer, H. (1969) *Symbolic Interactionism*. Englewood Cliffs, NJ: Prentice Hall.

Bramley, N. and Eatough, V. (2005) 'The experience of living with Parkinson's disease: An interpretative phenomenological analysis case study', *Psychology and Health*, 20: 223–235.

Brannen, J. (ed.) (1992) *Mixing Methods: Qualitative and Quantitative Research*. Aldershot: Avebury/Ashgate.

Breakwell, G.M. (1986) *Coping with Threatened Identities*. London: Methuen.

Breakwell, G.M. (1996) 'Identity processes and social changes', in G.M. Breakwell and E. Lyons (eds), *Changing European Identities: Social Psychological Analyses of Social Change*. Oxford: Butterworth Heinemann. pp. 13–27.

Brown, S.D. (2001) 'Psychology and the art of living', *Theory & Psychology*, 11: 171–192.

Broyard, A. (1992) *Intoxicated by My Illness, and Other Writings on Life and Death*. New York: Clarkson Potter.

Bruce, V. (2002) 'Changing research horizons', *The Psychologist*, 15: 620–622.

Bruner, J. (1990) *Acts of Meaning*. Cambridge, MA: Harvard University Press.

Burgess, R. (1984) *In the Field*. London: Hyman.

Burman, E. (1992) 'Feminism and discourse in developmental psychology: Power, subjectivity and interpretation', *Feminism & Psychology*, 2: 45–59.

Burman, E. (1995) ' "What is it?" Masculinity and femininity in cultural representations of childhood', in S. Wilkinson and C. Kitzinger (eds), *Feminism and Discourse: Psychological Perspectives*. London: Sage. pp. 49–67.

Burman, E. and Parker, I. (1993a) 'Introduction – discourse analysis: The turn to the text', in E. Burman and I. Parker (eds), *Discourse Analytic Research: Repertoires and Readings of Texts in Action*. London: Routledge. pp. 1–13.

Burman, E. and Parker, I. (eds) (1993b) *Discourse Analytic Research: Repertoires and Readings of Texts in Action*. London: Routledge.

Burr, V. (2003) *Social Constructionism* (2nd edition). London: Routledge.

Camp, D., Finlay, W.M.L. and Lyons, E. (2002) 'Is low self-esteem inevitable in stigma? An example from women with chronic mental health problems', *Social Science and Medicine*, 55: 823–834.

Carr, D. (1986) *Time, Narrative and History*. Bloomington, IN: Indiana University Press.

Carradice, A., Shankland, M. and Beail, N. (2002) 'A qualitative study of the theoretical models used by UK mental health nurses to guide their assessments with family caregivers of people with dementia', *International Journal of Nursing Studies*, 39: 17–26.

Chambers, N. (2006) 'A portfolio of academic, therapeutic practice and research work including an investigation of father absence'. Unpublished PsychD portfolio (Practitioner Doctorate in Psychotherapeutic and Counselling Psychology), University of Surrey.

Chapman, E. (2002) 'The social and ethical implications of changing medical technologies: The views of people living with genetic conditions', *Journal of Health Psychology*, 7: 195–206.

Charmaz, K.C. (1990) ' "Discovering" chronic illness: Using grounded theory', *Social Science & Medicine*, 30: 1161–1172.

Charmaz, K.C. (2006) *Constructing Grounded Theory: A Practical Guide Through Qualitative Analysis*. London: Sage.

Clarke, A.E. (2003) 'Situational analyses: Grounded theory mapping after the postmodern turn', *Symbolic Interaction*, 26: 553–576.

Coffey, A. and Atkinson, P. (1996) *Making Sense of Qualitative Data*. Thousand Oaks, CA: Sage.

Constantinople, A. (1973) 'Masculinity-femininity: An exception to a famous dictum?' *Psychological Bulletin*, 80: 389–407.

Coyle, A. (1996) 'Representing gay men with HIV/AIDS', in S. Wilkinson and C. Kitzinger (eds), *Representing the Other*. London: Sage. pp. 72–77.

Coyle, A. and Olsen, C. (2005) 'Research in therapeutic practice settings: Ethical considerations', in R. Tribe and J. Morrissey (eds), *Handbook of Professional and Ethical Practice for Psychologists, Counsellors and Psychotherapists*. Hove: Brunner-Routledge. pp. 249–262.

Coyle, A. and Rafalin, D. (2000) 'Jewish gay men's accounts of negotiating cultural, religious, and sexual identity: A qualitative study', *Journal of Psychology & Human Sexuality*, 12(4): 21–48.

Crites, S. (1986) 'Storytime: Recollecting the past and projecting the future', in T. Sarbin (ed.), *Narrative Psychology: The Storied Nature of Human Conduct*. New York: Praeger. pp. 152–173.

Cromby, J. and Standen, P. (1996) 'Psychology in the service of the state', *Psychology, Politics, Resistance*, 3(Spring/Summer): 6–7.

Cronin, A. (2001) 'Focus groups', in N. Gilbert (ed.), *Researching Social Life* (2nd edition). London: Sage. pp. 164–177.

Crossley, M. (2000a) *Introducing Narrative Psychology: Self, Trauma and the Construction of Meaning*. Buckingham: Open University Press.

Crossley, M. (2000b) 'Narrative psychology, trauma, and the study of self/identity', *Theory and Psychology*, 10: 527–546.

Crossley, M. (2000c) 'Deconstructing autobiographical accounts of childhood sexual abuse', *Feminism and Psychology*, 10: 73–90.

Crossley, M. (2003) 'Let me explain: Narrative emplotment and one patient's experience of oral cancer', *Social Science and Medicine*, 56: 439–448.

Crossley, M. (2004) 'Making sense of "barebacking": Gay men's narratives, unsafe sex and the "resistance habitus"', *British Journal of Social Psychology*, 43: 224–244.

Crossley, M. and Crossley, N. (2001) 'Patient voices, social movements and the habitus: How psychiatric survivors "speak out"', *Social Science and Medicine*, 52: 1477–1489.

Crossley, N. (1996) *Intersubjectivity: The Fabric of Social Becoming*. London: Sage.

Dallos, R. and Draper, R. (2000) *An Introduction to Family Therapy: Systemic Theory and Practice*. Buckingham: Open University Press.

Davies, B. and Harré, R. (1990) 'Positioning: The discursive production of selves', *Journal for the Theory of Social Behaviour*, 20: 43–63.

Davies, B. and Harré, R. (1999) 'Positioning and personhood', in R. Harré and L. van Langenhove (eds), *Positioning Theory*. Oxford: Blackwell. pp. 32–52.

Davies, M. (1997) 'Shattered assumptions: Time and the experience of long-term HIV positivity', *Social Science and Medicine*, 44: 561–571.

Denzin, N.K. and Lincoln, Y.S. (2005a) 'Introduction: The discipline and practice of qualitative research', in N.K. Denzin and Y.S. Lincoln (eds), *The SAGE Handbook of Qualitative Research* (3rd edition). Thousand Oaks, CA: Sage. pp. 1–32.

Denzin, N.K. and Lincoln, Y.S. (eds) (2005b) *The SAGE Handbook of Qualitative Research* (3rd edition). Thousand Oaks, CA: Sage.

Derrida, J. (1976) *Of Grammatology* (trans. G. Chakravorty Spivak). Baltimore, MD: Johns Hopkins University Press.

Dithey, W. (1984) *Descriptive Psychology and Historical Understanding* (English Translations 1977). The Hague: Martinas Mithaf.

Drew, P. (2003) 'Conversation analysis', in J.A. Smith (ed.), *Qualitative Psychology: A Practical Guide to Research Methods*. London: Sage. pp. 132–158.

Dunne, J. (1995) 'Beyond sovereignty and deconstruction: The storied self', *Philosophy and Social Criticism*, 21: 137–157.

Eatough, V. and Smith, J.A. (2006) ' "I feel like a scrambled egg in my head": An idiographic case study of meaning making and anger using interpretative phenomenological analysis', *Psychology and Psychotherapy: Theory, Research and Practice*, 79: 115–135.

Edley, N. and Wetherell, M. (1999) 'Imagined futures: Young men's talk about fatherhood and domestic life', *British Journal of Social Psychology*, 38: 181–194.

Edwards, D. and Potter, J. (1992) *Discursive Psychology*. London: Sage.

Elliott, R., Fischer, C.T. and Rennie, D.L. (1999) 'Evolving guidelines for publication of qualitative research studies in psychology and related fields', *British Journal of Clinical Psychology*, 38: 215–229.

Fallowfield, L. (2001) 'Participation of patients in decisions about treatment for cancer (editorial)', *British Medical Journal*, 323: 1144.

Field, D. and Copp, G. (1999) 'Communication and awareness about dying in the 1990s', *Palliative Medicine*, 13: 459–468.

Fielding, N. and Schreier, M. (2001) 'Introduction: On the compatibility between qualitative and quantitative research methods', *Forum Qualitative Sozialforschung/ Forum: Qualitative Social Research* [online journal], 2(1). Retrieved 15 May 2002, from http://qualitative-research.net/fqs-texte/1–01/1–01hrsg-e.htm

Fine, M. (1994) 'Working the hyphens: Reinventing self and other in qualitative research', in N.K. Denzin and Y.S. Lincoln (eds), *Handbook of Qualitative Research*. London: Sage. pp. 70–82.

Finlay, W.M.L. and Lyons, E. (2000) 'Social categorizations, social comparisons and stigma: Presentations of self in people with learning difficulties', *British Journal of Social Psychology*, 39: 129–146.

Finlay, W.M.L. and Lyons, E. (2001) 'Interviewing people with intellectual disabilities: A review of question phrasing, content and the use of self-report scales', *Psychological Assessment*, 13: 319–355.

Finlay, W.M.L. and Lyons, E. (2002) 'Acquiescence in people with mental retardation', *Mental Retardation*, 40: 14–29.

Fiske, S. and Taylor, S. (1991) *Social Cognition* (2nd edition). New York: McGraw Hill.

Flowers, P., Smith, J.A., Sheeran, P. and Beail, N. (1997) 'Health and romance: Understanding unprotected sex in relationships between gay men', *British Journal of Health Psychology*, 2: 73–86.

Forbat, L. (2005) *Talking about Care: Two Sides to the Story*. Bristol: Policy Press.

Foss, C. and Ellefsen, B. (2002) 'The value of combining qualitative and quantitative approaches in nursing research by means of method triangulation', *Journal of Advanced Nursing*, 40: 242–248.

Foster, C., Eeles, R., Ardern-Jones, A., Moynihan, C. and Watson, M. (2004) 'Juggling roles and expectations: Dilemmas faced by women talking to relatives about cancer and genetic testing', *Psychology and Health*, 19: 439–455.

Foucault, M. (1977) *Discipline and Punish: The Birth of the Prison*. London: Penguin.

Fowler, D.D. and Hardesty, D.L. (eds) (1994) *Others Knowing Others: Perspectives on Ethnographic Careers*. Washington, DC: Smithsonian Institution Press.

Frank, A. (1995) *The Wounded Storyteller: Body, Illness and Ethics*. Chicago, IL: University of Chicago Press.

Freud, S. (1909/1955) 'Notes upon a case of obsessional neurosis', in J. Strachey (ed. and trans.), *The Standard Edition of the Complete Psychological Works of Sigmund Freud* (Vol. 10). London: Hogarth Press. pp. 151–318.

Frosh, S., Phoenix, A. and Pattman, R. (2003) 'Taking a stand: Using psychoanalysis to explore the positioning of subjects in discourse', *British Journal of Social Psychology*, 42: 39–53.

Gergen, K.J. (1991) *The Saturated Self: Dilemmas of Identity in Contemporary Life.* New York: Basic Books.

Gibbs, G.R. (2002) *Qualitative Data Analysis: Explorations with NVivo.* Buckingham: Open University Press.

Gilhooly, K. and Green, C. (1996) 'Protocol analysis: Theoretical background', in J.T.E. Richardson (ed.), *Handbook of Qualitative Research Methods for Psychology and the Social Sciences.* Leicester: BPS Books. pp. 43–54.

Giorgi, A. and Giorgi, B. (2003) 'Phenomenology', in J.A. Smith (ed.), *Qualitative Psychology: A Practical Guide to Research Methods.* London: Sage. pp. 25–50.

Glaser, B.G. (1978) *Theoretical Sensitivity.* Mill Valley, CA: Sociology Press.

Glaser, B.G. (1992) *Emergence vs Forcing: Basics of Grounded Theory Analysis.* Mill Valley, CA: Sociology Press.

Glaser, B.G. and Strauss, A.L. (1965) *Awareness of Dying.* New York: Aldine.

Glaser, B.G. and Strauss, A.L. (1967) *The Discovery of Grounded Theory: Strategies for Qualitative Research.* New York: Aldine.

Golsworthy, R. and Coyle, A. (1999) 'Spiritual beliefs and the search for meaning among older adults following partner loss', *Mortality,* 4: 21–40.

Graham, H. (1986) *The Human Face of Psychology.* Milton Keynes: Open University Press.

Green, C. and Gilhooly, K. (1996) 'Protocol analysis: Practical implementation', in J.T.E. Richardson (ed.), *Handbook of Qualitative Research Methods for Psychology and the Social Sciences.* Leicester: BPS Books. pp. 55–74.

Hacking, I. (1990) *The Taming of Chance.* Cambridge: Cambridge University Press.

Harper, D.J. (1994) 'The professional construction of "paranoia" and the discursive use of diagnostic criteria', *British Journal of Medical Psychology,* 67: 131–143.

Harré, R. and Secord, P. (1972) *The Explanation of Social Behaviour.* Oxford: Blackwell.

Heartfield, J. (2002) *The 'Death of the Subject' Explained.* Sheffield: Sheffield Hallam University Press.

Heath, H. and Cowley, S. (2004) 'Developing a grounded theory approach: A comparison of Glaser and Strauss', *International Journal of Nursing Studies,* 41: 141–150.

Hegarty, P. (2003) 'Homosexual signs and heterosexual silences: Rorschach research on male homosexuality from 1921 to 1969', *Journal of the History of Sexuality,* 12: 400–423.

Hegarty, P. (2007) 'What comes after discourse analysis for LGBTQ psychology?' in E. Peel and V. Clarke (eds), *Out in Psychology: Lesbian, Gay, Bisexual, Trans and Queer Perspectives.* Chichester: Wiley. pp. 41–57.

Henriques, J., Hollway, W., Urwin, C., Venn, C. and Walkerdine, V. (1998) *Changing the Subject: Psychology, Social Regulation and Subjectivity.* London: Routledge.

Henwood, K. (1996) 'Qualitative inquiry: Perspectives, methods and psychology', in J.T.E. Richardson (ed.), *Handbook of Qualitative Research Methods for Psychology and the Social Sciences.* Leicester: BPS Books. pp. 25–40.

Henwood, K. and Pidgeon, N. (1992) 'Qualitative research and psychological theorizing', *British Journal of Psychology,* 83: 97–111.

Henwood, K. and Pidgeon, N. (1994) 'Beyond the qualitative paradigm: A framework for introducing diversity within qualitative psychology', *Journal of Community & Applied Social Psychology,* 4: 225–238.

Hepburn, A. and Wiggins, S. (2005) 'Size matters: Constructing accountable bodies in NSPCC helpline interaction', *Discourse & Society,* 16: 625–645.

Heron, J. (1996) *Co-operative Inquiry: Research into the Human Condition.* London: Sage.

Holloway, I. (1997) *Basic Concepts for Qualitative Research.* Oxford: Blackwell.

Hollway, W. (1989) *Subjectivity and Method in Psychology: Gender, Meaning and Science.* London: Sage.

Human Genetics Commission (2004) *Choosing the Future: Genetics and Reproductive Decision Making.* London: Human Genetics Commission.

Hutchby, I. and Wooffitt, R. (1998) *Conversation Analysis.* Cambridge: Polity Press.

James, W. (1890) *Principles of Psychology* (2 vols). London: Macmillan.

Jarman, M., Walsh, S. and DeLacey, G. (2005) 'Keeping safe, keeping connected: A qualitative study of HIV-positive women's experiences of partner relationships', *Psychology & Health*, 20: 533–553.

Jefferson, G. (1990) 'List construction as a task and resource', in G. Psathas (ed.), *Interaction Competence.* Lanham, MD: University Press of America. pp. 63–92.

Joffé, H. and Yardley, L. (2004) 'Content and thematic analysis', in D.F. Marks and L. Yardley (eds), *Research Methods for Clinical and Health Psychology.* London: Sage. pp. 56–68.

Kevles, D. (1968) 'Testing the army's intelligence: Psychologists and the military in World War 1', *Journal of American History*, 55: 565–581.

Kitzinger, C. and Wilkinson, S. (1996) 'Theorizing representing the Other', in S. Wilkinson and C. Kitzinger (eds), *Representing the Other.* London: Sage. pp. 1–32.

Kleinmann, A. (1988) *The Illness Narratives: Suffering, Healing and the Human Condition.* New York: Basic Books.

Krippendorf, K. (2004) *Content Analysis: An Introduction to its Methodology* (2nd edition). Thousand Oaks, CA: Sage.

Kvale, S. (1996) *Interviews: An Introduction to Qualitative Research Interviewing.* Thousand Oaks, CA: Sage.

Lewis, C.S. (1952) *Mere Christianity.* New York: Macmillan.

Lincoln, Y.S. and Guba, E.G. (1985) *Naturalistic Inquiry.* Newbury Park, CA: Sage.

Livia, A. (1996) 'Daring to presume', in S. Wilkinson and C. Kitzinger (eds), *Representing the Other.* London: Sage. pp. 33–42.

Lyons, E. (2000) 'Qualitative data analysis: Data display model', in G.M. Breakwell, S. Hammond and C. Fife-Schaw (eds), *Research Methods in Psychology* (2nd edition). London: Sage. pp 269–281.

Lyons, E., Chrysanthaki, T. and Barrett, M. (2006) 'The role of perceived discrimination and political trust in fostering social cohesion: The minority perspective', paper presented at the International Society of Political Psychology 29th Annual Scientific Meeting, Barcelona, Spain, 12–15 July.

Madill, A., Jordan, A. and Shirley, C. (2000) 'Objectivity and reliability in qualitative analysis: Realist, contextualist and radical constructionist epistemologies', *British Journal of Psychology*, 91: 1–20.

Mair, M. (1989) *Between Psychology and Psychotherapy.* London: Routledge.

Marks, D. (1996) 'Able-bodied dilemmas in teaching disability studies', in S. Wilkinson and C. Kitzinger (eds), *Representing the Other.* London: Sage. pp. 64–67.

Mason, J. (2002) *Qualitative Researching* (2nd edition). London: Sage.

Mayring, P. (2001) 'Combination and integration of quantitative and qualitative analysis', *Forum Qualitative Sozialforschung/Forum: Qualitative Social Research* [online journal], 2(1). Retrieved 15 May 2002, from http://qualitative-research.net/fqs-texte/1–01/1–01hrsg-e.htm

McAdams, D.P. (1993) *The Stories We Live By: Personal Myths and the Making of the Self.* New York: Morrow.

McAdams, D.P., Josselson, R. and Lieblich, A. (2001) *Turns in the Road: Narrative Studies of Lives in Transition.* Washington, DC: American Psychological Association.

McLean Taylor, J., Gilligan, C. and Sullivan, A.M. (1996) 'Missing voices, changing meanings: Developing a voice-centred, relational method and creating an interpretive community', in S. Wilkinson (ed.), *Feminist Social Psychologies: International Perspectives.* Buckingham: Open University Press. pp. 233–257.

McLeod, J. (1997) *Narrative and Psychotherapy.* London: Sage.

McLeod, J. (2000) *Qualitative Research in Counselling and Psychotherapy.* London: Sage.

Mead, G.H. (1934) *Mind, Self and Society.* Chicago, IL: Chicago University Press.

Miles, M.B. and Huberman, A.M. (1994) *Qualitative Data Analysis: A Sourcebook of New Methods* (2nd edition). London: Sage.

Millward, L.J. (2006) 'Focus groups', in G.M. Breakwell, S. Hammond, C. Fife-Schaw and J.A. Smith (eds), *Research Methods in Psychology* (3rd edition). London: Sage. pp. 274–298.

Moran, D. (2000) *Introduction to Phenomenology.* London: Routledge.

Moran-Ellis, J., Alexander, V.D., Cronin, A., Dickinson, M., Fielding, J., Sleney, J. and Thomas, H. (2006) 'Triangulation and integration: Processes, claims and implications', *Qualitative Research*, 6: 45–59.

Murray, M. and Chamberlain, K. (eds) (1999) *Qualitative Health Psychology: Theories & Methods.* London: Sage.

National Institute for Clinical Excellence (2004) *Guidance Manual: Improving Supportive and Palliative Care for Adults with Cancer.* London: National Institute for Clinical Excellence.

O'Connell, D.C. and Kowal, S. (1995) 'Basic principles of transcription', in J.A. Smith, R. Harré and L. van Langenhove (eds), *Rethinking Methods in Psychology.* London: Sage. pp. 93–105.

Oguntokun, R. (1998) 'A lesson in the seductive power of sameness: Representing Black African refugee women', *Feminism and Psychology*, 8: 525–529.

Palmer, R. (1969) *Hermeneutics.* Evanston, IL: Northwestern University Press.

Parker, I. (1992) *Discourse Dynamics: Critical Analysis for Social and Individual Psychology.* London: Routledge.

Parker, I. (1997) 'Discourse analysis and psychoanalysis', *British Journal of Social Psychology*, 36: 479–495.

Parker, I., Georgaca, E., Harper, D., McLaughlin, T. and Stowell-Smith, M. (1995) *Deconstructing Psychopathology.* London: Sage.

Payne, S. (1992) 'A study of quality of life in cancer patients receiving palliative chemotherapy', *Social Science & Medicine*, 35: 1505–1509.

Payne, S., Seymour, J.E., Chapman, A., Chau, R. and Lloyd, M. (2004) 'Attitudes and beliefs about end-of-life care in the Chinese community: Challenging stereotypes', *Palliative Medicine*, 18: 153.

Pidgeon, N. (1996) 'Grounded theory: Theoretical background', in J.T.E. Richardson (ed.), *Handbook of Qualitative Research Methods for Psychology and the Social Sciences.* Leicester: BPS Books. pp. 75–85.

Plummer, K. (ed.) (1981) *The Making of the Modern Homosexual.* London: Hutchinson.

Polkinghorne, D.E. (1988) *Narrative Knowing and the Human Sciences.* Albany, NY: State of New York University Press.

Pomerantz, A.M. (1986) 'Extreme case formulations: A new way of legitimating claims', *Human Studies*, 9: 219–230.

Popper, K.R. (1969) *Conjectures and Refutations.* London: Routledge and Kegan Paul.

Potter, J. (1996) *Representing Reality: Discourse, Rhetoric and Social Construction.* London: Sage.

Potter, J. (2003) 'Discourse analysis', in M. Hardy and A. Bryman (eds), *Handbook of Data Analysis.* London: Sage. pp. 607–624.

Potter, J. and Collie, F. (1989) ' "Community care" as persuasive rhetoric: A study of discourse', *Disability, Handicap & Society*, 4: 57–64.

Potter, J. and Wetherell, M. (1987) *Discourse and Social Psychology: Beyond Attitudes and Behaviour*. London: Sage.

Pratt, L.M. (1986) 'Fieldwork in common places', in J. Clifford and G.E. Marcus (eds), *Writing Culture: The Poetics and Politics of Ethnography*. Berkeley, CA: University of California Press. pp. 27–50.

Radley, A. and Chamberlain, K. (2001) 'Health psychology and the study of the case: From method to analytic concern', *Social Science & Medicine*, 53: 321–332.

Reason, P. and Rowan, J. (eds) (1981) *Human Inquiry: A Sourcebook of New Paradigm Research*. Chichester: Wiley.

Reicher, S. (2000) 'Against methodolatry: Some comments on Elliott, Fischer, and Rennie', *British Journal of Clinical Psychology*, 39: 1–6.

Rennie, D.L. (2000) 'Grounded theory methodology as methodical hermeneutics: Reconciling realism and relativism', *Theory and Psychology*, 10: 481–502.

Richards, L. (2000) *Using NVivo in Qualitative Research* (2nd edition). Melbourne: QSR International.

Richardson, J.T.E. (ed.) (1996) *Handbook of Qualitative Research Methods for Psychology and the Social Sciences*. Leicester: BPS Books.

Ricoeur, P. (1970) *Freud and Philosophy*. New Haven, CT: Yale University Press.

Rowlands, J. (2005) 'To tell the truth', *Cancer Nursing Practice*, 4(5): 16–21.

Sarbin, T.R. (ed.) (1986) *Narrative Psychology: The Storied Nature of Human Conduct*. New York: Praeger.

Schreier, M. and Fielding, N. (eds) (2001) 'Qualitative and quantitative research: Conjunctions and divergences', a special issue of *Forum Qualitative Sozialforschung/Forum: Qualitative Social Research* [online journal], 2(1). Retrieved 15 May 2002, from http://qualitative-research.net/fqs/fqs-eng.htm

Sedgwick, E. (1990) *The Epistemology of the Closet*. London: Penguin.

Senior, V., Smith, J.A., Michie, S. and Marteau, T.M. (2002) 'Making sense of risk: An interpretative phenomenological analysis of vulnerability to heart disease', *Journal of Health Psychology*, 7: 157–168.

Shepherd, R., Barnett, J., Cooper, H., Coyle, A., Moran-Ellis, J., Senior, V. and Walton, C. (forthcoming) 'Towards an understanding of British public attitudes concerning human cloning', *Social Science and Medicine*.

Shevlin, M. (2000) 'Surgery in a sewer? [Letter]', *The Psychologist*, 13: 181.

Shotter, J. (1993) *Cultural Politics of Everyday Life: Social Constructionism, Rhetoric and Knowing of the Third Kind*. Buckingham: Open University Press.

Shotter, J. (1997) 'The social construction of our inner selves', *Journal of Constructivist Psychology*, 10: 7–24.

Silverman, D. (1993) *Interpreting Qualitative Data*. London: Sage.

Simpson, M. (ed.) (1996) *Anti-Gay*. London: Freedom Editions.

Sinister Wisdom Collective (1990) 'Editorial', *Sinister Wisdom*, 42(4): 1–6.

Smith, B. and Sparkes, A.C. (2006) 'Narrative inquiry in psychology: Exploring the tensions within', *Qualitative Research in Psychology*, 3: 169–192.

Smith, J.A. (1993) 'The case study', in R. Bayne and P. Nicolson (eds), *Counselling and Psychology for the Health Professionals*. London: Chapman Hall. pp. 249–265.

Smith, J.A. (1996) 'Beyond the divide between cognition and discourse: Using interpretative phenomenological analysis in health psychology', *Psychology & Health*, 11: 261–271.

Smith, J.A. (1999) 'Towards a relational self: Social engagement during pregnancy and psychological preparation for motherhood', *British Journal of Social Psychology*, 38: 409–426.

Smith, J.A. (ed.) (2003) *Qualitative Psychology: A Practical Guide to Research Methods*. London: Sage.

Smith, J.A. (2004) 'Reflecting on the development of interpretative phenomenological analysis and its contribution to qualitative psychology', *Qualitative Research in Psychology*, 1: 39–54.

Smith, J.A. and Dunworth, F. (2003) 'Qualitative methods in the study of development', in K. Connolly and J. Valsiner (eds), *The Handbook of Developmental Psychology*. London: Sage. pp. 603–621.

Smith, J.A. and Osborn, M. (2003) 'Interpretative phenomenological analysis', in J.A. Smith (ed.), *Qualitative Psychology: A Practical Guide to Research Methods*. London: Sage. pp. 51–80.

Smith, J.A., Harré, R. and van Langenhove, L. (1995) 'Idiography and the case study', in J.A. Smith, R. Harré and L. van Langenhove (eds), *Rethinking Psychology*. London: Sage. pp. 59–69.

Smith, J.A., Flowers, P. and Osborn, M. (1997) 'Interpretative phenomenological analysis and the psychology of health and illness', in L. Yardley (ed.), *Material Discourses of Health and Illness*. London: Routledge. pp. 68–91.

Smith, J.A., Michie, S., Allanson, A. and Elwy, R. (2000) 'Certainty and uncertainty in genetic counselling: A qualitative case study', *Psychology & Health*, 15: 1–12.

Smith, J.A., Brewer, H., Eatough, V., Stanley, C., Glendinning, N. and Quarrell, O. (2006) 'The personal experience of Juvenile Huntington's Disease: An interpretative phenomenological analysis of parents' accounts on the primary features of a rare genetic condition, *Clinical Genetics*, 69: 486–496.

Smith, M. (2005) *Philosophy and Methodology in the Social Sciences*. London: Sage.

Spriggs, M. (2004) 'Commodification of children again and non-disclosure of preimplantation genetic diagnosis for Huntington's disease', *Journal of Medical Ethics*, 30: 538.

Sque, M. and Payne, S.A. (1996) 'Dissonant loss: The experience of donor relatives', *Social Science & Medicine*, 43: 1359–1370.

Strauss, A. and Corbin, J. (1990) *Basics of Qualitative Research: Techniques and Procedures for Developing Grounded Theory*. Thousand Oaks, CA: Sage.

Strauss, A. and Corbin, J. (1998) *Basics of Qualitative Research: Techniques and Procedures for Developing Grounded Theory* (2nd edition). Thousand Oaks, CA: Sage.

Tajfel, H. and Turner, J. (1986) 'The social identity theory of intergroup behaviour', in S. Worchel and W.G. Austin (eds), *Psychology of Intergroup Relations*. Chicago, IL: Nelson. pp. 7–24.

Taylor, C. (1989) *Sources of the Self: The Making of Modern Identity*. Cambridge: Cambridge University Press.

Taylor, S. and Bogdan, R. (1998) *Introduction to Qualitative Research Methods* (3rd edition). New York: Wiley.

Thomson, R. and Holland, J. (2003) 'Hindsight, foresight and insight: The challenges of longitudinal qualitative research', *International Journal of Social Research Methodology*, 6: 233–244.

Todd, Z., Nerlich, B., McKeown, S. and Clarke, D.D. (eds) (2004) *Mixing Methods in Psychology: The Integration of Qualitative and Quantitative Methods in Theory and Practice*. London: Routledge.

Triandis, H.C. (1996) 'The psychological measurement of cultural syndromes', *American Psychologist*, 51: 407–415.

Triandis, H.C., Leung, K., Villareal, M. and Clack, F.L. (1985) 'Allocentric vs. idiocentric tendencies: Convergent and discriminant validation', *Journal of Research in Personality*, 19: 395–415.

Turner, A.J. and Coyle, A. (2000) 'What does it mean to be a donor offspring? The identity experiences of adults conceived by donor insemination and the implications for counselling and therapy', *Human Reproduction*, 15: 2041–2051.

Turner, B. (1981) 'Some practical aspects of qualitative data analysis: One way of organising the cognitive processes associated with the generation of grounded theory', *Quality and Quantity*, 15: 225–247.

Turpin, G., Barley, V., Beail, N., Scaife, J., Slade, P., Smith, J.A. and Walsh, S. (1997) 'Standards for research projects and theses involving qualitative methods: Suggested guidelines for trainees and courses', *Clinical Psychology Forum*, 108: 3–7.

Ussher, J. (1991) *Women's Madness: Misogyny or Mental Illness?* London: Harvester Wheatsheaf.

Vignoles, V.L., Chryssochoou, X. and Breakwell, G.M. (2004) 'Combining individuality and relatedness: Representations of the person among the Anglican clergy', *British Journal of Social Psychology*, 43: 113–132.

Wallwork, J. and Dixon, J.A. (2004) 'Foxes, green fields and Britishness: On the rhetorical construction of place and national identity', *British Journal of Social Psychology*, 43: 21–39.

Warnock, M. (1987) *Memory*. London: Faber and Faber.

Weille, K.L. (2002) 'The psychodynamics of consensual sadomasochistic and dominant-submissive sexual games', *Studies in Gender and Sexuality*, 3: 131–160.

Wetherell, M. (1998) 'Positioning and interpretative repertoires: Conversation analysis and post-structuralism in dialogue', *Discourse & Society*, 9: 387–412.

Wetherell, M. and Potter, J. (1992) *Mapping the Language of Racism: Discourse and the Legitimation of Exploitation*. Hemel Hempstead: Harvester Wheatsheaf.

Wetherell, M., Taylor, S. and Yates, S.J. (eds) (2001a) *Discourse Theory and Practice: A Reader*. London: Sage/Open University Press.

Wetherell, M., Taylor, S. and Yates, S.J. (eds) (2001b) *Discourse as Data: A Guide for Analysis*. London: Sage/Open University Press.

White, H. (1987) *The Content of the Form: Narrative Discourse and Historical Representation*. Baltimore, MD: Johns Hopkins University Press.

Widdicombe, S. (1995) 'Identity, politics and talk: A case for the mundane and the everyday', in S. Wilkinson and C. Kitzinger (eds), *Feminism and Discourse: Psychological Perspectives*. London: Sage. pp. 106–127.

Wiggins, S. (2004) 'Good for "you": Generic and individual healthy eating advice in family mealtimes', *Journal of Health Psychology*, 9: 535–548.

Wilkinson, S. (1996) 'Feminist social psychologies: A decade of development', in S. Wilkinson (ed.), *Feminist Social Psychologies: International Perspectives*. Buckingham: Open University Press. pp. 1–18.

Wilkinson, S. (1997) 'Feminist psychology', in D. Fox and I. Prilleltensky (eds), *Critical Psychology: An Introduction*. London: Sage. pp. 247–265.

Wilkinson, S. and Kitzinger, C. (eds) (1996) *Representing the Other*. London: Sage.

Willig, C. (1995) ' "I wouldn't have married the guy if I'd have to do that": Heterosexual adults' accounts of condom use and their implications for sexual practice', *Journal of Community and Applied Social Psychology*, 5: 75–87.

Willig, C. (ed.) (1999) *Applied Discourse Analysis: Social and Psychological Interventions*. Buckingham: Open University Press.

Willig, C. (2001) *Introducing Qualitative Research in Psychology: Adventures in Theory and Method*. Buckingham: Open University Press.

Wooffitt, R. (2001) 'Analysing factual accounts', in N. Gilbert (ed.), *Researching Social Life* (2nd edition). London: Sage. pp. 324–342.

REFERENCES

Wynne, B. (2006) 'Public engagement as a means of restoring public trust in science: Hitting the notes but missing the music', *Community Genetics*, 9: 211–220.

Yardley, L. (1997) 'Introducing discursive methods', in L. Yardley (ed.), *Material Discourses of Health and Illness*. London: Routledge. pp. 25–49.

Yardley, L. (2000) 'Dilemmas in qualitative health research', *Psychology and Health*, 15: 215–228.

Yin, R. (1989) *Case Study Research* (rev. edition). Newbury Park, CA: Sage.

NAME INDEX

SUBJECT INDEX